Springer Studies in the History of Economic Thought

This series offers an outlet for research in the history of economic thought. It features scholarly studies on important theoretical developments and great economic thinkers that have contributed to the evolution of the economic discipline.

Springer Studies in the History of Economic Thought (SSHET) welcomes proposals for research monographs, edited volumes, textbooks and handbooks from a variety of disciplines that seek to study the history of economic thinking and help to arrive at a better understanding of modern economics. Relevant topics include, but are not limited to, various schools of thought, important pioneers and thinkers, ancient and medieval economic thought, mercantilism, cameralism and physiocracy, classical and neoclassical economics, historical, institutional and evolutionary economics, socialism and Marxism, Keynesian, Sraffian and Austrian economics, econometrics and mathematical studies as well as economic methodology and the link between economic history and history of economic thought.

All titles in this series are peer-reviewed. Scopus indexes the series and the volumes published in it.

For further information on the series and to submit a proposal for consideration, please contact Johannes Glaeser (Executive Editor Economics) Johannes.glaeser@springer.com.

Jan Greitens

Currency and Credit Money

A Comparative History of Early Monetary Theories (1358–1918)

Springer

Jan Greitens
Johann Wolfgang Goethe-Universität
Frankfurt, Germany

ISSN 2662-6098 ISSN 2662-6101 (electronic)
Springer Studies in the History of Economic Thought
ISBN 978-3-032-24112-2 ISBN 978-3-032-24113-9 (eBook)
https://doi.org/10.1007/978-3-032-24113-9

This Springer imprint is published by the registered company Springer Nature Switzerland AG
The registered company address is: Gewerbestrasse 11, 6330 Cham, Switzerland

Preface

Before I go on with this short history, let me make a general observation—the test of a first-rate intelligence is the ability to hold two opposed ideas in the mind at the same time, and still retain the ability to function.
—Fitzgerald (1936)

Questions about money have once again moved to the forefront of economic and political debate. The introduction of central bank digital currencies (CBDCs), the rise of private digital currencies like Bitcoin and stablecoins, and the growing popularity of Modern Monetary Theory (MMT) have all reignited an interest in the fundamental issues that have defined monetary theory since its inception. What is money? What determines its value? What are the proper roles of the state and private actors? Which normative visions of order, stability, and accessibility are embedded in competing conceptions of money? This book revisits such questions, seeking to make explicit the historical currents that have informed monetary debates up to the present day.

While exploring foundational perspectives on currency and credit money, this book provides an overview of key periods in the history of early monetary theory. Yet rather than attempting to synthesize the presented theories, the book furnishes a "panopticon" of diverse ideas, leaving opposing views unresolved. Moving chronologically, the book begins at the end of the scholastic period and concludes in the early twentieth century.

This book is a comprehensively revised translation of the third edition of the German-language textbook *Geld-Theorie-Geschichte* (Metropolis, 2024). As a supplement, I have also published a text compilation in which most of the discussed authors can be read in German or English (*Geld-Theorie-Geschichte: Ausgewählte Texte 1361 bis 1918*. Metropolis, 2019).

Frankfurt, Germany
January 2026

Jan Greitens

References

Fitzgerald, Francis Scott. 1936. The crack-up. *Esquire*. https://www.esquire.com/lifestyle/a4310/the-crack-up/

Greitens, Jan. 2024. Geld-Theorie-Geschichte. 3rd edition. Marburg: Metropolis Verlag.

Greitens, Jan (editor). 2019. Geld-Theorie-Geschichte. Ausgewählte Texte von 1361 bis 1918. Marburg: Metropolis Verlag.

Contents

Chapter 1
Introduction

It is our own fault that contemporary discussion of currency questions has gained nothing from the work of a century, and in part is not above, but below, the level of discussion in England at the time of the Bank Restriction Act (1797–1821). […] If we had the necessary ability and knowledge, and above all the kind of selflessness which loyally cultivates and develops what is at hand, instead of always striking attitudes of battle and discovery and anchoring all that we say to as personal a standpoint as possible, then our science could achieve what it should.—Schumpeter (1918, 150)

Much of the recent literature on the history of monetary thought is explicitly partisan, targeting specific audiences rather than trying to offer a broader perspective. This study is deliberately agnostic. Rather than synthesizing or favoring theories, the book wants to compare theories with each other. It thus takes a relativistic approach.

A core premise of the book that the complexity of historical realities gives rise to a variety of legitimate theories, each addressing specific issues and problems. Consequently, all theories must be considered within their historical context; in other words, they must also be reconstructed historically.

In line with this assumption, the book begins with three chapters that provide an important foundation for the reader to engage with the subsequent discussion. The first chapter addresses methodological issues. This is followed by a chapter on historical developments in monetary history in the eras in which the authors wrote.

A close reading of the presented works reveals that it is difficult to derive consistent monetary theories that are assignable to traditional economic schools of thought, as these schools primarily focus on historical periods and issues of value and price theory. No homogeneous theory of money exists within mercantilism, the classical period, or neoclassical economics.

This book therefore develops its own taxonomy (presented in Chap. 3) to categorize the authors' texts based on the theoretical questions they address and to distinguish certain traditions. An abridged version of this taxonomy was presented in a standalone paper (Greitens 2022).

J. Greitens, *Currency and Credit Money*, Springer Studies in the History of Economic Thought, https://doi.org/10.1007/978-3-032-24113-9_1

While this book rejects the notion that monetary theories can be assigned to traditional economic schools, schools are nevertheless used as an organizing principle, as they are useful for understanding chronological sequences as well as common geographical and historical backgrounds.

Notably, the book has several limitations. It focuses on the essence (or nature) and value of currency and credit money. Related topics, such as interest and exchange rates, are not systematically addressed. The authors were selected with the aim of providing readers with an overview of theory relevant to the chosen questions. The authors are not necessarily the "inventors" of the respective ideas, but rather their representatives. When selecting authors, a focus was placed on Germany and Europe. Due to the time periods covered, no female authors were included. With the aim of discussing early historical developments, the book begins in the early Renaissance and ends around the First World War, thus focusing exclusively on pre-Keynesian theories of money.

The authors are always discussed in relation to a specific text in which a central idea is expressed. Therefore, direct quotations figure prominently in this book. One aim is to provide readers with a direct experience of the authors' language; in this connection, terms are only modernized with caution. Naturally, we must limit ourself to excerpts, as it is not possible in this context to do justice to the full range of contributions made by each author.

References

Greitens. 2022. A structured approach for comparing monetary theories. *International Journal of Pluralism and Economics Education* 13 (3): 262–276.

Schumpeter, Joseph. 1918. Money and the social product. In *International Economic Papers 6*. 1956, 148–211. Translated by A. W. Marget of "Das Sozialproduct und die Rechenpfennige" *Archiv für Sozialwissenschaft und Sozialpolitik* 44:627–715.

Part I
Theoretical and Historical Foundations

Chapter 2
Methodological Considerations

In economics, any claim to originality is hardly possible, for one invariably finds even the most original lines of thought expressed more or less clearly in earlier writings, just as the modern theory of energy conservation was anticipated to a certain extent by a somewhat murky paragraph in Newton's Principia, even though Newton never formulated it in that way.—Fisher (1929, 11, my translation)

This book aims to compare monetary theories from a period spanning nearly 600 years. Numerous methodological questions are raised by the fact that the examined texts were written in highly divergent contexts, ranging from the types of money used, the broader economy in which they circulated, and the prevailing political conditions. What, then, can such a presentation achieve? What are the potential pitfalls associated with it?

This chapter accounts for the book's approach and is structured as follows:

- Firstly, it considers whether there has been progress in economics and, if so, whether it is fruitful to argue about theories from the past.
- Secondly, it discusses how to reconstruct theories and take the historical background into account.
- Thirdly, it discusses traditional schools of thought in economics and explains why they fit poorly as a means of classifying monetary theories.
- Fourthly, it spotlights important factors to consider when comparing theories from different historical periods.

2.1 Progress in Economics

Helmstädter proposes an approach that seeks to systematize three possible types of progress in economics (Helmstädter 1994, similar Blaug 2002):

J. Greitens, *Currency and Credit Money*, Springer Studies in the History of Economic Thought, https://doi.org/10.1007/978-3-032-24113-9_2

Cumulative Progress

Cumulative progress refers to the expansion of knowledge; knowledge builds on itself in an ongoing process of accumulation, like adding new bricks to a wall. In economics, for instance, this progress takes the form of improvements in data collection and processing, statistics, national economic accounting, and empirical research as a whole.

Substitutive Progress

Here, old knowledge is replaced by new knowledge, resulting in a renewal of understanding. Old approaches are classified as incorrect or outdated. To stay with the above analogy, no new bricks are used; old ones are replaced. From this perspective, science is understood as a continuous process of renewal. This conception corresponds to the intuitive idea of progress. In economics, this type of progress may take the form of improved methods: Through the formalization of models, the assumptions of a model and associated consequences can be presented with greater clarity; measurement and verification can also be improved.

Circular Progress

The concept of circular progress assumes that seemingly obsolete knowledge can return. Throughout history, similar problems have been raised repeatedly, not identical problems, but problems with different points of emphasis. Fundamental questions are discussed anew from different perspectives. Examples include the active or passive role of the state, questions of social justice, the nominalism or metallism of money, free trade or autarky, and the positive or negative role of state debt. Neumark even goes a step further: "The cyclical recurrence of certain content-related and methodological questions in our discipline, regardless of the temporal and spatial relativity of attempts to find solutions, suggests the existence of fundamental economic facts and problems, which can only be overcome theoretically and practically by choosing between two fundamentally contradictory alternatives" (Neumark 1975, 281, my translation). This type of progress is more strongly associated with value judgments, partly because they inform the selection of the important questions.

If there is only substitutive progress in economics, then the correct insights from the past are contained in modern theories, so there is no reason to engage with the history of theory, apart from personal interest. But in economics, all these types of progress can be found: cumulative progress in empirical research, substitutive progress in methods, and circular progress in fundamental ideas. The history of ideas primarily deals with topics in the area of circular progress, where competing approaches can reach similar conclusions using historically changing methods (e.g., Keynesianism and Neo-Keynesianism, or Classical, Neoclassical, and New Classical economics). As Schumpeter supposedly said: "Old friends come disguised to the party."

In monetary theory, similar questions are asked that fall under Helmstädter's definition of circular progress. The relationship between currency and credit money, money's intrinsic or extrinsic value, stability and elasticity in the monetary system, and between currency devaluation and economic stimulation, for example, have all been discussed repeatedly, albeit under different historical headings. These recurring themes make it useful to study historical monetary theories.

2.2 Analyzing Historical Theories

2.2.1 Conceptual History

One important consideration when dealing with historical theories is that language is time-dependent. This makes the history of concepts (*Begriffsgeschichte*) particularly important for comparing ideas from a period spanning nearly 600 years. Otto Brunner, who is considered an early figure in German conceptual history, insisted that historians should analyze the past on the basis of concepts contemporary with the era in question. The further back we go when harnessing terms from the past, the greater the gulf to current notions, to present-day conceptions of a market society. Brunner provides an example of the reconstruction of historical texts: "The historical demand for a source-based conceptual language comes up against the fact that the categories under which the times understood themselves do not meet our scientific requirements, but also that the concepts of modern science were developed on the basis of a reality that has only existed since the eighteenth century. The only option is to attempt, in full awareness of this fact, to reconstruct the internal structure of this past world, to separate the truly purely theoretical, universally valid elements of modern science from the elements of a contemporary analysis, and to make use of them to understand a different kind of past" (Brunner 1949, 62).

Modern conceptions of money, the market, or the state cannot be straightforwardly applied to earlier periods, as historically similar phenomena were embedded in fundamentally different semantic and institutional contexts. Medieval or early modern monetary concepts are therefore not merely primitive versions of modern theories, but expressions of distinct social, legal, and political orders that must be reconstructed and contextualized before meaningful comparison is possible.

2.2.2 *The Reconstruction of Past Ideas*

The concept of reconstruction is central to the history of economic thought. The aim is to trace and restore the past. "All texts of the past need to be reconstructed because they do not speak with one voice and are never unambiguous; even the authors of these texts are never in complete control of their own meaning" (Blaug 2001, 151).

The following section will discuss two approaches to reconstruction. Blaug (1990, 27–28) proposes the following two scientific methods: (1) historical reconstruction and (2) rational reconstruction. These methods are derived from a broader framework proposed by Richard Rorty (1984).

Rational Reconstruction

Here, a focus is placed on the ideas that inform the writing; the aim is to grasp the argument and identify errors. In other words, the "central concern is with the internal logic of a theory" (O'Brien 2007, 24).

"Concentration on theory does not rule out wider concerns. What it does rule out is relativism. [...] In its most extreme form relativism does little more than insist that economic theory is a 'Reflection' of contemporary historical events" (O'Brien 2007, 26). In this way, relativization involves the risk of treating logical errors as historically conditioned trivialities.

"My expressed doubt about rational reconstruction was that they threatened to make past ideas irrelevant since they often do little more than demonstrate how much more we now know than those fuddy-duddies of yesterday" (Blaug 2003, 607). Therefore, a purely rational reconstruction can lead to theories being misunderstood, time-bound questions being overlooked, and authors being wrongly belittled.

Historical Reconstruction

The historical reconstruction "attempts to give an account of past thinkers' systems of thought 'in their own terms,' that is, in terms these thinkers would have accepted as a correct description of what they had done" (Blaug 1990, 28).

A text should therefore be contextualized in relation to the problems and questions of its time, and its historical context disclosed. This includes both economic and theoretical historical aspects, for "if it is the task of economic history to describe the concrete manifestations of economic systems, one can try to determine dogmatically which schools of economic thought predominate and help to shape the style as a pattern for understanding events and as a guide to economic policy" (Schefold 2009, 17, my translation).

In line with this insight, each chapter in this book includes a short biographical description. To be sure, the theories of individual authors are influenced by their professional training, social environments, and national origins, but this does not necessarily cast into question their pursuit of truth or initial commitment to objectivity. The banker Ricardo viewed economic interrelationships differently than Thünen, who was a farmer with practical concerns. Similarly, the Englishman Malthus developed a pessimistic doctrine on population in overcrowded Great Britain, while the American Carey developed an optimistic doctrine in the sparsely populated New World (Kruse 1994, 4).

This book applies a combined methodological approach. Specifically, it aims to present both the author's perspective—the questions that the author himself wanted to answer—and to trace the logic of the argumentation in an ahistorical manner. This avoids the presentation falling into a condescending attitude that ostensibly lays claim to absolute truth; at the other extreme, it avoids excessive praise from a relativistic view. Nevertheless, this book takes a more historical approach than is common in the history of economic thought.

2.3 Schools of Economic Thought

Dividing theory into discrete schools of economic thought is not just difficult, it is also dangerous. It creates the false impression that all authors assigned to a school can be clearly and neatly categorized. The extent of agreement between authors can be easily overestimated. In addition, it can create the false impression that phases represent clean temporal divisions or linear developments. Schools are formed by historians of economic thought through a mixture of geographical or political similarities, certain structural factors, or broader intellectual history (Holub 2005, 56–58).

Theories of price and value are highly relevant for defining schools, yet theories of money are not. Indeed, schools are only appropriate for classifying monetary theories in specific cases. When authors are identified by their school of thought in the following, this is done to demonstrate that a separate taxonomy of monetary theory is more meaningful than a categorization based on schools. Nevertheless, the following chapters are named according to the standard school classification. This corresponds to typical reading habits, and the geographical and political contexts of the schools are instructive, as they illuminate the historical background against which the authors wrote. Nevertheless, the discussed authors will be classified according to the separate taxonomy of monetary theories on which the book is based.

2.3.1 Scholasticism

Scholasticism (from Latin *schola* = school), the philosophy of the High and Late Middle Ages, did not focus on economic questions. Instead, the questions that were pursued stemmed from theological considerations. Scholasticism revived Greek philosophy, particularly that of Aristotle, and applied it to economic issues, combining it with theological thinking. Economics was considered an ethical issue. The economy was approached normatively; the search was not for economic laws, but for behavioral norms. The concept of a stationary economy created by the will of God, which was to be preserved, was inherent. Scarcity was to be dealt with through asceticism and religiously motivated restraint.

In this book, Oresme and Biel originate from this period. As Biel is very much based on Oresme, both are quite similar in their view on money. Both started to gradually escape from the purely normative analysis of scholasticism as part of the dawning Renaissance.

2.3.2 Mercantilism

The rise of absolutism in the seventeenth and eighteenth centuries was closely connected to the formation of the modern state, including its territorial demarcation and consolidation. During this period, the expansion of state power, competition between European states, and the ruler's claim to absolute sovereignty reached their peak. Mercantilist writings (from French *mercantile* = commercial) shared a common orientation towards these state interests. A central assumption of economic thought at the time was that the increased utilization of idle resources could help to finance the state's growing expenditures. In this sense, mercantilism was an integral part of the broader process of state formation.

The guiding question was how to make one's own state richer and more powerful. Consequently, the focus lay on strengthening princely power rather than promoting the welfare of the population. After the era of Christian scholasticism, mercantilism represented a secularization of economics: that is, it was less a coherent theoretical school than a collection of economic policy doctrines, shaped by the diverse geographical and political contexts in which the authors lived. For princes, the key variables were a large population and sufficient money to finance courtly opulence and military might. Depending on the resources available, states developed differing economic policy recommendations.

The book covers the work of several authors from this period, in the following order: Copernicus, Bodin, Davanzati, Law, Locke, Galiani, Hamilton, and Cantillon. These authors are all very different and span a wide time period. Copernicus could be considered a (late) scholastic author, while Cantillon could also be considered an early classical author. The ideas of these authors were all anchored in a metal standard, even though they dealt with alternatives, such as paper money, to varying degrees. However, they have completely different ideas about how paper money can work. Some of them, such as Locke and Hamilton, hold clearly opposing views on paper money.

2.3.3 Cameralism

Cameralism (from Latin *camera* = chamber, meaning the prince's treasury) is often understood as the German form of mercantilism. In the Holy Roman Empire, the interests of individual princes and states took precedence, meaning that it was often the princes' officials who dealt with economic issues, as part of their official duties. While mercantilism focused on money and trade, cameralism focused on economic development.

Of all the thinkers in this book, only Justi can be clearly placed in this school. However, he might be considered a late-cameralist, as he was already influenced by liberal ideas, including those relating to monetary theory.

2.3.4 Classical Economics

Classical economic thought originated in England and Scotland, where the industrialization process began and fundamentally challenged older economic ideas. The rapid expansion of industry emphasized the increasing significance of the division of labor, competition, and foreign trade, all of which became key themes in classical economics. In this context, value theory played a pivotal role in shaping the classical school's abstract and deductive approach. Meanwhile, money, it was said, was regarded as a veil that did not alter the real processes of production and exchange (Humphrey 1991).

The book covers the work of several authors from this period: Hume, Thornton, Ricardo, Tooke, and Macleod. Together, they represent different stages in the development of monetary debates in Great Britain. Hume describes the prevailing specie system; Thornton and Ricardo discuss the introduction of inconvertible paper money; Tooke discusses the importance of purely credit money creation; and Macleod takes this idea to an extreme, proposing a monetary system based primarily on private credit money. Apart from language and geography, the authors have little in common. In fact, they oppose each other in their debates. Even the concept of money as a veil in classical economics must be sought out in their works.

2.3.5 The German Historical School

The German Historical School emerged from cameralism and the Romantic ideals of the early nineteenth century. In some respects, it was also a counter-movement to classical economics. This school emphasized the importance of institutions and the historical context of the economy, and was deeply rooted in German intellectual history. The integration of ethical questions was also a key feature. The "social question," which arose in the decades after the Napoleonic Wars due to widespread poverty, was the driving force. With a close connection to the state, people pursued a third way between capitalism and socialism, attempting to justify social policy scientifically.

This school is represented by Müller and Knapp in this book. Müller stands for the romantic roots of the historical school, while Knapp represents the late historical school. The two have less in common than is often claimed. Knapp rejects Müller's influence on his theory outright and is highly skeptical of Müller's speculative language. While Knapp clearly opposes metallism, Müller's position on this matter is unclear, as he attempts to achieve a synthesis.

2.3.6 Marx and Marxism

Karl Marx (1818–1883) offered a revolutionary response to the "social question." Drawing on the work of socialist thinkers such as Saint-Simon, Fourier, and Owen, and influenced by Hegelian philosophy and classical economics, Marx developed an economic theory centered on the labor theory of value. From this, he derived the concept of exploitation. Marx became the central reference point in socialist thought.

In this book, Hilferding also represents this school of thought. Marx derived money as a commodity in his analysis of the value form, while Hilferding interpreted Marx's sketches on credit money from the third volume of Capital. As Marx's analysis was unfinished, there are many different interpretations of money in Marxism.

2.3.7 Neoclassical Economics

Neoclassical economics shares many of the fundamental assumptions of classical economics, but in terms of methodology, it represents a significant development. It emerged in the late nineteenth century, during a period of high industrialization and rapid technological change. The analytical perspective shifted from a historical or societal view to an individualistic one, with economic actors modelled as rational individuals who maximize utility (households) or profit (firms), based on subjective value theories. At the center of neoclassical analysis is the problem of scarcity, along with the associated question of how limited resources can be allocated efficiently.

The book covers the work of Menger, Wicksell, Fisher, and Schumpeter from this period. A consistent approach to money is hard to find in neoclassical economics or among these authors. Many neoclassical economists are not interested in the subject at all. Menger, Fisher, and Wicksell take very different approaches to neoclassical monetary theory. However, Schumpeter could be placed in any period, as he was an eclectic thinker who drew from various strands of thought.

2.4 Serial Contextualism Between Episteme and Unit Ideas

This book compares ideas in monetary theory from the late Middle Ages to those of the recent past. This approach can be subjected to a fundamental criticism. Such a comparison presupposes the existence of timeless ideas, despite the fact that the need for historical reconstruction is strongly emphasized throughout this book. This criticism is most evident in the work of Michel Foucault, who argues that thinking is limited by the existing power structures of the time.

In his book *The Order of Things* (1966), Foucault declares that every historical period has underlying epistemic assumptions and ways of thinking that determine what constitutes truth and acceptable discourse on a given subject. "In any given culture and at any given moment, there is always only one episteme that defines the conditions of possibility of all knowledge, whether expressed in a theory or silently invested in a practice" (Foucault 1966, 168). As the books' subtitle—*An Archaeology of the Human Sciences*—suggests, Foucault wants to work like an archaeologist, excavating the past in layers.

Foucault's observation that thinking always takes place within power structures is of great importance to the history of economic thought. It would be a simplistic assumption to believe that transformations in policy regimes and economic ideas had no other effect apart from their acceptance (Guizzo 2021, 70). The acceptance of new ideas is closely linked to power structures. "Foucault's contribution consists in demonstrating that any scientific discourse can only be considered as the product of a certain period, that is, of a certain episteme: the genesis, legitimacy and readability of a certain scientific discourse are possible only from a determined episteme" (Herscovici 2023, 212).

This leads to a radically relativistic position that also rejects the narrative of progress in economics. Since economic theories were developed under different power structures, only synchronic comparisons are possible, not diachronic ones.

Foucault defines three epistemes for Western culture: the Renaissance, the Classical era, and the Modern era. However, as with all grand narratives, the closer you look, the more they fray. This classification, which is heavily influenced by a French perspective, does not sufficiently acknowledge genealogy (Herscovici 2023, 214), and conversely, it downplays differences within the epistemes (e.g., between Bodin and Davanzati, Foucault 1966, 169; or the emergence of Marxism, Foucault 1966, 261). Furthermore, transitions between epistemes are necessarily viewed in a simplified manner.

At the other extreme is Arthur Lovejoy and his *Great Chain of Being* (1936). According to Lovejoy, there is only a limited number of "unit ideas," a few fundamental concepts and elementary thoughts and arguments that recur time and time again. "Each age seems to evolve new species of reasonings and conclusions, even though upon the same old problems. But the truth is that the number of essentially distinct philosophical ideas or dialectical motives is [...] decidedly limited [...]. The seeming novelty of many a system is due solely to the novelty of the application or arrangement of the old elements which enter into it. When this is realized, the history as a whole should look a much more manageable thing" (Lovejoy 1933, 4).

Compared to Foucault, the logic here is reversed. This results in a radically positivist position. Comparisons across time are not just possible, but also desirable. Diachronic analysis is of particular interest, as it is more useful than synchronic analysis.

This book aims to take a middle ground. On the one hand, theories should be considered within their historical context to understand them in their time. Therefore, it is important not to ignore the historical contexts in which ideas circulate. However, contextualization tends toward a micro-perspective. Therefore, it is important to identify traditions and lines of thought. David Armitage's concept of "serial contextualism" provides the basis for this.

According to Armitage, Lovejoy's timeless unit ideas and diachronic histories are not reasonable in their current form. In most cases, the unit ideas have undergone a decisive revaluation at some point in the last 300 years. Armitage argues that Lovejoy's perspective that "the biography of an idea could be written as if it had a quasi-biological continuity and identity through time" is not adequate (Armitage 2012, 497).

Armitage proposes a transtemporal history. "Transtemporal history is not transhistorical: it is time-bound not timeless, to avoid the dangers of reification and denial of agency inherent in Lovejoy's abstract, atemporal history of ideas, for example. It also stresses the mechanisms of connection between moments and is therefore concerned with questions of concrete transmission, tradition and reception, again unlike the traditional history of ideas which assumed but did not investigate how ideas travelled materially and institutionally across time" (Armitage 2012, 498).

The approach taken in this book is therefore one of "serial contextualism." This entails "the reconstruction of a sequence of distinct contexts in which identifiable agents strategically deployed existing languages to effect definable goals such as legitimation and delegitimation, persuasion and dissuasion, consensus-building and radical innovation, for instance" (Armitage 2012, 498).

The book realizes this approach through the detailed historical contextualization of the examined works. Furthermore, rather than comparing theories in isolation, it compares them diachronically using a multidimensional, function-oriented classification framework—namely, the presented taxonomy of monetary theories.

References

Armitage, David. 2012. What's the big idea? Intellectual history and the Longue Durée. *History of European Ideas* 38:493–507.

Blaug, Mark. 1990. On the historiography of economics. *Journal of the History of Economics* 12 (1): 27–37.

Blaug, Mark. 2001. No history of ideas, please, we're economists. *Journal of Economic Perspectives* 15 (1): 145–164.

Blaug, Mark. 2002. Is there really progress in economics?: knowledge, truth and the history of economic thought. In *Is There Progress in Economics?* 21–41. Cheltenham: Edward Elgar Publishing.
Blaug, Mark. 2003. Rational vs. historical reconstruction—a counter-note on Signorino's note on Blaug. *European Journal of the History of Economic Thought* 10 (4): 607–608.
Brunner, Otto. 1949. *Adeliges Landleben und europäischer Geist*. Salzburg: Otto Müller.
Fisher, Irving. 1929. Fisher, Irving. In *Die Volkswirtschaftslehre der Gegenwart in Selbstdarstellungen*, vol. 2, 1–14. Leipzig: Verlag Felix Meiner.
Foucault, Michel. 1966. *The Order of Things*, 1994. New York: Vintage Books.
Guizzo, Danielle. 2021. Reassessing Foucault: power in the history of political economy. *International Journal of Political Economy.* 50 (1): 60–74.
Helmstädter, Ernst. 1994. Die Geschichte der Nationalökonomie als Geschichte ihres Fortschritts. In *Geschichte der Nationalökonomie*, 3rd ed., 1–13. Munich: Vahlen.
Herscovici, Alain. 2023. *Value, Historicity, and Economic Epistemology: An Archaeology of Economic Science*. Cham: Palgrave Macmillan.
Holub, Hans-Werner. 2005. *Eine Einführung in die Geschichte des ökonomischen Denkens*. In *Band I: Methodologische Vorbemerkungen, Altertum, Mittelalter*. München: Lit-Verlag.
Humphrey, Thomas M. 1991. Nonneutrality of money in classical monetary thought. *Economic Review* 77:3–15. Federal Reserve Bank of Richmond.
Kruse, Alfred. 1994. *Geschichte der volkswirtschaftlichen Theorien*. 6th ed. Berlin: Duncker & Humblot.
Lovejoy, Arthur. 1933. *The Great Chain of Being: A Study of the History of an Idea*. Cambridge: Harvard University Press.
Neumark, Fritz. 1975. Zyklen in der Geschichte ökonomischer Ideen. *Kyklos* 28 (2): 257–285.
O'Brien, Denis P. 2007. *The Development of Monetary Economics: A Modern Perspective on Monetary Controversies*. Cheltenham: Edward Elgar.
Rorty, Richard. 1984. The historiography of philosophy: four genres. In *Philosophy in History: Essays on the Historiography of Philosophy*, 49–75. Cambridge: Cambridge University Press.
Schefold, Bertram. 2009. Geschichte der Wirtschaftstheorie und Wirtschaftsgeschichte: Einleitung. *Jahrbuch für Wirtschaftsgeschichte.* 50 (1): 9–25.

[illegible] 2008. [illegible] New York: Palgrave Macmillan.

[illegible]

[illegible]

[illegible] New York: Vintage Books.

[illegible]

[illegible]

[illegible]

[illegible]

[illegible]

[illegible]

[illegible]

[illegible]

[illegible]

Chapter 3
Fundamentals in Monetary History

Studying the history of money is essential for any exploration of the history of monetary thought. Claassen (1980) illuminates why this is the case:

1. First, the practical problems that economic policymakers had to deal with shifted from era to era. In this sense, many monetary theorists attempted to use their theories to provide answers to the "questions of their time."
2. On the other hand, the monetary and credit system underwent manifold (evolutionary) transformations, so that monetary theories, insofar as they took this development into account at all, were often based on the prevailing state of the monetary and financial system of their time (Claassen 1980, 1, my translation).

This chapter provides a brief chronological overview of the history of money. The topics have been selected to support an understanding of the thinkers presented in later chapters. This overview is not intended to be exhaustive; instead, it focuses on the central questions addressed by the discussed thinkers. At the same time, this chapter does not provide detailed theoretical explanations of monetary phenomena, nor does it attempt to account for the origins of money. Like the later sections on individual authors, the discussion begins in the Middle Ages, and includes pertinent technical information on coinage.

3.1 The Middle Ages

With the fall of the Roman Empire, the established monetary system deteriorated. While the Roman standard of the *solidus* was copied and continued to be minted into the early Middle Ages, decentralized minting led to a steady decrease in the gold content of coinage. Additionally, silver coins remained in use, leading to a bimetallic system. The total amount of money in circulation also decreased, such that the economy ultimately moved backward toward a barter system.

J. Greitens, *Currency and Credit Money*, Springer Studies in the History of Economic Thought, https://doi.org/10.1007/978-3-032-24113-9_3

Charlemagne introduced a much-needed reorganization of the monetary system. This was based on the work of his father, Pippin. Minting was once again placed under royal supervision and private minting rights were abolished. In 793/794, a uniform coinage system (mononominalism) was introduced in the Frankish Empire, meaning that only denominations based on the Denar system of measurement and weight were used. Gold coinage was abolished, and a silver currency in the form of the standardized Denar was introduced (monometallism). From a Carolingian pound of 408 g of silver, 240 Denarii were minted for circulation, 12 to cover minting costs, and 12 for the prince (i.e., seigniorage). Consequently, the monetary situation gradually improved, and the Denar shaped the monetary system for the next 500 years (Spufford 1988, 7–35; Steinbach 2021, 184–186; North 2009, 8–13).

The Denar, which in English was called the penny, was codified as legal tender by the Capitular of the Synod of Frankfurt (794/795): "But concerning the denarius, you should certainly be aware of our decree that in every place, in every city, and in every market, those new denarius should circulate in the same way and be accepted by all, provided that they bear our name, are made of pure silver, and are of full weight." (Fig. 3.1)

From the eleventh century onward, increasing trade and the founding of new cities led to an increased monetization of the economy. The construction of bridges and cathedrals, the introduction of taxes, and the growing consumption and wealth in cities (especially Flanders and northern Italy) in the thirteenth century furthered this growth. This period of growth in cities, trade, and the monetary economy is known as the Commercial Revolution.

From the mid-thirteenth century onward, the right to mint coins in the Holy Roman Empire passed from the emperor to the individual territories within the empire, as set out in the *Statutum in Favorem Principum* (1231/1232).

Fig. 3.1 Denar of Charlemagne (Münzkabinett der Staatlichen Museen Berlin, 18202712, Lübke und Wiedemann)

Fig. 3.2 A gold florin from 1305 (Münzkabinett der Staatlichen Museen Berlin, 18205534, Lübke und Wiedemann)

During this time, the minting of gold coins began once again in the Mediterranean region. The most significant coins were the gulden, the florin (minted in Florence starting in 1252), and zecchino (minted in Venice starting in 1284), or ducat. The northern Italian cities were wealthy enough to keep the gold content of these coins stable over the long term, as they had sufficient access to precious metals. These high-quality coins were used widely for international trade (North 2009, 15, 28–30; Spufford 1988, 10–131; Steinbach 2021, 186–188) (Fig. 3.2).

From the resumption of gold coin production in the thirteenth and fourteenth centuries until the introduction of the gold standard around 1870, the prevailing standard was bimetallism, in which silver and gold coins circulated alongside each other. In international trade, merchants tried to exploit even the slightest changes in the gold-to-silver ratio by favoring either gold or silver currency in their transactions. Precious metal markets (with trading in bars/bullion) grew significantly in the early modern period and were highly integrated internationally. However, due to fluctuations in global precious metal production, bimetallic currency systems were constantly affected by the speculative export of gold or silver (Pilar 2013, 447).

In the fourteenth century, German cities obtained the right to mint gold coins; Lübeck took advantage of this right from 1340 onward. In 1356, the Golden Bull granted the Electors of the Holy Roman Empire the right to mint gold coins as well. This marked the transfer of the coinage prerogative, including for gold coins, from cities to the princes.

Various factors made the monetary system very complicated, thus increasing the importance of money changers. Key factors in this regard included the increase in gold coins alongside silver coins, the different coin standards used by divergent issuers, and the many substandard small coins and coin token (in addition to coins made of other materials, such as marten fur for leather money in Novgorod).

The Church's prohibition on charging interest were gradually loosened, as interest was increasingly interpreted as a legitimate return for risk and foregone profits.

As a result, systems of credit were able to develop. The bill of exchange was developed as a substitute for the risky and expensive transport of precious metals and became increasingly prevalent in long-distance trade.

In Tours, the minting of large pennies (*gros tournois*) began in the middle of the thirteenth century. These coins were valued at around 4:1 in relation to the normal penny. With this development, gold coins were now used for long-distance trade, large pennies for regional trade, and pennies for local trade.

The fourteenth century marked a break in the development of the monetary system, which had been growing in a fairly steady manner up to that point. During this crisis-ridden period, coins were frequently devalued and the price of precious metals increased. Declining revenues from minting rights accelerated the frequency of devaluations. Due to the large number of princes with minting rights, the minting system also became highly fragmented (Spufford 1988, 267–338; Steinbach 2021, 188–198; North 2009, 44–6).

A Short Primer on Coin Production

The minting of coins at this time essentially involved the following steps:

1. Smelting of metal and alloy production: The raw materials for the coin alloy were melted down from bars, old coins, or other metal scraps, and an alloy was produced based on the coin standard, which specified the ratio of precious metal to other metals.
2. Bar casting: The finished alloy was then cast into bars.
3. Hammering/rolling of the bar: In the ancient world and medieval period, the cast bars were hammered out to the thickness of the future coins; in the early modern period, by contrast, they were rolled out.
4. Cutting/punching of blanks: The coin blanks were then cut from the bar, which has been brought to the correct thickness, or punched out.
5. Minting: The blanks were then placed between the upper and lower coin dies, which were then pressed together with great force to imprint the coin image onto the blank. In the ancient world and medieval period, this process was carried out by hand with a hammer, with the lower die fixed in place and the upper die guided freely. Beginning in the early modern period, machines were increasingly used to mint large-format silver coins, such as thalers.

Beginning in the eighteenth century, coins were also knurled to give them a textured edge (Steinbach 2023, 81–82).

Seigniorage refers to revenue obtained by the government through the creation of money (*ius cudendae monetae*—the right to mint). Historically, this was a royal prerogative (*iura regalia*) that could be delegated to local princes in the form of minting rights. The word is derived from the French term *seigneur* ("feudal lord"). Seigniorage creates income due to the difference between the cost of coin production—including the value of the metal and minting expenses—and the nominal value of the issued coins. This difference was typically small, usually between 0.25 and 2.5% of a coin's nominal value. While the revenues from seigniorage were thus relatively modest under stable monetary conditions, it could become an important fiscal instrument during times of crisis and war, as it was possible to manipulate the metal content and weight of the coinage, allowing profits of up to 50% to be realized. However, such debasement risked a downward spiral of inflation and other ill effects, particularly in regions that were politically fragmented, such as in the German territories, where numerous princes with minting rights competed for revenue (Steinbach 2023, 92) (Fig. 3.3).

These manufacturing techniques often produced large fluctuations in the quality and weight of the finished coins. Accordingly, in a final step the coins were typically weighed. If they were too heavy, they were then trimmed at the edges (which was possible in the absence of knurling). Alternatively, if they were too light, they would be melted down. Uneven production quality underscored the need for improved coinage techniques. Significant improvements

Fig. 3.3 Maximilian Visiting the Mint (Hans Burgkmair, 1510): A medieval mint was managed by the master of the mint. In the background of this image, the emperor stands next to the master of the mint, who is writing in an open book and checking the coinage with a set of scales fixed to the wall. On the left the image depicts the cutting of blanks, in the middle the hammering of bars, and on the right the striking of coins using a free-moving upper coin die. A young apprentice hands the blanks to the coin hammerer, who places the minted pieces in a bowl. Behind the open window a smelting furnace emits smoke. The treasure chest in the foreground is used to store the finished coins

were introduced in a gradual fashion from the seventeenth century onward. For example:

- The caster poured the bars into metal molds instead of sand molds,
- the bars were processed with rollers instead of a hammer,
- coin blanks were cut with a spindle machine instead of scissors (Fig. 3.4),
- the setter embossed the coins with a spindle machine / balancier instead of a hammer (Fig. 3.5).
- In addition, knurling was introduced using a knurling machine (Fig. 3.6).

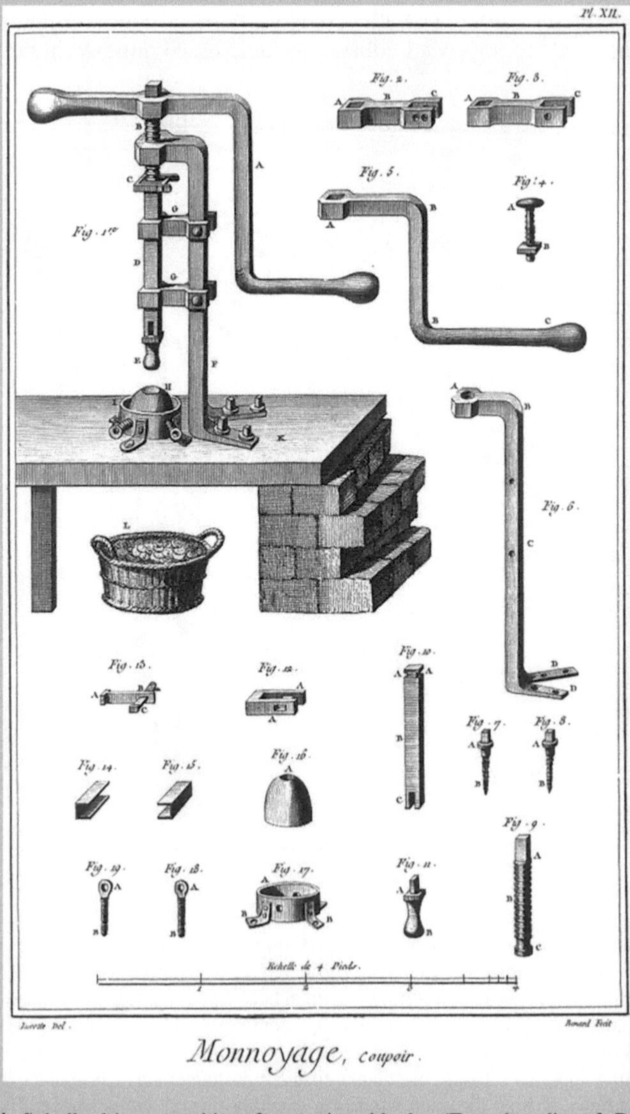

Fig. 3.4 Spindle-driven machine for cutting blanks (Encyclopedia of Diderot & d'Alembert, 1765)

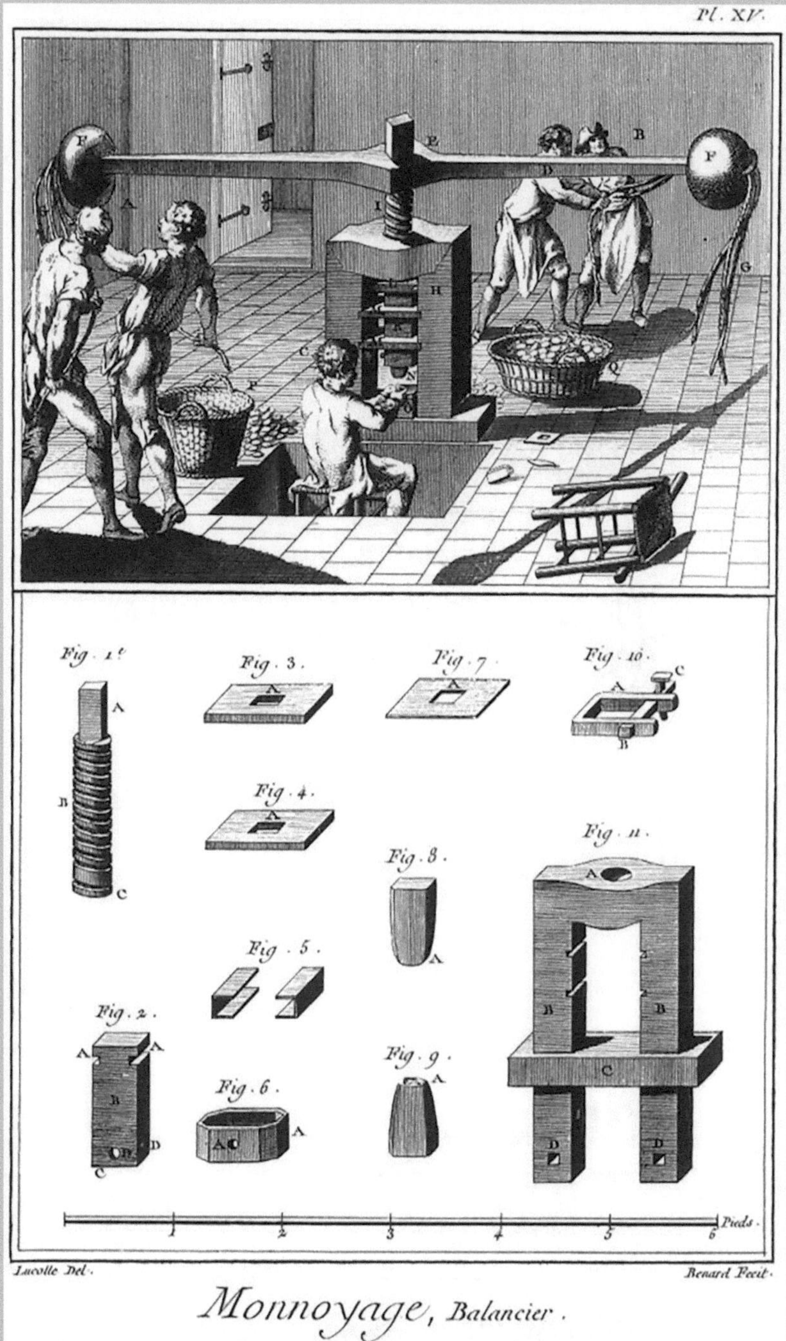

Fig. 3.5 Balancier press for minting coins (Encyclopedia of Diderot & d'Alembert, 1765)

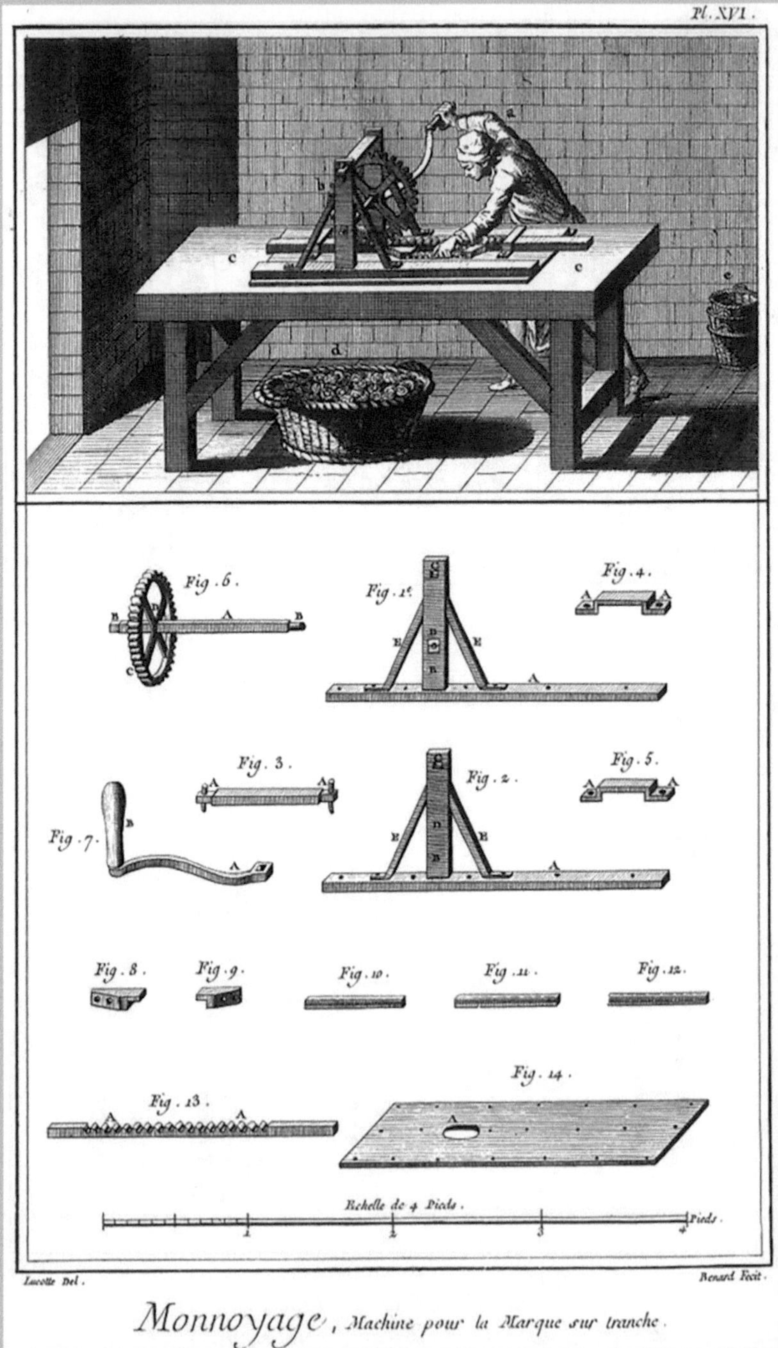

Fig. 3.6 Knurling machine for stamping the coin edge (Encyclopedia of Diderot & d'Alembert, 1765)

3.2 The Early Modern Period

Until the twelfth century, people did not experience famine and inflation as distinct phenomena. Money in the form of precious metals was considered a fixed standard, and the concept of generally dynamic monetary prices did not exist. It was only with the gradual dissolution of fixed ratios of exchange between goods in favor of market prices beginning in the eleventh century that famine and inflation were conceptualized as separate. Before the eleventh century, only *fames* (hunger) is mentioned in contemporary documents. It is not until the thirteenth century that the term *carista* (inflation) begins to appear in source documents. This shows that money was increasingly seen as a specific and independent phenomenon and not just as an ordinary commodity (Witthöft 2006, 449–451).

Letters of Exchange (Bills of Exchange)
During the Commercial Revolution of the Middle Ages, the growing need for means of payment led to the creation of new financial instruments. As coins were heavy and precious metals were scarce, transporting money was costly and risky. Consequently, merchants, particularly from the fourteenth century onward, began using bills of exchange as a form of cashless payment within their trading networks. A bill of exchange was a written order in which a merchant instructed a third party, typically based in a different city, to pay a specified sum to a beneficiary at a set time.

Thus, a bill of exchange functioned not only as a means of payment, but also as a credit instrument, bearing interest as compensation for time and risk. This method allowed merchants to access funds for purchases in trading centers without physically transporting money, and it had become widespread across the western Mediterranean and Western Europe by the fourteenth century.

From the thirteenth to the seventeenth centuries, exchange fairs, such as those held in Lyon and Frankfurt several times a year, enabled merchants to settle claims and counterclaims, with remaining balances paid in coin. In the sixteenth century, the practice of endorsement was introduced, whereby the right to redeem a bill of exchange could be transferred by writing a note on the back of it. As this could be repeated, with each previous owner remaining liable for payment, the instrument was both secure and flexible. This innovation effectively turned the bill into circulating paper—a form of merchant paper money that, although still tied to coinage, facilitated increasingly standardized and efficient cashless transactions (North 2009, 87).

Fig. 3.7 Thaler from the County of Schlick from 1525 (Münzkabinett der Staatlichen Museen Berlin, 18200819, Lübke und Wiedemann)

As a result of the Great Bullion Famine—a particularly large shortage of precious metals that occurred in Europe in the 1460s (Day 1978)—old mines were put back into operation and new silver veins were discovered in rapid succession. Important mining locations during this period included the Schwaz deposits in Tyrol; the silver districts of Schneeberg, Annaberg, and Buchholz in Saxony; and the Joachimstal silver mine in Bohemia (Fig. 3.7). Rising silver production meant that large silver coins could be minted with a value similar to the gold coins that formerly dominated long-distance trade. While previously there had been a shortage of currency, there was now an abundant supply of coinage, including in particular silver thalers, which were much heavier than medieval gold ducat but of equal value (North 2000, 83–85) (Fig. 3.8).

During the latter part of the sixteenth century, many European silver mines became unprofitable. This was mainly due to competition from mines in the Americas, where production was cheaper. Beginning in the 1530s, considerable silver deposits were identified in various locations in Mexico, and in 1545, the famous Silver Mountain of Potosí was discovered in the Viceroyalty of Peru. The name of this mine, which contained the world's largest known silver deposits, became synonymous with limitless wealth. In the mid-1550s, a more efficient amalgamation process was introduced, providing Europe with even more silver at lower costs (Fig. 3.9).

In the second half of the sixteenth century, the increasing supply of precious metals led to rising prices, a period known as the Price Revolution. While price increases had previously been attributed to currency depreciation, a new explanation was now necessary, as the supply of precious metals was increasing. Intra-European trade distributed precious metals throughout Europe, causing price increases to spread further east (Fig. 3.10).

Fig. 3.8 This altarpiece from 1521 in St. Annen Church (Annaberg-Buchholz) features images of silver mining in the Erzgebirge region

During the sixteenth century, several attempts were made to reorganize the currency system of the Holy Roman Empire. Before 1551, 113 types of gold coin were in circulation, issued by 63 authorities within the Empire as well as 50 from abroad. In addition, 134 types of silver coin were minted by 70 authorities within the Empire as well as 26 outside it. The *gold Rhenish guilder* was used as a unit of account for larger sums across the Holy Roman Empire (Volckart 2017, XXXIII, XXXIf). The vast majority of the Imperial Estates desired the standardization of the coinage system for two reasons: firstly, to simplify and promote trade, and secondly, to restrict trade in the coins themselves. The differences between nominal and metal values necessitated constant exchange and invited speculation.

The process of harmonizing the imperial currency was protracted: it began with the Augsburg Imperial Coinage Order of 1551, continued with the Diet of Augsburg in 1559, and concluded in 1566 once an agreement was reached with the Electorate of Saxony. A Saxon thaler with reduced silver content was established as the standard for minting thalers across the Empire; inferior thalers from certain territories

Fig. 3.9 Cerro del Potosí (Pedro de Cieza de León, Crónica del Perú, Parte primera, 1553)

were rejected, while others were incorporated into the system. Silver was the leading coinage metal.

Responsibilities for coinage were distributed among the imperial circles (*Reichskreise*). While this system did not regulate coinage standards and never achieved universal adoption, it did provide a stable governance structure for over 200 years. After the Kipper and Wipper period (1620–1622) during the Thirty Years' War, the system was reinstated. The most important coinage standard following the Thirty Years' War was the Leipzig Coinage Standard of 1690. Introduced by Electoral Saxony, Electoral Brandenburg, and the Duchy of Brunswick-Lüneburg, it aimed to combat coinage decay and the influx of foreign coins. Adopted by many territories, it ultimately became the imperial standard in 1738.

With the Imperial Coinage Regulations of the mid-sixteenth century and the subsequent shift of responsibility to the Imperial Circles, so-called Probation Days were held. At this regular event, the various Imperial Estates that had been granted the right to mint coins would convene to mutually test the quality of their coins in a process known as the Trial of the Pyx. The results were summarized in expert reports and published. These Probation Days and the associated assayers (*Kreiswardeine*) were crucial for monitoring and stabilizing the imperial coinage system (Volckart 2017, LXVIIf, LXXIII; Schön 2008, 467, 486, 493–494; Witthöft 1993) (Fig. 3.11).

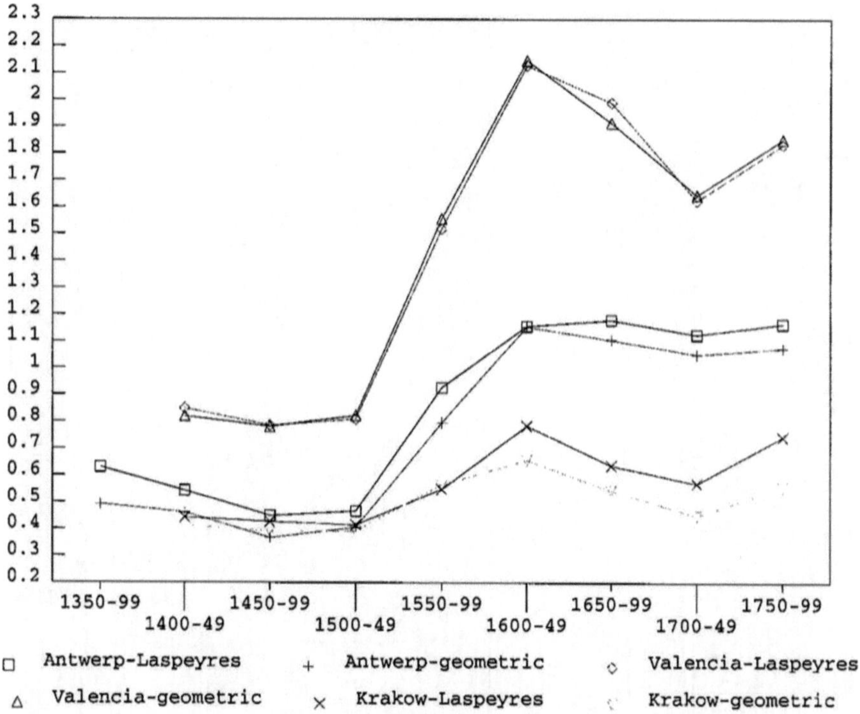

Fig. 3.10 Price indices in Valencia, Antwerp, and Kraków during the Price Revolution (Allen 2001, 425)

England made a gradual and unplanned transition from early modern bimetallism, in which silver played a leading role, to a gold standard, becoming the first European country to do so. This process began with the abandonment of seigniorage revenues in 1666. With the aim of increasing the quantity and quality of coins in circulation, the government allowed anyone to bring precious metals to the Royal Mint at the Tower of London to have coins produced free of charge. This reduced transaction costs, thus narrowing the "melting points"—that is, the thresholds at which exporting coins at their precious metal value became worthwhile. This encouraged the export of silver coins.

The price of gold in England fell due to large gold discoveries, especially in the Portuguese colony of Brazil. The Methuen Treaty (named after the English envoy in Lisbon, John Methuen), which was concluded between England and Portugal in 1703, opened the Portuguese (and by extension Brazilian) market to the English woolen cloth industry in exchange for a tariff reduction on Portuguese wines. The Portuguese trade deficit was paid by the export of gold, which significantly increased the gold supply in England. Gold from the English colonies in West Africa was the most important source of gold from 1664 to 1816. This gold was used to mint the

Fig. 3.11 Trial of the Pyx at the Probation Day of 1691: Frontispiece of Leucht, Christian Leonhard. 1692. Neuer Müntz-Tractat Von Approbirtén und devalvirten Guldinern: In the background, the masters of the mint are negotiating monetary policy, such as the coin minting quota. In the foreground, the three assayers of the imperial circles of Franconia, Bavaria, and Swabia are testing coins

Gresham's Law

Henry Dunning Macleod first coined the term Gresham's Law in 1858 (Macleod 1858, 476–477). Sir Thomas Gresham (1519–1579) was a founder of the London Stock Exchange and financial advisor to Queen Elizabeth. Just 3 days after her accession to the throne in 1558, he wrote to the Queen to explain that the deteriorating condition of her father Henry VIII's silver coins had caused an exodus of gold coins from England: "May it please your Majesty to understand that the first occasion of the foil of Exchange grew out of the act of the King's Majesty, your late father, in debasing his coin from 6 ounces fine to 3 ounces fine. Whereupon the Exchange fell from 19.8 to 18.4. And this was the cause of the export of all your fine gold out of this your realm" (Aldenham 1900, 431–432; MacFarlane 1845, 100–101).

The devalued silver coins were nominally worth more domestically than in the form of silver bars abroad. For gold coins, this relationship was inversed. Consequently, gold coins were taken abroad en masse. To address this problem, Elizabeth reformed the coinage system and reintroduced better coins.

Macleod illustrates this "Law" with a quotation from a pamphlet written during the Great Recoinage of 1696: "When two sorts of Coins are current in the same nation, of like Value by denomination, but not intrinsically, that which has the least Value will be current, and the other as much as possible hoarded, or exported. Which may be expressed more shortly thus: Bad money always drives good money out from circulation" (Macleod 1879, 64). Macleod summarizes this insight as follows: "The worst form of currency in circulation regulates the value of the whole currency, and drives all other forms of currency out of circulation" (Macleod 1896, 39).

Given a fixed nominal ratio of exchange between gold and silver coins, the bad money (i.e., with a metal value lower than the nominal value, in this case silver coins) displaces the good money (i.e., with a metal value higher than nominal value, in this case gold coins), the latter of which is exported or used as a store of value. It is from this observation that Gresham's Law is derived. Essentially, Gresham's Law states that "bad money drives out the good." Due to the conceptual similarities, Macleod later spoke of the "Law of Oresme, Copernicus, and Gresham" (Macleod 1896, 39; Balch 1908). It must be noted that under flexible exchange rates and full transparency, Gresham's Law does not apply.

Guinea, a coin named after the Gold Coast in West Africa (Kalkmann 1895, 2–14; Pilar 2013, 458) (Fig. 3.12).

As the full-weight silver coins were worth more as precious metal bars abroad than as coins in England—i.e., one received more for a gram of gold in England than on the continent—gold was imported to England in large quantities, while silver was exported. Silver coins increasingly disappeared from circulation, leaving

Fig. 3.12 Five Guineas from 1681 (Münzkabinett der Staatlichen Museen Berlin, 18227426, Sonnenwald)

gold coins available in abundance. Gold became the means of exchange for merchants, thus establishing a de facto gold standard in England. Although England had switched to a gold currency, it was not until 1774 that gold coins were declared legal tender. Silver minting was abandoned in 1798, and the gold standard was officially adopted in 1816 (Kalkmann 1895, 42–46; Pilar 2013, 459).

In the second half of the seventeenth century, complaints grew throughout Europe that the scarcity of money was hindering economic growth. Blame was directed first and foremost at the Dutch and British East India Companies, which imported goods from Asia in exchange for silver. In the German Empire, a shortage of silver led to a renewed debasement of silver coins below the standard established by the Leipzig Coinage Treaty of 1690. This debasement caused confusion while also eroding trust in the monetary system.

In the mid-eighteenth century, the larger and more economically powerful states of the Holy Roman Empire sought to introduce stable coinage outside of established imperial system. Prussia introduced the Graumann Reichsthaler in 1750, while Austria released the Conventionsthaler in 1748/53. Both countries sought to circulate these coins beyond their borders and increase seigniorage revenues. Austria was particularly successful with the Maria Theresa Thaler, which bore the image of Empress Maria Theresa and continued to be minted long after her death in 1780.

From around 1350 to the introduction of the gold standard in the 1870s, there were alternating phases of acute coin shortages, massive devaluations, and inflation, as well as periods of stability. Throughout this time, the problems of bimetallism—namely, fluctuations in the valuation of precious metals and the necessity of adjusting the official exchange ratios—were present. Paper money, whether private or state-issued, played an increasingly important role in compensating for these fluctuations.

Isaac Newton (1643–1727) as Master of the Royal Mint

Sir Isaac Newton (1643–1727) was appointed Warden of the Royal Mint in 1696, the same year as the failed reform effort known as the Great Recoinage. Three years later, he was named to replace the deceased Master of the Royal Mint. From the outset, Newton sought to stamp out fraud and prevent counterfeiting. To combat "culling," the selection and melting down of light coins, he promoted the introduction of machine-made coins called milled coins, which could be produced with almost identical technical properties. This reduced the rate of deviation from prescribed weights by around half (Craig 1963).

However, the most notable consequence of his work at the mint came in 1717 with his involvement in adjusting the "mint ratio"—that is, the legally defined relative value of gold to silver, which had been higher in England than on the Continent. This divergence meant that, despite the prohibition on exporting and melting coins, it was profitable to export the comparatively undervalued metal (silver) and import the comparatively overvalued one (gold). Eager to adjust the exchange rate, the government asked Newton for his opinion.

On August 12, 1717, Newton responded: "And to Compass this last there seems nothing more requisite than to take off about 10 d or 12 d [denarius, or penny] from the Price of the Guinea." Thus, while Newton wanted an adjustment of 10–12 pence, after consulting with the government, he apparently concluded that a reduction of 6 pence would be sufficient, as any greater reduction would be unacceptable to the public (Craig 1946, 106–109). "But if onely six pence were taken off at Present it wou'd diminish the Temptation to Export or Melt down the Silver Coyne, and the Effect wou'd shew hereafter, better than it can appear at Present with further Reduction would be most convenient for the Publick" (Newton 1717).

In another paragraph of Newton's letter, we find the following observation, which can be read as warning: "If things be let alone till Silver Mony be a little Scarcer the Gold will fall of it selfe, for People are allready backward in giving Silver for Gold, and will in a little time refuse to make Payments in Silver without a Premium, And this Premium will be an Abatement in the Value of the Gold, and so the Question is whether Gold shall be lowered by the Government or let alone till it falls of it selfe for the Want of Silver Monys" (Newton 1717).

In December, the government made a 6-pence adjustment, but this did not stop the outflow of silver, and the transition to gold continued.

The economic development that began in the early modern period would not have been possible without the rise of more complex institutional frameworks. This included the formation of a financial system. Initially, a focus was placed on improving public finances. Thanks to their developing financial systems, the leading states of the time—England and the Netherlands—were able to borrow large sums of money at low interest rates. This development is referred to as the Financial Revolution (Dickson 1967). A prerequisite was the constitutionally binding “credible commitment” of the ruler, restricted by parliament after the Glorious Revolution, to repay his debts and maintain institutional stability (North and Weingast 1989).

The Bank of England was founded in 1694, 6 years after the Glorious Revolution and 2 years before the Great Recoinage, both of which were initiated by William III. His progressive policies shaped the English Financial Revolution. William III’s financial difficulties resulted in merchants being granted the royal privilege of establishing a chartered private note bank in the form of a joint-stock company, in exchange for a cheap loan. Unlike the Bank of Amsterdam, the Bank of England could issue banknotes not only against bullion, but also by discounting commercial bills. These notes were convertible into coins. Combined with its monopoly on issuing notes within a 60-mile radius of the City of London and the prohibition of any other joint-stock banking in England, this innovation enabled the Bank of England to acquire a prominent position in the English banking system during the second half of the eighteenth century, gradually leading to a two-tier financial system. The state’s borrowing was carried out via the Bank of England, and its banknotes began to dominate payment transactions. The issuance of paper money also compensated for weaknesses in the coinage system (Tilly 2003, 56–60).

These new institutions were created by the wealthy bourgeoisie, who held enlightened, capitalist ideas, as well as through legal regulations. The absolute authority previously claimed by rulers was thus limited. This development was associated with the emergence of structures that subsequently made it possible to finance private investments—a prerequisite for industrialization.

3.3 The Era of the Gold Standard

For a long time, England was the only country with a gold standard. Following the discovery of gold in California and elsewhere in the nineteenth century, almost all European countries gradually adopted the gold standard. This era came to an end with the outbreak of the First World War. Due to the declining demand for silver as a coin metal, silver prices collapsed within a few years.

Gradually, banknotes began to replace coins in circulation. In England, banknotes exceeded coins by the mid-nineteenth century. In Germany and France, however, coins remained the dominant means of payment well into the twentieth century. Alongside coins and banknotes, another form of credit money became increasingly significant in the nineteenth century—namely, book or giro money. By the eve of the First World War, over 80% of the money supply in England consisted of bank deposits. This figure was 68% in the German Empire and 44% in France (Hesse 2013, 152).

Until 1914, almost all central banks in Europe held a monopoly on note issuance. A certain proportion of this issuance had to be backed by gold and other assets to ensure redeemability: this reserve ratio was one-third in England, France, and Germany. Gold continued to form the basis for note issuance, and there was an obligation to redeem banknotes for gold. However, when the war began in 1914, demand for money increased and, as a result, gold redeemability was suspended (North 2009, 145–180).

References

Aldenham, Lord. 1900. *A Colloquy on Currency*. London: Wilson.

Allen, R. C. 2001. The great divergence in European wages and prices from the Middle Ages to the First World War. *Explorations in Economic History* 38:411–447.

Balch, Thomas Willich. 1908. The law of Gresham, Copernicus and Gresham. *Proceedings of the American Philosophical Society* 47:18–29.

Claassen, Emil-Maria. 1980. *Grundlagen der Geldtheorie*. 2nd ed. Berlin: Springer.

Craig, John. 1946. *Newton at the Mint*. Cambridge: Cambridge University Press.

Craig, John. 1963. Isaac Newton and the Counterfeiters. *Notes and Records of the Royal Society of London* 18 (2): 136–145.

Day, John. 1978. The Great Bullion Famine of the Fifteenth Century. *Past & Present* 78:3–54.

Dickson, Peter G. M. 1967. *The Financial Revolution in England: A Study in the Development of Public Credit, 1688–1756*. London: Macmillan.

Hesse, Jan-Ottmar. 2013. *Wirtschaftsgeschichte*. Frankfurt: Campus.

Kalkmann, Philipp. 1895. *Englands Übergang zur Goldwährung im achtzehnten Jahrhundert*. Strassburg: Verlag von Karl J. Trübner.

MacFarlane, Charles. 1845. *The Life of Sir Thomas Gresham*. London: Charles Knight.

Macleod, Henry Dunning. 1858. *Elements of Political Economy*. London: Longman.

Macleod, Henry Dunning. 1879. *Economics for Beginners*. New York: Homans.

Macleod, Henry Dunning. 1896. *The History of Economics*. London: Bliss.

Newton, Isaac. 1717. *Response to an order to report on gold and silver coin in Britain*. MINT 19/2/111-16. National Archives. https://www.newtonproject.ox.ac.uk/view/texts/normalized/MINT00322.

North, Michael. 2000. Münzpolitik in der ersten Hälfte des 16. Jahrhunderts: Das Heilige Römische Reich und Sachsen im europäischen Kontext. In Schefold, Bertram (Hrsg.) (2000): Vademecum zu drei klassischen Schriften frühneuzeitlicher Münzpolitik, Düsseldorf: Verlag Wirtschaft und Finanzen, S. 82–98.

North, Michael. 2009. *Kleine Geschichte des Geldes*. München: Beck.

North, Douglass, and Barry R. Weingast. 1989. Constitutions and commitment: the evolution of institutions governing public choice in seventeenth-century England. *The Journal of Economic History* 49 (4): 803–832.

Pilar, Nogues-Marco. 2013. Competing bimetallic ratios: Amsterdam, London, and Bullion Arbitrage in mid-eighteenth century. *The Journal of Economic History* 73 (2): 445–476.

Schön, Gerhard. 2008. Die Münzprobationstage im Alten Reich. *Abhandlungen der Braunschweigischen Wissenschaftlichen Gesellschaft* 61:465–496.

Spufford, Peter. 1988. *Money and Its Use in Medieval Europe*. Cambridge: Cambridge University Press.

Steinbach, Sebastian. 2021. *Einführung in die Wirtschaftsgeschichte. Band 3: Mittelalter*. Verlag: W. Kohlhammer.

Steinbach, Sebastian. 2023. *Numismatik. Eine Einführung in Theorie und Praxis*. 2nd ed. Stuttgart: Verlag W. Kohlhammer.

Tilly, Richard. 2003. *Geld und Kredit in der Wirtschaftsgeschichte*. Stuttgart: Franz Steiner Verlag.

Volckart, Oliver. 2017. Einleitung. In *Eine Währung für das Reich. Die Akten der Münztage zu Speyer 1549 und 1557*, XXX–LXXXVI. Stuttgart: Franz Steiner.

Witthöft, Harald. 1993. Die Münzordnung und das Grundgewicht im Deutschen Reich vom 16. Jahrhundert bis 1871/72. In *Geld und Währung vom 16. Jahrhundert bis zur Gegenwart*, 45–68. Stuttgart: Steiner.

Witthöft, Harald. 2006. Über Korn und Brot – Geld und Münze. *Vierteljahrschrift für Sozial- und Wirtschaftsgeschichte* 93 (4): 438–479.

Chapter 4
Key Concepts in Monetary Theory

This essay stems from the conviction [...] that currency policy is a field in which there is no sense whatever in approaching practical problems before we have become clear on the fundamental questions of money and have removed the paralysing influence of differences of principle. More than elsewhere, practice here must and can rest on theoretical understanding.—Schumpeter (1918, 149)

In 1864, Bruno Hildebrand advocated a stage theory of economic development. The methods by which goods are exchanged is the determining criterion of this theory: "Either goods are exchanged directly for other goods, or the noble metals, money, are used as a medium of exchange, or finally, goods are exchanged for the promise to repay the same or an equal value in the future, i.e., for credit. [...] Based on these three possible types of transactions, three economic systems develop: the natural economy, the monetary economy, and the credit economy" (Hildebrand 1864, 4, my translation).

The natural economy, which is a barter economy, is his starting point. "The monetary economy can therefore only develop once prosperity has already been achieved, when people produce more than they need. The credit economy, on the other hand, can only emerge when regulated monetary transactions are fully developed, but the sluggishness of money circulation is already being felt and the need for simplification of means of payment has been awakened. Before that, credit transactions are only an exception to the rule and a consequence of momentary insolvency" (Hildebrand 1864, 4, my translation). The stages follow one another, but are not strictly chronological; rather, they develop through gradual transitions.

Hildebrand's approach emphasizes the importance of a monetary economy and raises key questions in monetary theory. Why does money exist, and what is the relationship between money in the narrower sense (currency) and money in the broader sense (credit)? This section will outline some fundamental terms relating to the authors to be presented.

J. Greitens, *Currency and Credit Money*, Springer Studies in the History of Economic Thought, https://doi.org/10.1007/978-3-032-24113-9_4

4.1 The Functions of Money

"Money is that money does" (Walker 1878, 405). This theory-less, tautological and somewhat helpless-sounding sentence, which is attributed to various economists—first and foremost Francis Walker—puts the question of what money actually does at the beginning of monetary theory, rather than starting with abstract definitions. Therefore, the usual introduction to monetary theory is functional, describing some characteristics of money without providing a broader definition of its nature or essence. The most common approach is to divide the functions that are supposed to define money into four categories. These categories will serve as the basis for the following discussion.[1]

- *Medium of exchange*: Money is a general medium of exchange, intended to simplify the exchange of goods by acting as intermediating good, as a commodity in circulation.
- *Means of payment*: Money serves as a standard of deferred payment used to give credit or pay debts. It is not about the exchange of goods, but the necessary financial transactions required to allow an exchange to fall apart in time and value.
- *Store of value*: Money is used to transfer purchasing power from the present to the future. The degree of liquidity is used to differentiate between money, which is used to store purchasing power, and other assets, which are used to achieve revenue.
- *Unit of account*: Money is used to compare the value of commodities and steer or manage economic operations. In this role, money serves to make the value of goods comparable. This comparability provides signals for directing economic exchange. In the sense of Max Weber, money as a unit of account is the "most comprehensive means of economic calculation, that is, the most formally rational means for the orientation of economic action" (Weber 1921, 173). This is an abstract function of money, rather than a concrete one, because money does not have to be present in any concrete form for this function to be carried out.

The functions of money as a medium of exchange and a means of payment are often confused. As a medium of exchange, money solves the problem of the double coincidence of wants. All goods can be exchanged for the generally accepted medium of exchange, and the prices of goods are expressed in relation to it. In contrast, the function of money as a means of payment facilitates the decoupling of transactions. Transactions fall apart in terms of value and time. Therefore, credit is essential for a complex economy based on the division of labor. The functions of medium of exchange (as currency) and means of payment (as credit money) have always been performed jointly.

From today's perspective, it seems that the four functions that define money in Europe apply cumulatively to the euro. However, this is by no means necessary;

[1] Karl Knies (1885) was the first economist in Germany to develop a monetary theory based on the functions of money. In terms of the historical approach of this book, see Feliu (2019).

historically, it was the exception rather than the rule. For instance, medieval pennies served as a medium of exchange and a unit of account, but due to frequent debasement of the coinage, they were only of limited use as a store of value. Medieval accounting coins were often high-value and used in trade as a unit of account, but they were rarely minted as they were too large and impractical. In eighteenth-century England, the silver shilling remained the unit of account, even though hardly any silver coins were in circulation during the transition to the gold standard. The few silver coins that remained in circulation served as a store of value and were often melted down for this purpose, but they were no longer used as a medium of exchange. The stones on the island of Yap were too heavy to be used as a medium of exchange, but they served as a pledge or token of payment. Cigarettes could fulfil the function of a medium of exchange on the black markets of post-war Germany, but not as a unit of account or store of value.

4.2 Forms and Quantities of Money

> *In no other case is it difficult to distinguish between an object and a claim to it, but in the case of money, claims can serve as money substitutes. I cannot ride on a claim to a horse and everybody realizes that the creation of such a claim does not increase the available quantity of horses and that it would be inadmissible double-counting to put a horse and a claim thereto on the same level. But with a claim to money, I can in certain circumstances do exactly the same as with the object to which the claim gives tide.*—Schumpeter (1918, 167)

Money includes the narrower concept of currency, or money as a medium of exchange (in Schumpeter's analogy, the horses), issued by a central bank. Credit money is the means of payment (in Schumpeter's analogy, the claims to horses) and are generally accepted as money. They are usually issued by commercial banks and temporary.

Currency is the official means of payment that is legally accepted. As legal tender, currency enables the final and definitive settlement of an obligation. In contrast, private credit money is a promise to pay currency, representing a deferral of final settlement. In this sense, currency acts as a medium of exchange, even if it is not a commodity itself. While currency is issued by the state, credit money is created by private entities in response to demand. As it usually represents a claim on currency, credit money is linked to the currency. Whereas credit money always originates from private credit, currency can consist of commodity money (e.g., gold), can be created through loans (as in the open market operations of central banks), or can be issued directly by the state as fiat money.

Lorenz von Stein identifies these three forms of currency. In addition to coins made of precious metals or commodities, credit papers (especially banknotes) issued by a chartered bank can be recognized as legal tender. This is the *Bankfundation*, meaning currency is founded/based on credit by (public) banks. The third form is state paper money, which is issued directly by state authorities through the *Steuerfundation* (founded/based on taxation). The quantity of this state paper money is supposed to be limited by the tax payments to be made (Stein 1858, 60).

Currency is the safest and most liquid form of money. In contrast, credit money carries risks relating to the issuer and its general acceptance. While the quantity of currency can be controlled by the relevant authority, the quantity of credit money, which is created through a decentralized process by many private institutions, can only be controlled indirectly. Consequently, currency is typically associated with the principle of stability, while credit money is linked to the principle of elasticity.

- Stability: The so-called "currency principle" aims to preserve the value of money and maintain stability. To achieve this, the money supply must be kept restricted, which carries the risk of the economy being under-supplied with money. This concept is based on currency.
- Elasticity: The so-called "banking principle" is to provide money elastically for all transactions and investments. To achieve this, the money supply must be elastically adjustable, which carries the risk of excessive money creation and financial crises. This concept is based on credit money.

A central bank cannot create money elastically for companies and households with which it has no business relationship. However, without the elasticity of the monetary system, the currency can become unstable due to increased volatility in interest and exchange rates. Today's two-tier monetary system can be understood as the result of a historical and institutional development of this conflict of objectives and legitimate demands placed on the monetary system. The central bank that issues currency is responsible for maintaining stability (as the "bank of banks" and "lender of last resort"), while commercial banks that issue credit money are responsible for maintaining elasticity (Banerjee et al. 2025).

Both principles are part of the explanation of money and the money system fluctuates between these poles: historically, theoretically, and politically. Claassen defined this contrast as the central question of monetary theory. "Since the beginning of the nineteenth century and up to the present day, two fundamentally different concepts of money can be identified: one is based on a 'narrow' concept of money, while the other also treats so-called money substitutes as monetary factors" (Claassen 1980, 1, my translation).

To correctly understand historical monetary theories, it is also important to consider the legal traditions regarding money. Whether a currency is considered a commodity (metallistic) or not (nominalistic) is heavily influenced by historical legal frameworks. Since the Middle Ages, the common law tradition in England has mainly adopted a nominalistic understanding of money, meaning that changes in the currency standard are irrelevant for domestic credit contracts. In England's constitutional landscape, for instance, the monarch had the authority to diminish the silver content of coins. A credit contract (*mutuum*) referred to the nominal value (*valoris impositus* or *aestimatio*) rather than the intrinsic value (*valoris intrinsicus*), i.e., the amount of silver. Therefore, the concept of money was not determined by the metal itself. This favors the borrower over the lender, who has to factor in the risk of a currency reform during the term of the loan (Fox 2016b Nominal Values; Fox 2016a Mixt Monies). In the continental European civil law tradition, however, the metallistic understanding of money and the principle of commodity value have persisted. Following a currency reform, the court most often upheld the view that the old metal value of the coins (*ad aestimatio antique*) was to be repaid on a loan, rather than an abstract value. Money was generally understood as metal with an intrinsic value (Dondorp 2016; Schott 2016).

The term *inflation* originally did not refer to rising prices, but rather to an increase in the amount of circulating medium. Until modern times, this was the common understanding. It was not until 1865 that Alexander Del Mar first used the term *inflation* (from Latin: *inflare* = to inflate) to refer specifically to price increases. It was not until the beginning of the twentieth century that the concept of inflation as a general rise in prices became established. Nevertheless, this book uses the term *inflation* ahistorically in the modern sense (Fig. 4.1).

4.3 Classifying Monetary Theory

Various attempts to categorize monetary theory have been made since the nineteenth century. An obvious distinction between monetary theories is how money is defined. A narrow definition of money as currency, which means physical or state money, contrasts with the broader, liquidity-oriented definition, which includes money surrogates, such as liquid forms of credit (credit money). This division is based on the mid-nineteenth century currency-banking school debate in England, where *quantity-oriented* representatives of the currency principle and *liquidity-oriented* supporters of the banking school competed against each other.[2]

The best-known classification of monetary theories is *nominalism* versus *metallism*: “By theoretical metallism we denote the theory that it is logically essential for money to consist of, or to be ‘covered’ by, some commodity so that the logical source of the exchange value or purchasing power of money is the exchange value or purchasing power of that commodity, considered independently of its monetary role” (Schumpeter 1954, 288).

Metallism does not necessarily refer to metals but commodities that are used as money, which for practical reasons were mostly precious metals. Nominalism (cartalism) “may best be defined by the corresponding negatives. Thus, we shall speak of theoretical cartalism wherever we find denial of the proposition that it is logically essential for money to consist of, say, gold, or to be promptly convertible into gold” (Schumpeter 1954, 288). Nominalism and metallism alternate repeatedly in history. “Metallism and nominalism [form] theoretical opposites in money theory, but in essence both are needed to understand historical practices” (Schefold 2008, 38).

[2] The description of taxonomy follows Greitens (2022).

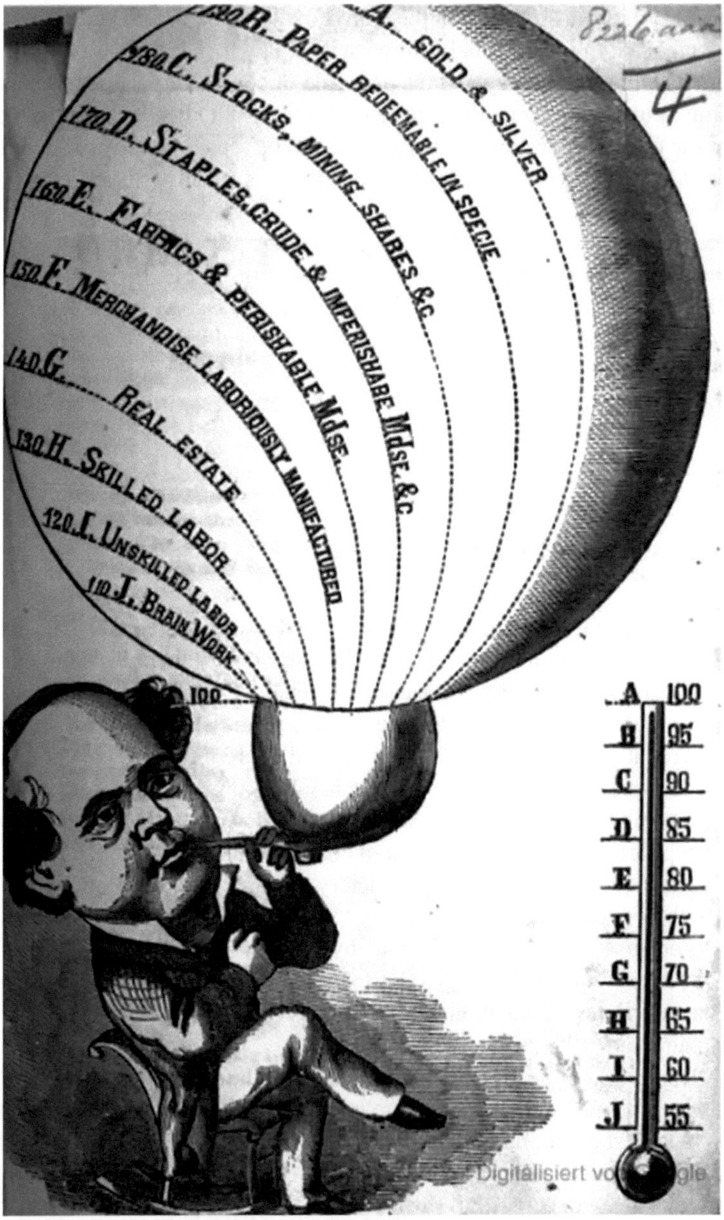

Fig. 4.1 Inflation as rising prices (del Mar 1864, Frontispiece): "The Bubble represents the expansion of paper currency. The figure 100 at the brim of the pipe indicates the level of prices before expansion—for instance, a dollar's worth of Gold, or Merchandise, or Labor. The figures 110 to 200, at the side of the bubble, represents the relative inflation of the articles opposite to them—a relation that will be maintained as long as the expansion continues. (…) But when one thing is forced down below its natural level, something else flies up, or vice versa, and the aggregate sum of all the increased prices will continue to be the same, without the inflation itself increases or diminishes"

This easy classification, however, was too simple to effectively classify monetary theories.

In 1908, Altmann classified monetary theories according to the questions they raised. He distinguished between qualitative-static theories, which investigate the nature/essence and monetary functions, and quantitative-dynamic theories, which investigate monetary value and why it changes. Theories about the essence of money are closely tied to the origins of money. According to Altmann, the essence of money refers to the preconditions that an object must fulfil to be able to execute monetary functions, i.e., the qualitative level, which then forms the basis for the value of money.

In 1934, Ellis conducted a synthesis of classifications. As an advocate of Knapp's nominalism/cartalism, and thus well acquainted with the latter's taxonomy of money (Knapp did not develop a monetary theory taxonomy), Ellis (1934) classified theories into nominalistic and metallistic. Additionally, he utilized Altmann's separation into the essence and origin of money from theories on the determinants of the purchasing power of money. Ellis used terms like *formalistic* and *naturalistic* to describe different views on the essence of money, and *authoritarian* and *economic* to describe different monetary value theories (Ellis 1934, 11).

In contrast to Knapp's work, Ludwig von Mises distinguished between *catallactic* and *acatallactic* theories. The former means "to locate the nature of money in circulation" (Mises 1917, 199, my translation) and "explain its value in the form of the laws of exchange" (Mises 1917, 199, my translation). Catallactic theories are accessible to economic value theories and thus to economic theories in a narrower sense. By contrast, the latter term means seeking legal, historical, or sociological justification for money. For Mises, Knapp viewed barter as irrelevant to the emergence of money and that the state alone has the power to determine, by proclamation, legal means of payment, and thus money. Mises (1924, 509) argued that his theory was not accessible to economic value theories, noting that "never has there been a more miserable and empty representation of monetary history." The term catallictic goes back to Richard Whately (1832) who wanted to coin economics with the name catallictic as the "Science of Exchanges" (Whately 1832, 6).

4.3.1 Classification Based on Monetary Functions

Werner Ehrlicher (1965) uses the four functions of money—as a medium of exchange, means of payment, store of value, and unit of account—as a basis for categorizing monetary theories that address the nature or essence of money. He classifies monetary theories according to their most relevant function. However, identifying the primary function of a monetary theory is not always straightforward, as the functions of money are often interrelated and cannot be separated. Nevertheless, it is precisely this ambiguity that raises the question of what the central problem or theme of each theory really is.

- If the essence of money is primarily determined by its function as a store of value, then the theory emphasizes "the commodity character of money for its origin, function, and in particular, for its explanation of value" (Ehrlicher 1965, 233, my translation). Such theories are metallistic, which means that "money [...] can only be a commodity where its value is protected by its intrinsic value, i.e., has a value that exists independently of the use as money" (Ehrlicher 1965, 233, my translation).
- If the essence of money is primarily determined by the medium of exchange function, then the theory views the primary role of money as the most marketable commodity for intermediate exchange, i.e., the functional theory of money (Ehrlicher 1965, 233, my translation). Thus, this theory emphasizes that money must be a commodity; however, this commodity loses its original role and intrinsic value in the usage as money.
- If the essence of money is primarily determined by its function as a means of (deferred) payment, then the theory is based on the legal setting or commercial usage that credit requires. For example, the convention theory of money, states that "money owes its origin and validity to an agreement of man to accept a certain good as a means of payment" (Ehrlicher 1965, 233, my translation).
- If the essence of money is primarily determined by the unit of account function, then the theory's "focus is not on the individual concrete exchange, but on the abstract quantitative relations behind them on another logical level" (Ehrlicher 1965, 234, my translation). For example, the token theory of money views money as a coupon or certificate for a proportion of the production corresponding to one's own contribution, similar to a cloakroom ticket. The essence and value of money does not lie in a concrete exchange, but in an abstract monetary circuit approach, which connects income, production and prices.

Ehrlicher assumed a logical connection between the essence of money and the value of money with the monetary functions. For example, if the means of payment is considered the most essential function of money, the convention theory applies, and the monetary value is necessarily determined by the Quantity Theory of Money.

However, Ehrlicher's approach has two main drawbacks. First, the assignment of theories to specific primary functions is not clearly feasible, as these functions are often interrelated and cannot be separated. Second, the vagueness of terms like *commodity theory*, *token theory*, and *income theory* may lead to misunderstanding, since these terms are not uniformly understood, even when more known.

Utilizing Ehrlicher's (1965) approach as the starting point for developing a monetary theory taxonomy, the first step is to classify monetary theories into the nominalism and metallism categories as described earlier. The store of value and medium of exchange functions are both connected to metallism since both require money to be a commodity, while the means-of-payment and unit-of-account functions do not. At first, the focus is on currency, i.e., private credit money is disregarded. Ehrlicher added another classification, created by Altmann (1908): the essence of money and the value of money. The following description follows a horizontal order, first addressing the question of the essence of currency, then the value of currency, and finally credit money (Fig. 4.2).

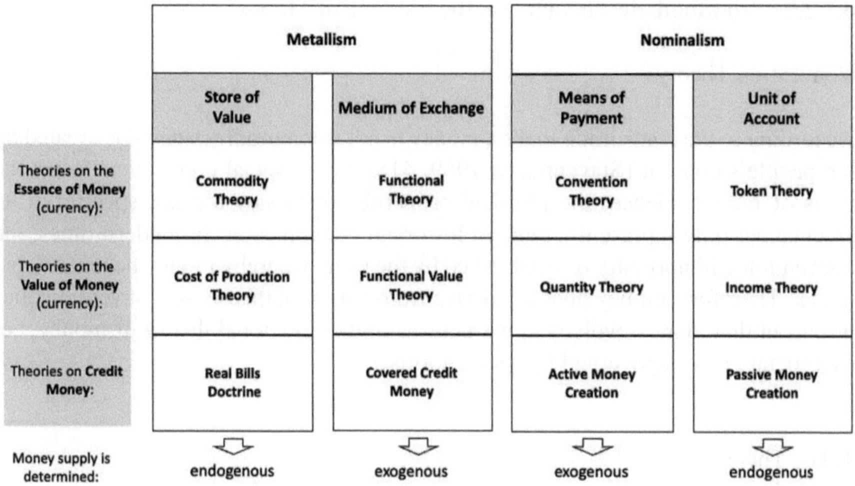

Fig. 4.2 Function-oriented taxonomy of monetary theories

4.3.2 *The Essence of Money*

4.3.2.1 Metallistic Theories on the Essence of Money

Commodity Theory

In the commodity theory of money, precious metals form the crux of the monetary system, and their value is determined according to an objective value theory (Brandl 2015, 3). Precious metals, like other commodities, are subject to economic laws and, therefore, cannot have a monetary value independent of the value of the coin as metal (Stavenhagen 1969, 419). All theories that emphasize the essence of money in its physical properties, emphasize money's function as a store of value. According to Roscher (1897, 331, my translation), "false definitions of money can be divided into two main groups: those considering it to be more than and those considering it to be less than a commodity."

Functional Theory

The functional theory of money describes the essence of money not by the physical properties of the money commodity, but by its use value (Stavenhagen 1969, 42). The essence of money is viewed in its economic role, i.e., as a medium of exchange. Money is the most marketable good that is used for intermediary exchange to surmount the coincidence-of-wants problem. Although this theory is metallistic, the neoclassical subjective value theory applies here, i.e., the valuation of a monetary commodity based on its function of facilitating exchange (Brandl 2015, 32).

4.3.2.2 Nominalistic Theories on the Essence of Money

Convention Theory

According to the convention theory, money is not a commodity since it is created by the people's consent (Stavenhagen 1969, 418), i.e., a social convention forms the basis of money. Hence, the physical properties of money are not specific to its essence but only represent a random historical phenomenon. In modern times, the convention will normally be established by the state, whereby money becomes legal tender. Therefore, money does not derive from barter. In this sense, convention does not mean that money evolves in markets, as in the functional theory of money, but as a social process governed by social norms.

Token Theory

This theory refers to economic exchange in the circuit of money and goods. Accordingly, everyone receives a quantity of goods equivalent to their contribution to production in society. Therefore, money is considered a token or certificate of added value. Money is an instrument for the allocation of goods, just like a ticket at a theater. This form of money can be without any intrinsic value, but must be denominated with reference to a certain quantity of goods (Brandl 2015, 36).

4.3.3 The Value of Money

For Ehrlicher, the essence of money refers to why something is used as money, and why it has any value. The value of money refers to the mechanics of how value is determined. The value of money can be derived from the essence of money, and the logically following monetary value theories are a continuation of the previous function-related theories regarding the essence of money. Going beyond Ehrlicher, the question of whether the quantity of money is determined exogenously or endogenously is added.

4.3.3.1 Metallistic Theories on the Value of Money

Cost of Production Theory

The cost of production theory is a theory on the value of money that corresponds to the commodity theory of money (Ehrlicher 1965, 233). Since money is a commodity, its value is also subject to general economic laws. The cost of production of each quantity of a commodity determines its value; thus, the value of money must also relate to its production costs (Stavenhagen 1969, 443). Money cannot have any value independent of the value of the commodities used as money. Advocates of this theory worry about the manipulation of money's value (e.g., light coins with lower silver content than claimed, such that the nominal value deviates from the commodity value) and the negative consequences that can produce.

The quantity of full coins in circulation will always be adjusted endogenously. When prices are low, it will be profitable to produce more gold or silver, which, through its positive effect on the money supply, will raise prices until its expected profitability decreases to that of other goods. When prices are too high, the commodity used as money will leave monetary circulation and be hoarded.

Functional Value Theory

When the essence of money is related to its medium of exchange function, its value is determined by the utility received by using the money commodity as money. This value is based on its ability to circulate and its function as a medium of exchange, which refers to the purchasing power of money (Stavenhagen 1969, 421–422). And, as Mises (1924, 130) wrote, "The subjective use-value of money, which coincides with its subjective exchange value, is nothing but the anticipated use-value of the things that are to be bought with it. The subjective value of money must be measured by the marginal utility of the goods for which the money can be exchanged."

This functional value and cost of production theories both describe money as a valuable commodity, which is why both these theories belong to metallism. Since the value of money is explained in the functional value theory by its subjective-use value, an excessive quantity of money will reduce the use-value received from the commodity used as money and increase prices. However, the money commodity will not, as in the cost of production theory, leave circulation to serve its original purpose. Therefore, the quantity of money as a medium of exchange is limited by the availability of the commodity, meaning exogenously determined, since the quantity of money does not necessarily respond to fluctuations in the circulation of goods.

4.3.3.2 Nominalistic Theories on the Value of Money

Quantity Theory

From the perspective of the means-of-payment function, money is based on a convention, which is why money need not have an intrinsic value. Therefore, the value of money is determined by the amount of money in circulation vis-a-vis the volume of transactions. The Quantity Theory of Money is one of the oldest economic theories. Since the Price Revolution of the 1500s, it has established a causal relationship between the quantity of money and the price level in various forms. The most common representation of this theory is Irving Fisher's equation of exchange, which includes the amount of money in circulation (M), the velocity of money (V, i.e., the frequency in which money is used for transactions), the transaction volume (T, or in the monetarist simplification, income Y), and the price level (P). It is assumed that if V is constant and exogenously defined by payment habits, a more rapid increase in M vis-a-vis output leads to inflation. An exogenous change in the money supply leads to endogenous adjustments in the price level, which, in turn, determines the monetary value (also known as the transaction volume quantity theory).

Income Theory

This theory rejects the one-sided causality between money supply and prices, and assumes that changes in the money supply can only affect price levels when used for spending. Therefore, an effective money supply must be determined based on income levels and the disposition of income (Stavenhagen 1969, 444). Thus, this theory is also known as the *income type of quantity theory*. Subsequently, "even from the standpoint of the most rigorous quantity theory, not only that the quantity of gold money determines prices, but also that in principle prices likewise determine the quantity of gold money; that the purchasing power of money or its value 'depends' upon the quantity of gold, but at the same time that the quantity of gold 'depends' upon the purchasing power of money" (Schumpeter 1918, 199).

An exogenous change in prices, caused by real scarcities, will lead to an endogenous adjustment of the money in circulation. It is important to identify what money is used for, whether consumption or investment. Income spent on consumption leads to an elastic adjustment of money supply at market prices.

4.3.4 Credit Money Theories

Ehrlicher did not address giro money or money surrogates and other types of currency substitutes (here generally referred to as *credit money*), although they are quantitatively the most significant types of money. Thus, to have a broader understanding of money, it is important to consider credit money theories as well.

Can the Ehrlicher functional classification, based on monetary functions, be extended to credit money theories? In principle, any form of credit money is a (potential) means of payment. However, in determining the value of credit money, monetary theories diverge and can be assigned to different primary monetary functions. Credit money theories also follow a specific understanding of the essence of the underlying currency.

4.3.4.1 Metallistic Credit Money Theories

Real Bills Doctrine

This is one of the oldest credit money theories, based on the use of bills of exchange, dating back to Smith (1776, 236): "When a bank discounts to a merchant a real bill of exchange drawn by a real creditor upon a real debtor, and which, as soon as it becomes due, is really paid by that debtor, it only advances to him a part of the value which he would otherwise be obliged to keep by him unemployed and in ready money for answering occasional demands. The payment of tire bill, when it becomes due, replaces to the bank the value of what it had advanced, together with the interest."

Here, credit only represents commodities in exchange and does not have an independent role. As long as credit is short-term, valuable, and risk-free, bills of exchange only represent commodities that are like the commodity itself, i.e., in the sense of the commodity theory, money. The volume of credit is determined endogenously by the goods in circulation, and the value of credit money depends on the value of the commodities that are represented by it, i.e., the value of bills of exchange depend on the circulating commodities.

Covered Credit Money

Under the gold standard, credit money was pegged to gold as a value-securing good. Banks were required to hold gold reserves to cover the lending and creation of paper money, thus restricting the expansion of credit money. Banks are assumed to be pure intermediaries that collect deposits and lend them out as loans, even when loans are only partially covered. Therefore, the volume of credit money is determined exogenously by the quantity of the commodity to which it is attached. In this theory, the pegging of currency to commodities like gold is essential. The best-known concept in this context is the money multiplier in the tradition of Phillips (1920).

4.3.4.2 Nominalistic Credit Money Theories

Active Credit Money Creation

These theories focus on money-creating institutions, especially banks. The creation of private credit money depends on bank initiatives and does not reflect any previous or simultaneous processes in the real economy, which are a reaction to the supply of credit by banks. Credit does not passively follow the processes of a real economy despite all the restrictions (e.g., demand for loans or the availability of collateral). In this sense, credit money is exogenously determined by banks (acatallactic, according to Mises 1917, 199).

Passive Credit Money Creation

From this perspective, the creation of credit money is a complex issue between production, consumption, and the derived demand for credit. A bank's credit money creation tends to be passive and follows the demand and intention of non-banks to use credit money. Thus, credit money is endogenously determined by the behavior and demand of economic agents (catallactic according to Mises 1917, 199).

4.4 Systemizing Credit Money Theories

In addition to this taxonomy, a few other concepts are useful for understanding the monetary theories that will be presented. These relate to credit money and have been systematized very convincingly by Wagner (1937) from the perspective of the history of economic thought. This following section briefly introduces three concepts relevant to the authors.

4.4.1 The Development Theory of Credit

Wagner (1937, 227–342) refers to his Development Theory of Credit in more precise terms as the theory of "additional credit." He sees the purpose of credit in enabling new forms of production and thus in increasing output. His starting point is the concept of a quasi-stationary, traditional economy that changes little. In this economy, the production of the previous period is either consumed and used for replacement investments in the current period. Money only serves as a medium of exchange and credit transactions do not occur.

Development means investing in new forms of production and introducing new technologies, which leads to a different use of production factors. Implementation requires capital, but in the form of credit, as free means of production are unavailable in the static cycle. This credit provides entrepreneurs with the purchasing power to acquire the necessary means of production and pave the way for development. Without additional credit, the cycle's expansive tendencies cannot be realized. The monetary factor determines the pace and extent of economic development.

This development theory can be traced back to mercantilism, in which the circulation of money is considered the driving force behind economic development. In this book, Law, Hamilton and Schumpeter present a Development Theory of Credit money based on the concept of cash-in-advance.

4.4.2 Indifference Theory

According to the Indifference Theory (Wagner 1937, 17–50), money is merely a medium of exchange. Additional credits cannot be used to expand production. This is based on the idea of the "money veil," the classical dichotomy, which states that money has no fundamental influence on the real economy. "There cannot, in short, be intrinsically a more insignificant thing, in the economy of society, than money [...]. It is a machine for doing quickly and commodiously, what would be done, though less quickly and commodiously, without it [...] The introduction of money does not interfere with the operation of any of the Laws of Value laid down in the preceding chapters" (Mill 1848, 8). The Indifference Theory denies the importance of credit. Credit is merely a "neutral" element in the cycle, providing a technical service.

Essentially, the Indifference Theory implicitly assumes that every capital owner would manage its own capital. Credit is a private economic process by which economic goods are transferred from one economic agent to another, typically to an entrepreneur without capital. This transfer may be significant in private economic terms, but irrelevant in macroeconomic terms. In the sense that it does not change the picture of the creditless and moneyless barter economy, credit is indifferent.

In this book, Locke, Cantillon, Hume and Ricardo are associated with this theory of Wagner's. However, one might question whether they truly offered an Indifference Theory as defined by Mill, given that they all attribute some significance to money, albeit through the exchange rate.

4.4.3 The Social-Legal Theory of Credit

The Social-Legal Theory of Credit, as defined by Wagner (1937, 51–71), takes a more sociological perspective. The economy breaks down into a multitude of legally independent individual businesses, each pursuing its own interests. However, because of the division of labor, they are also dependent on each other for the organic unity of the national economy and are therefore interdependent as parts of a social whole. Consequently, there is a contradiction between the legal order of the economy and its social character that must be reconciled for the economy to function. The task of exchange and credit is to resolve this contradiction.

Credit is thus the result of the private organization of labor, which breaks down social productive capital into individual economies that are then reunited through credit. While maintaining the legal organization of the economy, credit restores the inherent socio-economic unity. "That is why credit transactions represent a higher level of socialization and a reduction in the individualistic independence of individual households" (Knies 1885, 173, my translation)."

Wagner derives this theory from romanticism, which places a key focus on society as a whole. The German historical school builds on this idea without developing it into an economic theory. In this book, Müller is associated with this theory.

4.5 Summary

From a functional perspective, the following strands of monetary theory can be distinguished:

- The theories that focus on money's function as a store of value see money as a commodity, whereby the money only represents this commodity. Credit, as well, is merely a representation of a valuable commodity.
- The theories that focus on money's function as a medium of exchange see money as a commodity, but assume that the value of money and its use are solely determined by its function as a medium of exchange. The scarcity of the money commodity is important, not its physical form. This scarcity must also apply to credit money.
- The theories that focus on money's function as a means of payment see money as an agreement. Money is created through a social and legal convention.
- The theories that focus on money's function as a unit of account use money for managing the economy. Its creation is dependent on the economic cycle and the demand for money.

The taxonomy cannot be transferred into a chronological structure (e.g., from metallism to nominalism) because this would imply a less obvious progress than one might expect.

It is important to emphasize the limitations that a taxonomy necessarily has. First, this comparison focuses on economic thought rather than the empirical manifestations or concrete forms of money that exist (or have existed). Second, it is impossible to create a comprehensive system for categorizing monetary theories from the history of economic thought. Due to the wide range of monetary theories, no taxonomy can be fully comprehensive. The categories presented in this chapter overlap and depend on different perspectives. This systematization cannot do justice to every author; it is only an approximation. Nevertheless, it can help clarify the central assumptions and statements of the theories. This taxonomy is intended primarily to facilitate a systematic examination of the texts, exposing their underlying assumptions and traditions. It allows us to examine the structure of a monetary theory and determine which concept of money supply the authors adhere to and which function is central to them.

The theories of the origin of money will not explicitly be considered further because they are generally overestimated in terms of their importance for theoretical explanations. As Schumpeter said: "This view is an interesting example of the epistemologically so important fact which we meet at every step in the social sciences, that the historical beginnings of a phenomenon by no means always show it in its simplest and purest form, so that an attempt to get at the essential nature of the problem by genetic treatment may easily be misleading. The historical origin of money certainly lies in the value of the money commodity, but its essential nature lies elsewhere. It is, of course, clear that in primitive conditions only money made of an intrinsically valuable material can obtain its definite market valuation and continue to circulate" (Schumpeter 1918, 157).

References

Altmann, S. P. 1908. Zur deutschen Geldlehre des 19. Jahrhunderts. In *Die Entwicklung der deutschen Volkswirtschaftslehre im neunzehnten Jahrhundert*, vol. 1, 1–67. Leipzig: Duncker & Humblot.

Banerjee, Ryan Niladri et al. 2025. *Elasticity in the monetary system.* BIS Bulletin No. 101.

Brandl, Felix. 2015. *Von der Entstehung des Geldes zur Sicherung der Währung*. Wiesbaden: Springer Gabler.

Claassen, Emil-Maria. 1980. *Grundlagen der Geldtheorie*. 2nd ed. Berlin: Springer.

Del Mar, Alexander. 1864. *The Great Paper Bubble; or, the Coming Financial Explosion*. New York.

Dondorp, Harry. 2016. The effect of debasements on pre-existing debts in early modern jurisprudence. In *Money in the Western Legal Tradition: Middle Ages to Bretton Woods*, 247–266. Oxford: Oxford University Press.

Ehrlicher, Werner. 1965. Geldtheorie. *Handwörterbuch der Sozialwissenschaften* 4:231–258.

Ellis, H. 1934. *German Monetary Theory, 1905–1933*. Cambridge: Harvard University Press.

Feliu, Gaspar. 2019. Money and currency. In *Money and Coinage in the Middle Ages*, Reading Medieval Sources, vol. 1, 21–40. Leiden: Brill.

Fox, David. 2016a. The case of Mixt Monies (1604). In *Money in the Western Legal Tradition: Middle Ages to Bretton Woods*, 224–243. Oxford: Oxford University Press.

Fox, David. 2016b. The enforcement of nominal values to money in the medieval and early modern common law. In *Money in the Western Legal Tradition: Middle Ages to Bretton Woods*, 203–223. Oxford: Oxford University Press.

Greitens. 2022. A structured approach to compare monetary theories. *Journal of Pluralism and Economics Education* 13 (3): 262–276.

Hildebrand, Bruno. 1864. Naturalwirthschaft, Geldwirthschaft und Creditwirthschaft. *Jahrbücher für Nationalökonomie und Statistik* 2:1–24.

Knies, Karl. 1885. *Das Geld: Darlegung der Grundlehren von dem Gelde*. 2nd ed. Berlin: Weidmannsche Buchhandlung.

Mill, John Stuart. 1848. *Principles of Political Economy*, 1909. London: Longmans.

Mises, Ludwig von. 1917. Zur Klassifikation der Geldtheorie. *Archiv für Sozialwissenschaft und Sozialpolitik* 44 (1): 198–213.

Mises, Ludwig von. 1924. *The Theory of Money and Credit*. Translated by H. E. Batson. Indianapolis: Liberty Fund, 1981.

Phillips, Chester A. 1920. *Bank Credit*. New York: Macmillan.

Roscher, Wilhelm. 1897. *Die Grundlagen der Nationalökonomie*. Stuttgart: Cotta.

Schefold, Bertram. 2008. Die Bedeutung des Problems der Wertformenlehre und der Transformation von Werten in Preise für das Kapital. In *Marx-Engels Jahrbuch*, 34–91. Berlin: Akademie Verlag.

Schott, Clausdieter. 2016. German Law Faculties and Benches of Jurymen (Schöffenstühle) on loans and inflation. In *Money in the Western Legal Tradition: Middle Ages to Bretton Woods*, 284–294. Oxford: Oxford University Press.

Schumpeter, Joseph. 1918. Money and the social product. In *International Economic Papers 6*, 1956, 148–211. Translated by A. W. Marget of "Das Sozialproduct und die Rechenpfennige". *Archiv für Sozialwissenschaft und Sozialpolitik* 44:627–715.

Schumpeter, Joseph. 1954. *History of Economic Analysis*. Edited from manuscript by Elizabeth Boody Schumpeter. New York: Oxford University Press.

Smith, Adam. 1776. *An Inquiry into the Nature and Causes of the Wealth of Nations*. Metalibri, 2007.

Stavenhagen, Gerhard. 1969. *Geschichte der Wirtschaftstheorie*. 4th ed. Göttingen: Vandenhoeck & Ruprecht.

Stein, Lorenz von. 1858. *Lehrbuch der Volkswirthschaft*. Wien: Braumüller.

Wagner, Valentin F. 1937. *Geschichte der Kredittheorien*. Eine dogmen-kritische Darstellung. Vienna: Springer.

Walker, Francis. 1878. *Money*. New York: Henry Holt.

Weber, Max. 1921. *Economy and Society: A New Translation,* 2019. Translated by Keith Tribe. Cambridge: Harvard University Press.

Whately, Richard. 1832. *Introductory Lectures on Political Economy: Delivered in Eastern Term*. 2nd ed. London: Fellowes.

Part II
Scholastic Authors

Chapter 5
Nicolaus Oresme (1325–1382): The Quality Theory of Money

5.1 Biography[1]

Nicolaus Oresme was born around 1325 in Caen, Normandy. He was probably the son of a farmer. Thanks to his talents, however, he rose from these humble origins to pursue a career in the clergy. Records show that by 1348, he was a theology student at the Collège de Navarre. He probably obtained a doctorate in theology, becoming headmaster of the Collège in 1356.

During the captivity of King John II ("John the Good") Oresme entered into the service of the Dauphin of France, who would later become King Charles V. He maintained close contact with the Dauphin throughout his life. Acting on the Dauphin's behalf, Oresme helped negotiate the ransom of John II, who was being held captive in England at the time. In 1362, he became a canon of Rouen Cathedral and, in February 1363, of the Sainte-Chapelle in Paris. In 1363, he was part of a delegation to the papal court in Avignon. It is unclear how Oresme managed to gain this position at the court and begin a career in the church, a career which appears to have served the interests of the king more than those of the pope.

In Paris, his colleague was Jean Buridan, a philosopher 20 years his senior and the university rector. Oresme's work shows Buridan's influence. At the request of Charles V, Oresme translated Aristotle's *Politics*, a work about Greek city-states, from Latin into French. The translation was clearly intended as the foundation of a program for prudent governance. In 1377, Oresme was appointed bishop of Lisieux, a position he held until his death in 1382.

[1] This biography follows Tietmeyer and Lindenlaub (2004, 125) and Schefold (2016, 83–84).

J. Greitens, *Currency and Credit Money*, Springer Studies in the History of Economic Thought, https://doi.org/10.1007/978-3-032-24113-9_5

5.2 Selected Text

Oresme, Nicholas. 1358. "Treatise on Money." Translated by Charles Johnson. *A Source Book on Early Monetary Thought*. Cheltenham: Edward Elgar Publishing. 2020. 70–88.

5.3 Historical Background

The Commercial Revolution, which began in the eleventh century and unfolded alongside profound social and intellectual changes, brought about by urbanization and commercialization. During this period, the use of money increased, and it became the universal standard. As the economy became increasingly monetized, reflection on issues related to money increased in turn.

After an extended period of rising prosperity, the fourteenth century was marked by crisis. Fundamental economic and political questions arose as a result of the Hundred Years' War over a divided France; the Black Death, which exacted an enormous death toll from 1347 onward; and the conflict associated with the establishment of the papacy in Avignon.

In order to finance state expenditures—including in particular the enormous cost of waging war—it was common at this time to debase coins by issuing them with a significantly lower precious metal content. Unlike in modern economics, where monetary and fiscal policy are seen as distinct, these two areas were viewed as the same in the Middle Ages. The right of coinage was also considered a legitimate and lucrative source of income. As early as 1303/04, bishops and nobles in France issued a declaration against the coin debasement of King Philip IV, who was later described as the *counterfeit king* due to his intensive use of this method of financing (Mäkeler 2003, 64).

In order to finance the Hundred Years' War, which began in 1337, the French King Philip VI resorted to debasing the coinage, resulting in significant devaluations. By 1342, the silver content of the French *gros tournois* had fallen to roughly half its 1336 level. Philip VI's son, King John II, ascended the throne in 1350. After a pause, fighting resumed in 1355, resulting in John II being captured by the English at the Battle of Poitiers in 1356. He was released in 1360 in exchange for territorial concessions and ransom payments, which in turn had to be financed by further devaluation. Between 1337 and 1360, there were over 80 instances of coin debasement, which led to unrest on several occasions (Mäkeler 2003, 65–68; Spufford 1988, 305–307) (Fig. 5.1).

The coin reform of 1360, which was probably influenced by Oresme, marked the beginning of a period of stability. John II introduced the *franc à cheval* (cheval means "horse" in French; the coin depicts the mounted king), to which the silver coins were pegged. This had been demanded for a long time by the nobility because, as large landowners, they received rents that were nominally fixed. State financing had to

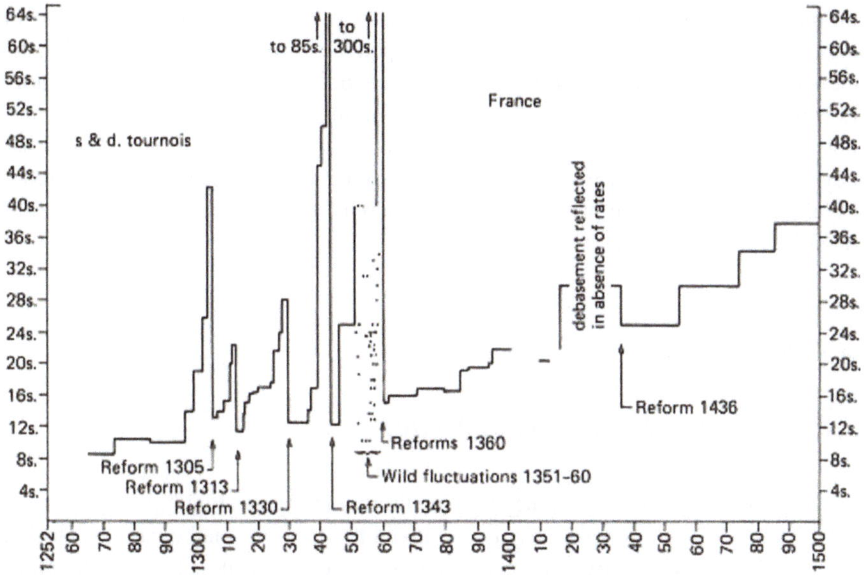

Fig. 5.1 Changes in the value of the French coinage (Spufford 1988, 297)

Fig. 5.2 Franc à cheval from 1360 (Münzkabinett der Staatlichen Museen, 18205198, Lübke und Wiedemann)

evolve from a reliance on customs duties and seigniorage to a more reliance on taxes. Therefore, John also announced the introduction of a tax called the *taille*, from which the nobles were exempt (Mäkeler 2003, 68–78; Spufford 1988, 307–308) (Fig. 5.2).

Nicole Oresme began engaging with monetary theory very early in his career. As early as 1355, he started drafting a treatise on money. Between March 1357 and May 1358, he elaborated on this work, producing the first known systematic treatise on money and minting written within the Latin Christian world, titled *Tractatus de mutatione monetarum*. This work was shaped by three sessions of the Estates General, during which the future of currency policy was debated. Remarkably, Oresme did not limit himself to the scholarly Latin version expected of a university master; he also composed a French adaptation. In doing so, he deliberately reached beyond a learned audience to a broader readership, including members of the French royal court, with whom he was becoming increasingly connected (Mäkeler 2003, 69–70; Kaye 2024, 730) (Fig. 5.3).

5.4 Discussion

5.4.1 The Quality Theory of Money

Initially, Oresme introduces money as a medium of exchange, highlighting its practical advantages, such as being easy to count and transport in small quantities, despite its high value. Gold and silver are scarce and cannot be produced artificially. Therefore, money is defined as a valuable commodity; accordingly, even alloys used for hardening coins are to be viewed with suspicion. The value of coins is determined by the weight of the precious metals they contain. Due to the scarcity of precious metals, Oresme argues against their use for anything other than money (Oresme 1358, 70–71).

Oresme advocated a strict metallistic theory of money, emphasizing that its value depends on its precious metal content rather than its use as a medium of exchange. According to Oresme, money should be scarce yet still sufficiently available (Mäkeler 2003, 71; Lapidus 1997, 30–31).

The right to mint coins is held by those determined by the community or the Estates General (*communitas*) for the benefit of the entire community (pro bono *communitatis*). As the highest authority, the prince receives the right to mint coins and must guarantee their weight and quality to protect the people from inferior currency. Oresme asserts that the prince does not own the money; he is not its originator. However, he must faithfully oversee it. Accordingly, the image on the coin does not signify the prince's ownership, but rather his responsibility to ensure the coin's quality on behalf of the community. Coins should be highly stable and the exchange ratio between gold and silver coins should correspond to that of the underlying metals (Oresme 1358, 72–73). Accordingly, Oresme advocates a *quality theory of money* (Schefold 2016, 91).

5.4.2 Alterations in Coinage

For Oresme, the production of slightly inferior coins in order to cover minting costs is permitted. However, Oresme is critical of all other forms of coinage alteration, distinguishing between five types (Oresme 1358, 74–78):

Fig. 5.3 Frontispiece of Oresme' coinage treatise (Traité de la première invention des monnaies, Bibliothèque nationale de France)

- Change of form: only permitted as a means of combatting counterfeiting or due to the gradual deterioration of coins in circulation.
- Change of ratio: establishment of a new value relationship between the coins; this is only permitted for adjustments to the gold–silver market ratio.
- Change of name: only permitted if the actual metal content of the coin changes.
- Change of weight: resetting of the coin weight is not permitted.
- Change of material: the introduction of a different coin material is only permitted in extreme cases, such as when a coin metal is in abundant supply.

Thus, for Oresme, only changes that maintain the quality of the coins in circulation are permitted: "An alteration can justly be made for one of two reasons. One is, if a foreign prince or false coiners maliciously copy or counterfeit the moulds or die of the money and there is found in the realm a forged, false money, like the good in colour and form. [...] Another reason might be if perchance the old money was too much injured by age or reduced in weight. Its currency should then be forbidden and the new and better money should be given a different stamp, so that the common people should be able to know one from the other" (Oresme 1358, 74). If the prince wants to change the coin standard for other reasons, this is necessarily motivated by the "greedy and disgraceful enhancement of his own profit" (Oresme 1358, 86).

"I am of opinion that the main and final cause why the prince pretends to the power of altering the coinage is the profit or gain which he can get from it [...]. I propose therefore to give fuller proof that such gain is unjust. For every change of money, except in the very rare cases which I have mentioned, involves forgery and deceit, and cannot be the right of the prince, as has previously been shown. Therefore, from the moment when the prince unjustly usurps this essentially unjust privilege, it is impossible that he can justly take profit from it. Besides, the amount of the prince's profit is necessarily that of the community's loss. But whatever loss the prince inflicts on the community is injustice and the act of a tyrant and not of a king, as Aristotle says. And if he should tell the tyrant's usual lie, that he applies that profit to the public advantage, he must not be believed, because he might as well take my coat and say he needed it for the public service. [...] Again, if the prince has the right to make a simple alteration in the coinage and draw some profit from it, he must also have the right to make a greater alteration and draw more profit, and to do this more than once and make still more, and also to make one or more compound alterations, constantly making more profit in the ways already described" (Oresme 1358, 78).

For Oresme, alterations to the coinage deprive subjects against their will. They bring the prince a profit that is as comprehensive and general as plunder or fraudulent exploitation. These actions are worse than usury, leading to many great misfortunes. The prince thereby loses his honor and becomes a tyrant. "It is exceedingly detestable and disgraceful in a prince to commit fraud, to debase his money, to call what is not gold, gold, and what is not a pound, a pound, and so forth" (Oresme 1358, 81). "Consequently, to propose to take from him the power of altering the coinage, is an attack on the honour of the king, a disherison of the prince, it is indeed impoverishing him and robbing him of his magnificence, not only unjustly, but

Fig. 5.4 The cauldron of justice (Coutumes de Toulouse, 1296, Bibliothèque nationale de France)

disgracefully to the whole community which cannot with decency have a prince unless he maintains his dignity" (Oresme 1358, 84).

According to contemporary legislative sources, the punishment for coin counterfeiting was cruel, with penalties becoming harsher from the thirteenth century onward. Counterfeiters who were captured were often themselves "melted"—that is to say, they were executed by boiling in a *cauldron of justice*. Oresme thus insinuates that the death penalty should be imposed for a prince's illegitimate debasement of coins (Fig. 5.4).

5.4.3 The Economic Consequences of Debasing the Coinage

According to Oresme, the consequences of bad coinage can be divided into three categories: (1) impacts on income and wealth distribution; (2) impacts on economic development; and (3) impacts on the affairs of the state (Tietmeyer and Lindenlaub 2004, 128–129):

1. Impacts on income and wealth distribution: Alterations to the coinage impoverish the subjects of a state; for Oresme, no tax could be more oppressive or extensive. Only those who speculate and those who exchange money benefit from

constant alterations to the coinage. Those who are informed in advance can also exploit hidden devaluations of money for their own benefit.

"Some sections of the community are occupied in affairs honourable or profitable to the whole state, as in the growing of natural wealth or negotiating on behalf of the community. Such are churchmen, judges, soldiers, husbandmen, merchants, craftsmen and the like. But another section augments its own wealth by unworthy business, as do money changers, bankers or dealers in bullion: a disgraceful trade [...]. These men, then, who are as it were unwanted by the state, and some others such as receivers and financial agents, etc., take a great part of the profit or gain arising from changes in coinage and by guile or by good luck, draw wealth from them, against God and Justice, since they are undeserving of such riches and unworthy of such wealth. [...] The persons above mentioned, whose business is contemptible and largely fraudulent, get a large part of it. Again, when the prince does not announce beforehand the date and the scheme of the alteration which he means to make, some persons, by their own cunning or through their friends, secretly foreknow it, and buy up merchandise with the weak money to sell again for the sound, get rich quickly and make an excessive and undue profit against the lawful course of normal trade. And this seems to be a kind of monopoly to the prejudice and damage of all the rest of the community" (Oresme 1358, 81).

Therefore, any changes to the coinage should be decided by the community and made public. The role of the prince is to carry out the decisions.

2. Impacts on economic development: For Oresme, alterations to the coinage cause lenders to lose, which leads to a decline in credit issuance. This weakens economic development. This is accompanied by the export of precious metals and the import of poor-quality coins, which, in the long term, leads to a shortage of coin metal and, consequently, money in the country. Imports can no longer be financed, and trade comes to a standstill: "Again, such alterations and debasements diminish the amount of gold and silver in the realm, since these metals, despite any embargo, are carried abroad, where they command a higher value. For men try to take their money to the places where they believe it to be worth most. And this reduces the material for money in the realm" (Oresme 1358, 81–82).

   Good money is exported, while bad money remains in circulation. This principle later became known as Gresham's Law. Precious metals flow out of the country because merchants avoid states with unstable or chaotic currencies. However, Oresme offers no analysis of the effects that result from exchange rate fluctuations under a bimetallic standard, of the relationship between current and capital accounts, or of the movement of precious metals (Schefold 2016, 100).

3. Impacts on the affairs of the state: There is a loss of awareness of injustice, as the king is seen as a tyrant. The losers are the "honorable" parts of society, namely churchmen, judges, soldiers, husbandmen, merchants, craftsmen and recipients of nominal income (Tietmeyer and Lindenlaub 2004, 130–132). By altering the coinage those "who are the best sections of the community, are impoverished by

it; so that the prince in this way damages and overburdens the larger and better part of his subjects and yet does not receive the whole of the profit" (Oresme 1358, 81).

Oresme views coin debasement as permissible under two circumstances: in the event of emergencies, such as war or ransom payments, and in the event of precious metal shortages. However, even in these cases, the measures to be taken should be decided by the community, not the prince alone.

5.5 Evaluation

Prior to Oresme, no systematic or theoretical economic writings are known to have existed from the early Middle Ages. As a result of the Commercial Revolution of the late Middle Ages and the expansion of the monetary economy from the thirteenth century onwards, normative economics was gradually replaced by positive, explanatory economics. While elements of Oresme's thought can be traced back to antiquity, including in particular Aristotle, his writings mark the beginnings of a scientific and specifically economic monetary literature that addresses not only moral but also economic issues. Within the normative system of scholasticism, his writing provides political, social, and economic analysis and argumentation. Adopting the Aristotelian view, Oresme states that a coin is a specific weight of precious metal, the quantity and purity of which is certified by the issuing authority's stamp. Currency does not belong to the issuing authority, but to the public who use it to exchange goods. Therefore, the prince has no right to alter the standard. Oresme also marks a beginning of metallism as a school of thought in monetary theory. For him, money is a commodity that fulfils the function of a medium of exchange. However, he takes the idea of stability so far that he becomes a proponent of the store of value position, developing a strict quality theory around it. Based on this theory, Oresme deduces that the prince is responsible for the quality of the coins on behalf of the community, a notion that is very modern (Lapidus 1997, 27–31).

It is striking that Oresme makes no mention of credit or bills of exchange, despite the fact that they were widely used by Italian bankers from the beginning of the fourteenth century onwards. Instruments of credit money are not discussed in Oresme's work.

However, it is also important to understand Oresme in the context of his role as a political figure. Oresme presents his arguments as if they were in the interest of the overwhelming majority of the population, although they appear to have been perceived differently by specific groups. The community he is talking about does not include everyone, but rather the nobility. As recipients of a fixed income, they benefit from a stable currency and are less affected, or not at all, by the emerging reliance on taxation as a means of public finance, thanks to tax exemptions. Oresme's views were probably widespread in these circles, which is why he was seen as the theoretical proponent of a movement by the nobility against John II's coinage policy. From 1360 onward, his ideas became the new paradigm under Charles V, suggesting the nobility and Charles V had arrived at a consensus. As the arguments advanced by the proponents of a soft currency have not been preserved, we cannot explore the full debate (Spufford 1988, 290–310).

Taxonomic Classification
To Oresme, coinage is a medium of exchange, but he focuses on its function as a store of value. He has no theory on the value of money; this value is largely predetermined for him. His understanding of the money supply is narrow, so he only considers currency in the form of coinage, while neglecting credit instruments such as bills of exchange.

References

Kaye, J. 2024. Mensurantur enim omnia nummismate: The impact of money and monetization on vital new directions in scholastic philosophy, ca. 1250–1350. In *The Palgrave Handbook of Philosophy and Money*. Cham: Palgrave Macmillan.

Lapidus, André. 1997. Metal, money and the price. *History of Political Economy* 29 (1): 21–53.

Mäkeler, Hendrik. 2003. Nicolas Oresme und Gabriel Biel. Zur Geldtheorie im späten Mittelalter. *Scripta Mercaturae* 37 (1): 56–94.

Oresme, Nicholas. 1358. "Treatise on Money." Translated by Charles Johnson *A Source Book on Early Monetary Thought*. Cheltenham: Edward Elgar Publishing. 2020. 70–88.

Schefold, Bertram. 2016. *Great Economic Thinkers from Antiquity to the Historical School*. Translated from the series Klassiker der Nationalökonomie. Routledge.

Spufford, Peter. 1988. *Money and Its Use in Medieval Europe*. Cambridge: Cambridge University Press.

Tietmeyer, Hans, and Dieter Lindenlaub. 2004. Nicolaus Oresme und die geldpolitischen Probleme von heute. In *Vademecum zu einem Klassiker der mittelalterlichen Geldlehre*, 125–146. Düsseldorf: Verlag Wirtschaft und Finanzen.

Chapter 6
Gabriel Biel (1410–1495): At the Crossroads of Pragmatism and Dogmatism

6.1 Biography[1]

Gabriel Biel was born around 1410 in Speyer. By the time he enrolled at the University of Heidelberg in 1432, he was already serving as a priest in his hometown. He received his master's degree in 1438 and, about 5 years later, began studying theology at Erfurt, completing his studies in 1457. Biel then served as a cathedral preacher in Mainz, undertook two journeys to Rome, and supported the establishment of monasteries before entering monastic life himself at Butzbach in 1469.

In 1476, Count Eberhard of Württemberg appointed him to assist with the reform of the church in Württemberg. Biel contributed to the founding of the University of Tübingen and began teaching theology there in 1484. By 1492, he was recorded as the first provost of the newly established St. Peter's Monastery on the Einsiedel near Tübingen.

In 1493/94, Württemberg minted hellers, pfennigs, and shillings whose value fell short of that stipulated in agreements with neighboring regions. The discrepancy may have been linked to rising expenditures, including the costly reunification of the divided Württemberg lands in 1482 and the elevation of Count Eberhard to duke in 1495. Biel likely alluded to these issues when he delivered a lecture on the coinage system in Tübingen in 1495, the year of his death.

Biel is regarded as one of the most prominent late scholastic thinkers, often described as the last of his kind, and he became an important point of reference for Martin Luther in his critique of scholasticism.

[1] This biography follows Mäkeler (2003) and Berthold (1891).

J. Greitens, *Currency and Credit Money*, Springer Studies in the History of Economic Thought, https://doi.org/10.1007/978-3-032-24113-9_6

6.2 Selected Text

Biel, Gabriel. 1516. *Treatise on the Power and Utility of Moneys.* University of Pennsylvania Press. 1930.

6.3 Historical Background

Biel developed his thoughts on money as only one aspect of a larger subject. The Treatise on the Power and Utility of Moneys *(Tractatus de potestate et utilitate monetarum)*, published in 1516, is an excerpt from the *Collectorium* circa *quattuor libros Sententiarum*, a four-volume work printed in Oppenheim in 1501 by Biel's student, Wendelin Steinbach, following Biel's death.

The *Collectorium* is Biel's most important work, representing a comprehensive synthesis of scholasticism. The Treatise on the Power and Utility of Moneys was the only work to be printed separately from the *Collectorium*; in this work, Biel wrote about the falsification of coins, among other topics (Kötz 2016, 74–77).

The Treatise was published amid renewed financial crisis in Württemberg during the 1510s. In 1514, a series of peasant uprisings occurred in Württemberg as part of the Poor Konrad Movement. The duke was presented with a petition that complained about the low quality of the coinage. On 29 June 1514, Duke Ulrich acknowledged that bad money was damaging the common good. As part of this debate, Biel's treatise on coinage had to be printed outside Württemberg, in 1516 in the Free Imperial City of Oppenheim, which was known for its liberal printers. A few years later, monetary conditions such as those in Württemberg contributed to the Peasants' War of 1525. The Holy Roman Empire launched formal discussions on a standardized imperial coinage in the 1550s due to the destabilizing social and economic effects of debased and inferior coins (Rössner 2025). (Fig. 6.1).

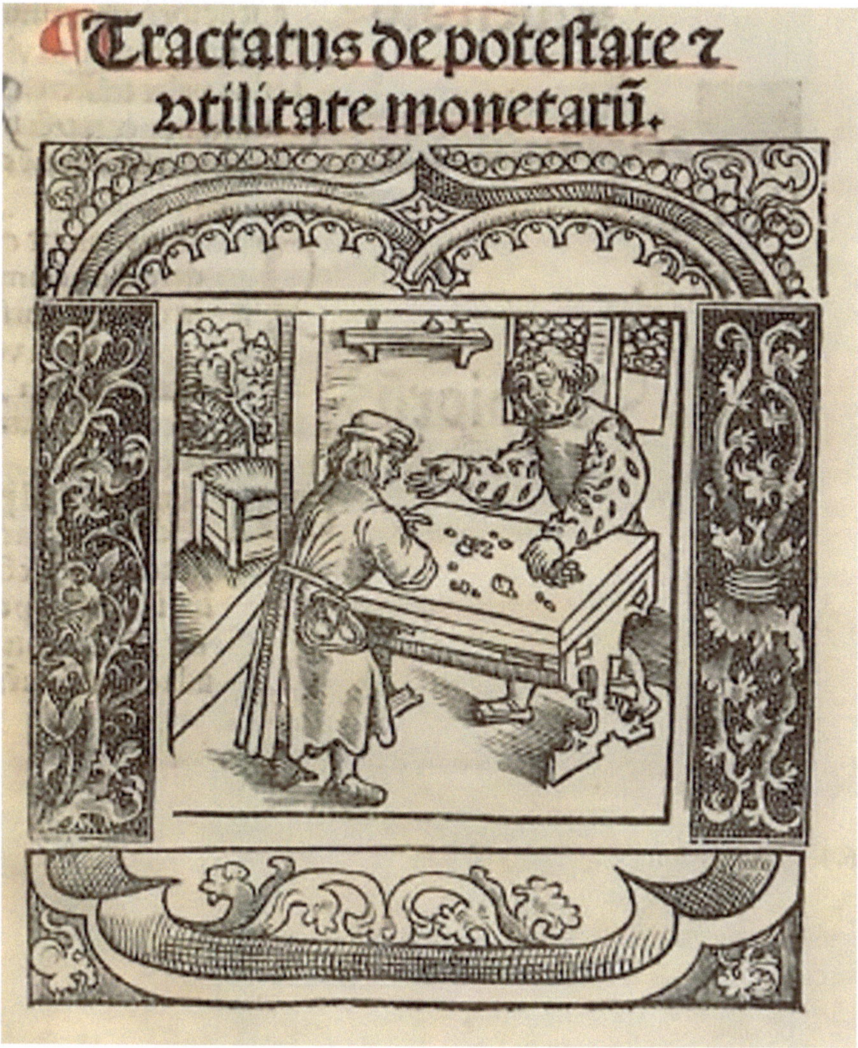

Fig. 6.1 Coin exchange after a currency reform and devaluation (Frontispiece of the Tractatus de potestate et utilitate monetarum)

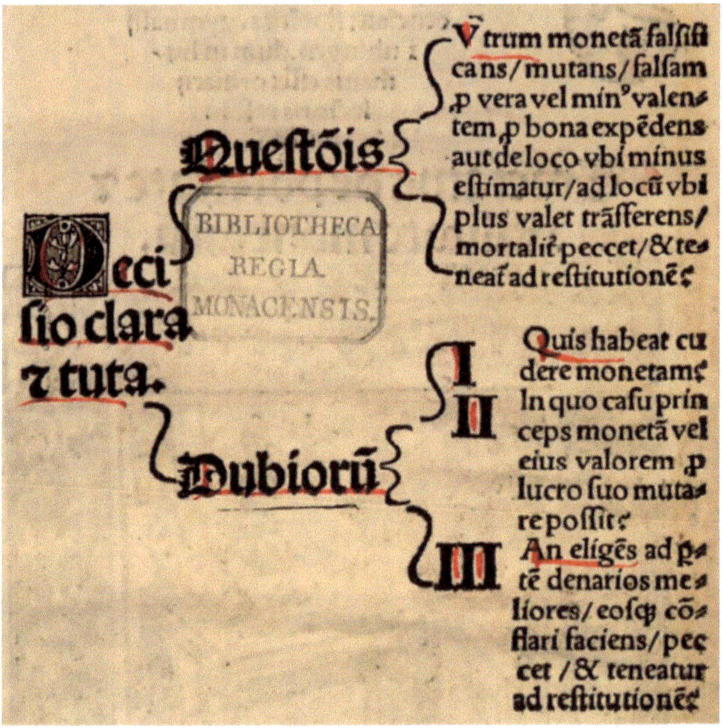

Deci
ſio clara
& tuta.

Queſtõis

Vtrum monetã falſifi
cans/mutans/falſam
ꝑ vera vel min⁹ valen-
tem ꝑ bona expẽdens
aut de loco vbi minus
eſtimatur/ad locũ vbi
plus valet trãſferens/
mortalit peccet/& te-
neat ad reſtitutionẽ?

Dubiorũ

I Quis habeat cu
dere monetam?
II In quo caſu prin
ceps monetã vel
eius valorem ꝑ
lucro ſuo muta-
re poſſit?
III An eligẽs ad ꝑ-
tẽ denarios me-
liores/eoſq̃ cõ-
flari faciens/pec
cet/& teneatur
ad reſtitutionẽ?

Fig. 6.2 *Introduction to the* Tractatus de potestate et utilitate monetarum *with the questions to be addressed*

6.4 Discussion

My translation (Fig. 6.2):

Clear and certain agreement
[between the]
Question,
whether someone commits a grave sin and is obliged to make amends if he counterfeits coins, changes their value by giving inferior money for good money, or if he takes it to a place where it has more value?
[and the to be clarified]
Doubts

I. Who is entitled to mint coins?
II. In which case can the master of the mint change the coins to his own advantage?
III. Is it a sin and does it require amends if someone sorts out the better coins and melts them down?

For Biel, money originated from exchange of goods, which it facilitates. The value of the coins guaranteed by the prince with minting rights stems from the amount of metal a coin contains and must match its assigned nominal value. No subordinate power should be permitted to mint coins without permission. According to Biel, as with Oresme, the minting of coins must benefit the community and be done by the ruler, who lends his name to guarantee the coins' value.

Counterfeiting can involve changes to the composition, total weight, or appearance of a coin. In this way, the counterfeit coin deviates from the established and publicly announced fine weight of the coin. According to Biel, if this harms a person or the community, it is essentially theft and a mortal sin. The counterfeiter must therefore compensate the victim (Biel 1516, 25–26).

While Biel largely reiterated Oresme's arguments, he introduced at least two significant extensions. In the context of the Great Bullion Famine of the fifteenth century, he explicitly justified devaluations due to the scarcity of materials, as they could not be obtained at the previous price. Furthermore, he argued that moving money from an area where its value is lower to an area where its value is higher does not constitute a sin. This seems to legitimize arbitrage with respect to both the bimetallic ratio and divergent price levels (Parsons 2024, 762).

Biel argues that, provided the community consented, rulers should be permitted to devalue the currency in times of necessity—such as during war—in order to generate seigniorage revenue, since this was the quickest means of raising funds. However, he insists that, once the emergency has passed, the former quality of the money is to be restored. Thus, Biel goes much further than Oresme in allowing the deterioration of the coinage, for he links monetary policy to economic scarcity and the political demands of the common good (Kötz 2016, 78; Kötz 2012, 141; Mäkeler 2003, 83–84).

6.5 Evaluation

Like Oresme, Biel believes that alterations to the coinage are harmful to the community, but he is less dogmatic and thus more realistic. He believed that alterations could be necessary given changes in the value of the underlying precious metals. For Biel, it is permissible to melt down individual coins. He also believes that the ruler has the right to levy extraordinary taxes in the form of coin devaluations, as this allows the burden of raising revenue to be quickly and easily distributed among all subjects. Biel is a moderate metallist. In contrast to Oresme, whom he recognizes as the ultimate authority in this field, Biel argues to a greater extent from a moral standpoint (Mäkeler 2003, 82, 90; Kötz 2016, 82). Biel played a pivotal role in spreading Oresme's ideas about money, particularly in German-speaking regions. He thus contributed to their integration into cameralism (Rössner 2018, 105–106).

Taxonomic Classification
Biel follows in the footsteps of Oresme, focusing on the function of money as a store of value. Like Oresme, he only considers coinage; his limited understanding of the money supply fails to take credit money into account.

6.6 Summary of Scholastic Monetary Theories

The Commercial Revolution, which brought about the increasing monetization of the economy, including frequent devaluations of the coinage in the fourteenth century, raised questions about the essence and value of money for the first time since antiquity. Without developed financial instruments, money was only a commodity; the value of coinage was seen as determined by its precious metal content.

Questions arose as to the proper relationship between the nobility and the king in the domain of coinage, and about how the ongoing costs of the court and particularly of war were to be financed. This phase also marked a transition to tax financing.

The recurring contradictions between calls for stable coinage and frequent devaluations can be explained by the perpetual shortage of precious metals in relation to the rising monetization of the economy and associated financing needs.

References

Berthold, Georg. 1891. Biel, Becher und Weiss, drei pfälzische Volkswirte. *Mitteilungen des historischen Vereines der Pfalz* 15:150–242.

Biel, Gabriel. 1516. *Treatise on the Power and Utility of Moneys*. University of Pennsylvania Press. 1930.

Kötz, Stefan. 2012. Geldtheorie an der Universität Tübingen um 1500. In *Die Universität Tübingen zwischen Scholastik und Humanismus. Tübinger Bausteine zur Landesgeschichte*, 117–160. Ostfildern: Thorbecke.

Kötz, Stefan. 2016. The last scholastic on money. In *Money in the Western Legal Tradition*, 71–89. Oxford: Oxford University Press.

Mäkeler, Hendrik. 2003. Nicolas Oresme und Gabriel Biel. Zur Geldtheorie im späten Mittelalter. *Scripta Mercaturae* 37 (1): 56–94.

Parsons, J. 2024. Philosophy of money in Renaissance France. In *The Palgrave Handbook of Philosophy and Money*, 755–775. Cham: Palgrave Macmillan.

Rössner, Philipp Robinson. 2018. Monetary theory and cameralist economic management. *Journal of the History of Economic Thought* 40 (1): 99–134.

Rössner, Philipp Robinson. 2025. Peasants, wars and evil coins: towards a 'monetary turn' in explaining the 'revolution of 1525'. *German History* 43 (1): 1–23.

Part III
Mercantilist Authors

Chapter 7
Nicolaus Copernicus (1473–1543): The Dignity of the Coin

7.1 Biography[1]

Nicolaus Copernicus was born on February 19, 1473, in Thorn. His father, a merchant from Kraków, had settled in Thorn, but died in 1483. After his death, Copernicus and his siblings came under the guardianship of their maternal uncle, Lucas Watzenrode, who later became bishop of Warmia.

From 1488 to 1491, Copernicus attended the gymnasium in Kulm, and from 1491 to 1495 he studied at the University of Kraków, although he did not complete a degree. In 1497, his uncle secured him a position in the cathedral chapter of Warmia, a post he held for the rest of his life. Between 1496 and 1501, Copernicus studied law at the University of Bologna, where he embraced the spirit of humanism, earning a master's degree in 1499. He continued his studies in medicine at Padua from 1501 to 1503, but for financial reasons obtained his doctorate in canon law at Ferrara. Though never ordained as a priest, he did receive minor orders as required of cathedral canons.

From 1504 to 1510, Copernicus lived at the episcopal residence in Heilsberg, and thereafter at the cathedral castle in Frauenburg. In 1504, while accompanying his uncle to an estates assembly in Elbing, he first encountered issues of monetary policy. Within the cathedral chapter, Copernicus built a solid career: he served repeatedly as chancellor, administered various estates, and even acted as vicar of the diocese during the interregnum of 1523.

Copernicus died of a stroke on May 24, 1543. According to tradition, on that very day he received a copy of his recently published masterpiece, *De revolutionibus orbium coelestium.*

---

[1] This biography follows Stasiewski (1973).

J. Greitens, *Currency and Credit Money*, Springer Studies in the History of Economic Thought, https://doi.org/10.1007/978-3-032-24113-9_7

7.2 Selected Text

Copernicus, Nicolaus. 1526. "Monete cudende ratio." Memorandum of 1526.[2] Translated by Edward Rosen and Erna Hilfstein. *A Source Book on Early Monetary Thought*. Cheltenham: Edward Elgar Publishing. 2020. 96–102 (Figs. 7.1 and 7.2).

7.3 Historical Background

The Teutonic Order's power in the Baltic region declined steadily throughout the fifteenth century. Following conflicts with the Polish king, the Second Peace of Thorn in 1466 resulted in Warmia, Gdańsk, and other areas being separated from the Order's territory. The bishops of Kulm and Warmia abandoned the Order's protection to become vassals of the Polish crown. However, the relationship between this "Royal (Polish) Prussia" and Poland was unclear and fluctuating. From the Peace of Thorn in 1466 until the Union of Lublin in 1569, during which time it largely lost its autonomy, the area enjoyed a semi-autonomous, contested status. Consequently, the assembly of estates played a significant role in administration. In 1489, Lucas Watzenrode, the uncle of Nicolaus Copernicus, was appointed bishop of Warmia against the will of the Polish king (Hubatsch 1973, 138–146).

During the Polish–Teutonic War (1519–1521), Albrecht of Brandenburg, the last Grand Master of the Teutonic Order, tried to consolidate his political power through military action. While the Diocese of Warmia sought to remain neutral, it became a primary battlefield. Albrecht financed the war through seigniorage—specifically, through debasement of the coinage (Fig. 7.3).

Following the defeat of the Knights in the war, Albrecht embarked on a radical new course of action. He transformed the Order's territory into a secular duchy governed hereditarily by the House of Hohenzollern. He also introduced the Reformation and, on April 10, 1525, recognized the Polish King's authority through the Treaty of Kraków. The Polish king Sigismund wanted to solve the pressing currency problems by Pentecost of the following year (Hubatsch 1973, 148–150; Volckart 1997, 431).

The Grand Master of the Teutonic Order had held minting rights since 1226. However, from 1410 onward, as the Order declined, the precious metal content of the coins decreased, particularly during the Polish–Teutonic War. Following the Peace of Thorn in 1466, the King of Poland, the Grand Master of the Teutonic Order, and the cities of Thorn, Gdańsk, and Elbląg were granted the right to mint coins. The Teutonic Order was particularly responsible for the continuous devaluation of the currency through the introduction of increasingly lightweight coins. A variety of highly different and increasingly poorly minted coins circulated

[2] Sommerfeld (1978) is certain that it was written in 1526, but others think it could have been written between 1525 and 1528.

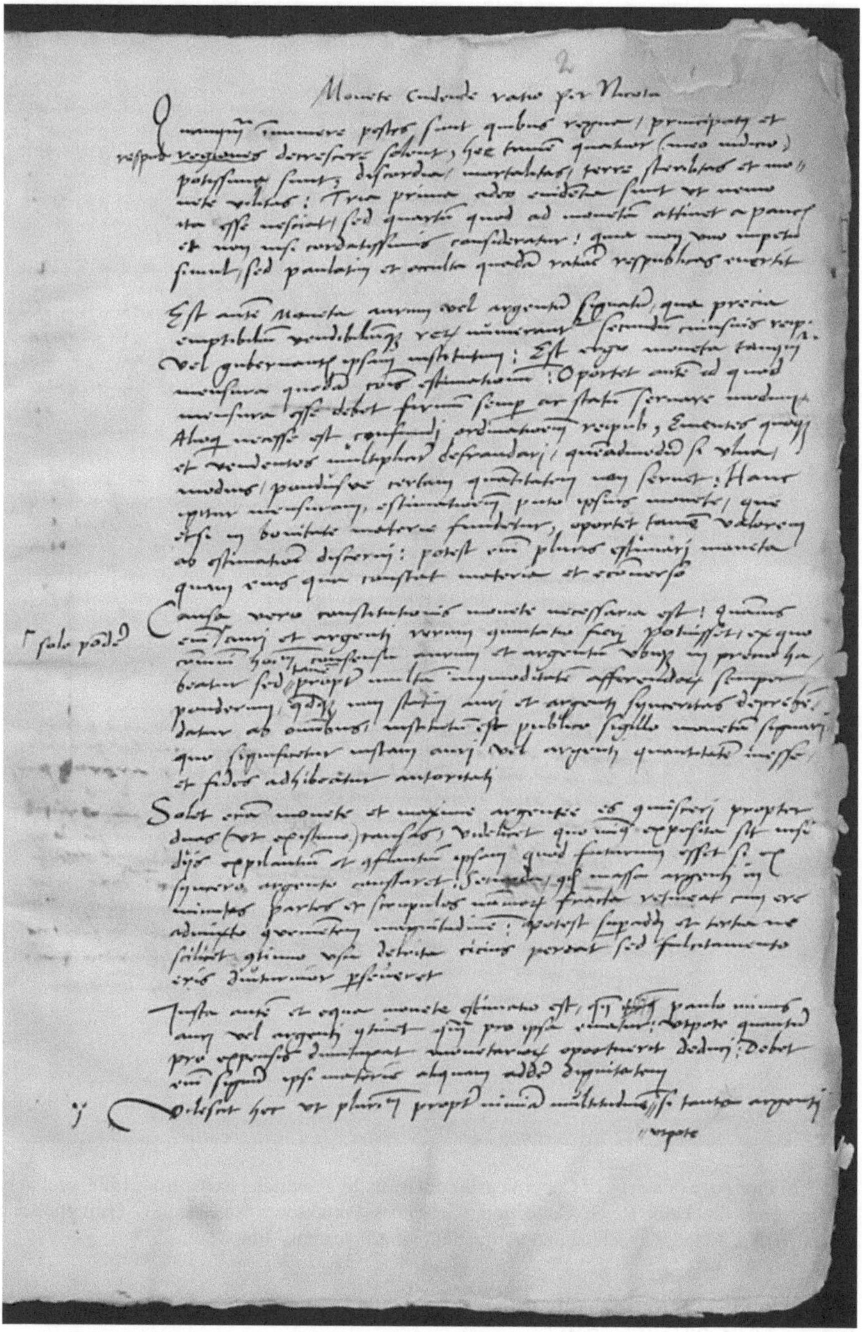

Fig. 7.1 First page of a copy of Copernicus's coin treaty from the Felix Reich Collection from 1526 (Geheimes Preußisches Staatsarchiv, XX. HA, HBA, No. 752)

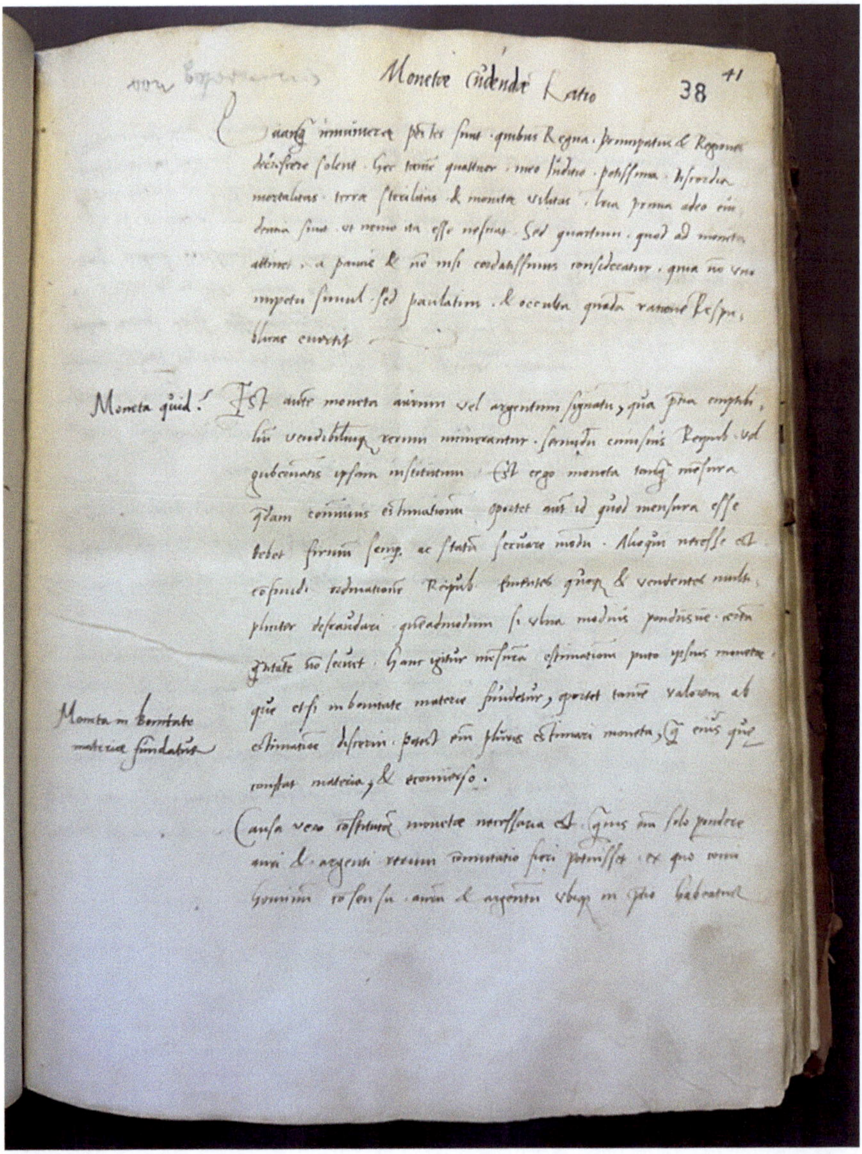

Fig. 7.2 First page of a copy of Copernicus's coin treaty by Friedrich Fischer from 1528, probably a copy from the Felix Reich Collection (Geheimes Preußisches Staatsarchiv, Ostpreußische Folianten, No. 12868, Gutachten und Verhandlung mit Polen das Münzwesen)

throughout the region, causing prices to rise significantly (Kellenbenz 1973, 84–86; Jastrow 1914, 736) (Fig. 7.4).

As early as 1519 and 1522, the estates of Royal Prussia were negotiating a uniform coin standard with Poland. As part of his duties, Copernicus encountered the

Fig. 7.3 ¼ Thaler of the Teutonic Order from 1521 (Arto Gorbatšuk). An emergency coin from the Polish–Teutonic War with a low silver content and a counterstamp to reduce its face value

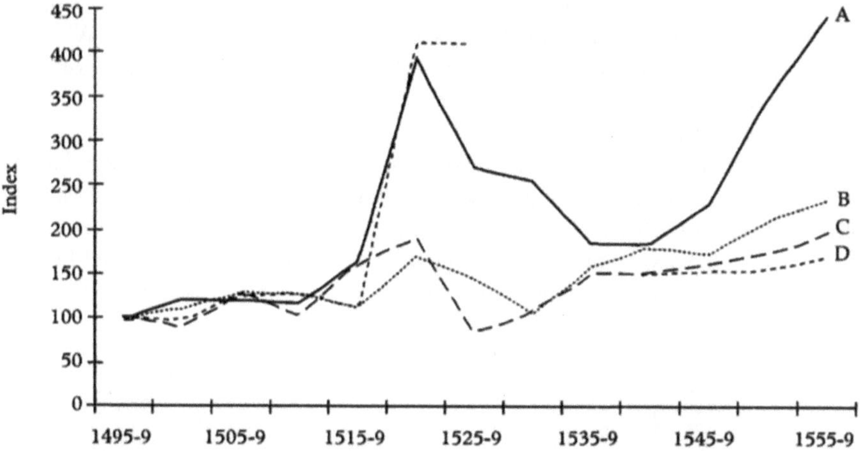

Fig. 7.4 Commodity prices in Prussia from 1495 to 1559: A = Grain, B = Wood products, C = Spices, D = Import goods (Volckart 1997, 438)

issue of inflation. He carefully considered the resulting economic problems in a study that is an early purely empirical discussion of the monetary question. It is also remarkable for its secular spirit, since it contains no theological arguments or quotations from the Bible. Completed on August 15, 1517, Copernicus described it as his *Meditata* (private reflections). He wrote it in Latin, presumably with the intention of circulating it among his colleagues and friends. At the request of the West Prussian Estates, Copernicus prepared a German translation in 1519 (Czartoryski 1985, 169).

At a meeting of the Prussian Estates in March 1522, a spokesman for the Polish crown expressed the king's desire to introduce a uniform currency throughout his empire, including Prussia. Coincidentally, Copernicus was present at the meeting, representing his bishop in the negotiations. Afterward, he added his thoughts on aligning the Prussian and Polish coins to the text. At another meeting of the West Prussian Estates in October 1522, the decision was made to link the Prussian and Polish currencies. By the end of 1523, Gdańsk had finally been authorized to mint shillings in accordance with Copernicus's proposal (Czartoryski 1985, 169–170; Kellenbenz 1973, 81–82, 86).

With the conversion to a secular duchy in 1525, the coinage conditions also had to be renegotiated. The Polish king attempted to enforce the Polish coin standard. Ludwig Dietz, the Royal Polish Master of the Mint, demanded a regular and fixed profit for the Polish crown from the new coinage to be produced. The Estates wanted to resist this demand. The Treaty of Kraków stipulated that a settlement should be reached by Pentecost 1526 (Czartoryski 1985, 170–171; Kellenbenz 1973, 85–86).

In spring 1526, the third and final version of the memorandum was published for use at the Royal Prussian Estates Assembly. Here, Copernicus employed the clearest language and most precise terminology. The main proposal was to reduce the number of mints to a single one, if possible. The Diocese of Warmia had no coinage rights and was therefore not interested in coin profits; on the contrary, it suffered greatly from the currency manipulations of those entitled to mint coins. While the majority of council members tried to push through the proposals, the Polish King succeeded in establishing the lower-value Polish coinage as the standard (Sommerfeld 1978, 13–15, 130).

Implementation took several years, and required a series of negotiations; Copernicus remained involved in these deliberations. The resolutions of the Malbork convocations in 1528 established one of the largest and most uniform currency areas in Europe in the sixteenth century: it encompassed Poland, Lithuania, and Prussia, and compatibility with the coins of the late Hanseatic League was assured (Fig. 7.5).

Fig. 7.5 Dreigröscher by Albrecht von Brandenburg-Ansbach from 1535 (Münzkabinett der Staatlichen Museen Berlin, 18230886, Saczewski)

7.4 Discussion

7.4.1 Coinage in General

Copernicus begins his work by describing the four greatest dangers to the state in a passage that appears to be inspired by the Four Horsemen of the Apocalypse (who represent war, death, conquest, and famine): "Although there are countless scourges which in general debilitate kingdoms, principalities, and republics, the four most important (in my judgment) are dissension, abnormal mortality, barren soil, and debasement of the currency. The first three are so obvious that nobody is unaware of their existence. But the fourth, which concerns money, is taken into account by few persons and only the most perspicacious. For it undermines states, not by a single attack all at once, but gradually and in a certain covert manner" (Copernicus 1526, 96). Through this, Copernicus highlights the particular significance of his subject: the debasement of currency (Fig. 7.6).

First, he defines money in the traditional metallistic way: "Coinage is imprinted gold or silver, by which the prices of things bought and sold are reckoned according to the regulations of any state or its ruler. Therefore money is, as it were, a common measure of values" (a*estimatio*/appraisal)[3] (Copernicus 1526, 96). However, for Copernicus, in contrast to his contemporaries, money is not just important as a means of exchange, but also as a unit of account. To fulfill these functions, money must be both reliable and stable: "That which ought to be a measure, however, must always preserve a fixed and constant standard. Otherwise, public order is necessarily disturbed, with buyers and sellers being cheated in many ways, just as if the yard, bushel, or pound did not maintain an invariable magnitude" (Copernicus 1526, 96).

This raises the question of the precious metal content of a coin and the nominal value. "Hence this measure is in my opinion the coin's face value. Although this is based on the metal's purity, nevertheless intrinsic value must be distinguished from face value. For the denomination of a coin may exceed its metallic content, and the other way around" (Copernicus 1526, 96).

The minting of coins is done for convenience and to certify their quality: "Coinage was introduced for a necessary reason. Things could have been exchanged for gold and silver by weight alone, because mankind's common judgment prizes gold and silver everywhere. But to carry weights around all the time was very inconvenient. The purity of the gold and silver, moreover, was not instantly recognizable by everybody. Accordingly, people ordained that a coin should be marked with a universally recognized symbol to indicate that it contained the proper amount of gold or silver, and to instill confidence in its reliability" (Copernicus 1526, 96).

But now Copernicus introduces a new distinction: "intrinsic value [*valor*/value] must be distinguished from face value [*aestimatio*/appraisal]. For, the denomination of a coin may exceed its metallic content, and the other way around" (Copernicus

[3] (*Latin word used by Copernicus*/literal English translation): (*aestimatio*/appraisal); (*valor*/value); (*dignitas*/dignity).

Fig. 7.6 The Four Horsemen of the Apocalypse (Albrecht Dürer, 1498)

1526, 96). A coin can therefore contain not only too little precious metal, but also too much. "The face value of a coin is just and proper when the coin contains slightly less gold or silver than may be bought with it, since only the expenses of the minters should be deduced. For, the symbol should add some value to the metal"

(Copernicus 1526, 96). This is the normal case: Coinage adds *dignitas*/dignity to the *valor*/value of metal. The *aestimatio*/appraisal with which the coins circulate should be high enough to cover the costs of the precious metal and minting, while leaving a small profit. This prevents good coins from being exported or melted down immediately.

The difference between the underlying value of the metal (*valor*/value) and the face value (*aestimatio*/appraisal) represents the *dignitas*/dignity. Following Sommerfeld (1978, 75–76), this leads to the following equation: *aestimatio*/appraisal = *valor*/value + *dignitas*/dignity. The *aestimatio* is therefore the exchange value, relevant in circulation, which has detached itself from the precious metal's value (*valor*), giving it a nominalistic coloring. The *dignitas* represents the difference from the metal's value and can therefore only be derived from the function of money.

Different assessments have been made regarding this interpretative distinction between *aestimatio*/appraisal and *valor*/value (Reis and Hinderliter 1979, 300–303). For the Marxist Sommerfeld, *dignitas* can be objectively determined from labor values (Sommerfeld 1978, 133). Jastrow, however, claims that Copernicus introduced *dignitas*/dignity out of embarrassment and that the concept lacked a strong theoretical basis (Jastrow 1914, 743–745). Rothbard interpreted Copernicus "neo-classically" and saw *aestimatio*/appraisal as being determined by supply and demand (Rothbard 1995).

By separating the *aestimatio*/appraisal into *dignitas*/dignity and *valor*/value, the *aestimatio*/appraisal can fluctuate for two reasons. "Money loses its value [*aestimatio*/appraisal] most of all through excessive abundance, if so much silver is coined as to heighten people's desire for silver bullion more than for coined money. For in this way the coinage's market value vanishes [has lost its *dignitas*/dignity] when with it it is not possible to buy as much silver as the money itself contains, and is found a greater advantage in destroying the coin by melting the silver. The solution is to mint no more coinage until it recovers its par value and becomes more desirable than silver (Copernicus 1526, 96–97)." Here, the *aestimatio*/appraisal loses through a negative *dignitas*/dignity, and this is brought about by over-minting. In this way, even "full-value" coins can lose their value when there is an excess in coin production, when they are over-minted (Sommerfeld 1978, 137).

Conversely, the appraisal may decrease if the content of the precious metal decreases. "This face value [*aestimatio*/appraisal] is corrupted in many ways. Firstly, the metal alone may be defective, when for the same weight of coin more than the right amount of copper is alloyed with the silver. Secondly, the weight may be defective, even though the proportion of copper and silver is correct. Thirdly, and this is the worst, both defects may be present at the same time. The value [*aestimatio*/appraisal] of a coin deteriorates also by itself as the coin is worn down through long use. Only for this reason should it be renewed and replaced. This is indicated if somewhat less silver is found in the coin than is bought with it. This is the condition in which depreciation of the coinage is properly perceived" (Copernicus 1526, 97).

The question is whether this already constitutes a Quantity Theory of Money, as Copernicus may suggest: “But, being inattentive, we do not realize that the dearness of everything is produced by the debasement of the coinage” (Copernicus 1526, 97). This is also answered differently. Rothbard, for example, would agree with this view, for he asserts that Copernicus “became the first person to set forth clearly the *Quantity Theory of Money*, the theory that prices vary directly with the supply of money in the society” (1995). Jastrow, by contrast, advocates a contrary perspective: “If one wanted to attribute to the thinker everything that falls under his words, regardless of whether he was aware of it or not, one could still credit him with anticipating many later discoveries. [...] Similarly, it seems to me impossible to portray Copernicus as an early proponent of the quantity theory based on the observation that a coin loses value when minted beyond demand” (1914, 478, my translation).

According to Copernicus, there are two possible reasons why the *aestimatio*/appraisal deteriorates.

1. Firstly, *valor*/value may decrease. This is the standard metallistic interpretation, which had previously been formulated by Oresme. The metal content decreases, either intentionally by the master of the mint or through use and degradation. Economic agents export the higher-quality coins to pay for imported goods or melt them down. Thus, the quantity of coins is determined endogenously by their use as money or as a precious metal, depending on circulation needs. In a second step, the master of the mint who has saved precious metal by minting undervalued coins will presumably use the saved silver to increase the money supply exogenously.
2. Secondly, *dignitas*/dignity can deteriorate and even become negative. Here, the quantity even of full-value coins can lead to a decline in *aestimatio*/appraisal. This negative dignity results from over-minting. In this case, money is understood in nominalistic terms. The excessive quantity of coins issued by the master of the mint leads to a loss of *aestimatio*/appraisal in terms of the Quantity Theory of Money. In a second step, economic agents will melt down the coins and exploit the higher value of the pure metal, thereby reducing the money supply endogenously.

Copernicus presents two forms of depreciation and their interactions. In this respect, Copernicus could be considered the founder of both the Quantity Theory of Money and the endogenous, Income Theory of Money tradition. However, what is fascinating is how he interweaves insights and handles the resulting complexity.

In this specific historical context, the aim was to limit the number of coins in circulation by restricting the number of mints. “An excessive multiplicity of coinage should be avoided” (Copernicus 1526, 102). At the same time, Copernicus wanted to ensure that the precious metal content of the coins did not fall too low by keeping seigniorage within a reasonable and stable range.

7.4.2 The Development of Prussian Coinage

Copernicus begins by recounting the period around 1400, when the coins of the Teutonic Order contained a high proportion of silver. He then describes how the silver content gradually decreased, to the point where, due to over-minting, their value even fell below their denomination. Copernicus describes the consequences in dramatic terms: "But woe to you, O Prussia, you who pay the penalty for a maladministered state by your ruin, alas! Thus, although the money's market value and intrinsic value were gradually vanishing at the same time, nevertheless there was absolutely no interruption in the coining of money. The costs of minting did not cover the difference by which the later coinage would be equalized with the older coinage. Hence, a coinage always worse than the previous coinage was superimposed on it. This depressed the worth of the earlier coinage and drove it out, until the shilling's face value coincided in due proportion with the groat's intrinsic value, and 24 light marks were equivalent to 1 pound of silver" (Copernicus 1526, 98).

This is followed by a passage that is often cited as the first written articulation of Gresham's Law: "Then what remains in the absence of help except that hereafter Prussia, drained of gold and silver, will have an exclusively copper currency? Consequently, imports of foreign merchandise and all foreign trade will soon end. For what foreign merchant will want to exchange his goods for copper coins? Lastly, which of our merchants will be able to buy foreign merchandise in foreign lands with the same money? Yet those in authority scornfully disregard this immense misfortune of the Prussian state. To their very dear country they owe, not to mention the deepest devotion, after piety to God, even their very lives. Yet by their thoughtless indifference they let their country slip wretchedly downhill further and further day after day and crash" (Copernicus 1526, 98–99). In the context of the other explanations, Copernicus is somewhat clearer about the consequences of the problem of different currencies than Oresme was.

Copernicus sees no economic advantages to a weak currency. Indeed, it places a particular burden on those with fixed incomes. "But maybe someone will argue that cheap money is more convenient for human needs, forsooth, by alleviating the poverty of people, lowering the price of food, and facilitating the supply of all the other necessities of human life, whereas sound money makes everything dearer, while burdening tenants and payers of an annual rental more heavily than usual" (Copernicus 1526, 99).

Like Oresme before him, Copernicus also points out the negative distributional effects: "While, then, such grave evils beset Prussian money and consequently the whole country, its calamities benefit only the goldsmiths and those who know the purity of metal by experience. For from the mixed coinage they collect the old pieces, from which they melt down the silver and sell it. From the inexperienced public they constantly receive more silver with the coinage. But after those old shillings now disappear completely, the next best are selected, while the inferior mass of money remains behind" (Copernicus 1526, 99).

Thus, in sum, Copernicus notes: "If they will have regard for the common good, they will surely be unable to deny that sound money benefits not only the state but also themselves and every class of people, whereas debased coinage is harmful. Although this is quite clear for many reasons, we learn that it is so also through experience, the teacher of objective truth. For we see that those countries flourish the most which have sound money, whereas those which use inferior coinage decline and fall" (Copernicus 1526, 99).

7.4.3 Copernicus's Proposals for Reform

Copernicus derived his reform proposals from his description of the effects of inflation: "Therefore, if it is decided to let Prussia at last recover at some future time from its previous depression by restoring its currency, the most urgent task will be to avoid the confusion arising from the differences between the various mints where the coinage is to be struck. For, multiplicity interferes with uniformity, and maintaining standardized production in several mints is harder than in one. It would therefore be advantageous to have for all of Prussia one common mint producing coinage of every denomination. [...] If, however, this could not be done because of the opposition of the Duke of Prussia on the grounds that he wants to have his own mint, let two places be designated at the most, one in his Royal Majesty's territory and the other in the Duke's domain. [...] Let both coinages be subject to royal control, and by His Majesty's order be used and accepted throughout the entire kingdom. This arrangement will produce no small effect on the reconciliation of attitudes and participation in trade" (Copernicus 1526, 100). The two princes should mint the coins without wanting to profit from them by generating seigniorage income. The ratio of gold and silver coins should be in line with the precious metal exchange rates, and any changes to the coinage system must be agreed upon by all the Estates.

7.5 Evaluation

Although Copernicus was a church representative, his text is entirely shaped by his observations on the economic function of money. According to Sommerfeld, it is "the striving of the Renaissance scientist for a departure from theological and feudal-juridical constraints (1978, 130, my translation)." It is the rationality of his economic thinking and the rigor of his analysis of money that are particularly striking.

The distinction between *valor*/value and *aestimatio*/appraisal paves the way for a distinction between nominalism and metallism, and thus also for the Quantity Theory of Money. Even if Copernicus could not yet fill this without an economic value theory, the "over-minting" of full-value coins and their conceptual interpretation represent a decisive step forward. In other respects, Copernicus follows in Oresme's footsteps with his call for full-value coins, his description of Gresham's Law, and his acknowledgment of the negative consequences of currency devaluation.

Taxonomic Classification
Copernicus addresses the issue of the value of money. On the one hand, he follows the tradition of "good" coinage, focusing on their function as a stable medium of exchange. However, he also considers the issue of over-minting, which requires money to be more than just a commodity. Money is also a means of payment whose value is co-determined by its *dignitas*/dignity. As he does not deal with credit money, Copernicus has a narrow understanding of the money supply, relating only to currency.

References

Copernicus, Nicolaus. 1526, "Monete cudende ratio." Memorandum of 1526. Translated by Edward Rosen and Erna Hilfstein. *A Source Book on Early Monetary Thought*. Cheltenham: Edward Elgar Publishing. 2020. 96–102.

Czartoryski, P. 1985. Copernicus and the money question. In *Nicholas Copernicus Minor Works*, 167–215. London: Palgrave Macmillan.

Hubatsch, Walther. 1973. Das westliche Preußen und das Ermland zur Zeit des Copernicus. In *Nicolaus Copernicus zum 500. Geburtstag*, 138–154. Cologne: Böhlau Verlag.

Jastrow, Ignaz. 1914. Kopernikus' Münz- und Geldtheorie. *Archiv für Sozialwissenschaft und Sozialpolitik* 38:734–751.

Kellenbenz, Hermann. 1973. Die Vorschläge des Nicolaus Copernicus zu einer Reform des preußischen Münzwesens. In *Nicolaus Copernicus zum 500. Geburtstag*, 81–96. Cologne: Böhlau Verlag.

Reiss, Timothy J., and Roger H. Hinderliter. 1979. Money and value in the sixteenth century: the Monete Cudende ratio of Nicholas Copernicus. *Journal of the History of Ideas* 40 (2): 293–313.

Rothbard, Murray. 1995. Copernicus and the quantity theory of money. *Austrian Perspective on the History of Economic Thought*. https://mises.org/library/copernicus-and-quantity-theory-money.

Sommerfeld, Erich. 1978. *Die Geldlehre des Nicolaus Copernicus*. 2nd ed, 2003. Berlin: Neunplus.

Stasiewski, Bernhard. 1973. Nicolaus Copernicus als ermländischer Domherr. In *Nicolaus Copernicus zum 500. Geburtstag*, 63–80. Cologne: Böhlau Verlag.

Volckart, Oliver. 1997. Early beginnings of the quantity theory of money and their context in Polish and Prussian monetary policies, c. 1520–1550. *Economic History Review* 50 (3): 430–449.

Chapter 8
Development of the Quantity Theory of Money

In his *History of Economic Analysis*, Joseph Schumpeter discusses the historical development of the Quantity Theory of Money. Schumpeter divides early theories into two groups, referring to the first as the crude, naive, or metallistic version of the quantity theory, and to the second as the nominalistic or cartalistic quantity theory (he prefers the term *theorem* because it only explains the exchange value of money). Schumpeter asserts that solely the latter group treats the problem as a distinct monetary phenomenon while also making a statement about the value of money (Schumpeter 1954, 312).

To illustrate the difference, Schumpeter presents two scenarios within a pure gold currency. He starts with the naive or metallistic quantity theory: “Let us embrace, for a moment, uncompromising metallism and consider the case of perfect gold monometallism—gold metallism such that gold can move freely in and out of the monetary system—from this standpoint. Gold being a commodity like any other, the value in terms of commodities of the golden monetary unit will fall, other things being equal, if gold production increases, just as the price of eggs will fall, other things being equal, if egg production increases. Any rise in prices in terms of gold that may occur is here explained as a consequence of increased supply. Let us note that the extent of this fall (in the value of gold) will simply depend upon the shape of the demand schedule for gold as a commodity in terms of some other standard, and that the operative ‘quantity’ in question is the total amount of the increase. In consequence, there is no reason to suppose that, however equal the other things, the fall will be proportional to the increase. […] But recognition of the relevance of ‘quantity’ to the value of money in this sense and for this reason has no more to do with the Quantity Theory of Money than that the word quantity occurs in both arguments” (Schumpeter 1954, 312).

He then points out the differences to the nominalistic Quantity Theory of Money. In this second case, Schumpeter expands the presented assumptions. Now the existing pile of goods is unchangeable and the money available to buyers must be used immediately and completely for the purchase of these goods. If gold production

J. Greitens, *Currency and Credit Money*, Springer Studies in the History of Economic Thought, https://doi.org/10.1007/978-3-032-24113-9_8

increases, the prices of goods for the share of gold entering the money circulation must increase proportionally. “It is the increase in this quantity which, the purchasing power of the total monetary stock remaining constant, is the immediate cause of the resulting fall in the exchange value of the monetary unit. And this fall will be the same as if this stock, without being increased, had been split into units of smaller gold content, because in either case there is now less of every commodity per coin” (Schumpeter 1954, 313).

Even when explained with an example based on gold money, this version of the Quantity Theory of Money is quasi-nominalistic. “But it is one of the strong points of the quantity theory that it can be applied to the case of paper money without any auxiliary construction. [...] This logical affinity of the quantity theorem with theoretical cartalism should be borne in mind: the theorem essentially amounts to treating money not as a commodity but as a voucher for buying goods, though not everyone who does consider money in this light need accept the specific schema offered by the quantity theorem. It is the more important to remember this point because later developments tended to obliterate it” (Schumpeter 1954, 313).

In the case of a gold-based currency, a price increase can be caused by a fall in the value of gold or silver as a commodity and/or a shift in the balance between goods and money. During the Price Revolution of the fifteenth and sixteenth centuries, when silver was produced and delivered to Europe much more cheaply than before, the authors were unable to identify the specific cause. However, this is different in the case of paper money, where it is clear that a price increase is caused by an increase in the amount of paper money in circulation.

A large number of authors wrote about these issues during the Price Revolution. These include Copernicus, who has already been discussed, as well as Azpilcueta de Navarro from the School of Salamanca, Thomas Gresham in England, Jean Bodin in France, Bernardo Davanzati in Florence, and anonymous authors in Saxony. While the Saxon coin dispute (1530/1) is argued with naive quantity theory, Copernicus's work already goes beyond this. The following section briefly introduces Bodin and Davanzati as two authors who exemplify Schumpeter's distinction (O'Brien 2000, 267, 272; Arestis and Howells 2002, 193–196).

8.1 Jean Bodin (1530–1596): Gold and Silver from the New World

8.1.1 Biography[1]

Jean Bodin came from a middle-class background and at first entered a Carmelite monastery. After a few years, however, he abandoned the plan of becoming a monk. Between 1550 and 1560 he is documented in Toulouse, first as a student and later as

[1] This biography follows O'Brien (1997, 11–14).

a lecturer. From 1561 onward, he worked as a lawyer in Paris and became politically active. He narrowly survived the St. Bartholomew's Day Massacre in 1572 and withdrew from active politics in 1576. Afterward, he served as a prosecutor in Laon, where he died in 1596 during one of the many plague epidemics.

Among his most important works are the influential *Six livres de la république* (1576), through which he established his reputation as a political theorist, and his treatise on witch trials, *La Démonomanie des sorciers* (1580). Bodin is regarded as a political thinker on the threshold of modernity and was seen in his own time as a "universal genius." Today, he is primarily remembered as a leading theorist of absolutism.

8.1.2 Selected Text

Bodin, Jean. 1568. *Response to the paradoxes of Malestroit.* Translated and edited by Henry Tudor and R.W. Dyson. Bristol: Thoemmes Press. 1997.

8.1.3 Historical Background

The book starts with the developments that followed the introduction of New World silver from the Potosí mines in the sixteenth century European Price Revolution. In 1566, Jean de Malestroit wrote the treatise *Les paradoxes du seigneur de Malestroit sur le faict des monnoyes publiés* about the rising prices. In it, he formulated two paradoxes. "First Paradox: That we are wrong to complain that the price of everything in France has increased, because no prices have increased during the past 300 years" (Malestroit in Bodin 1568, 41). Malestroit therefore argues that the price of gold has not increased and that the quantity of gold remains constant. "Second Paradox: That much can be lost on an écu or other gold and silver money, even though it is paid out at the same rate as that at which it was received" (Malestroit in Bodin 1568, 44). He believes that the rising prices are only caused by the increasingly inferior quality of the coins being minted (O'Brien 2007, 19; O'Brien 2000, 276).

8.1.4 Discussion

In 1568, Bodin responded with the treatise *Réponse de J. Bodin aux paradoxes de M. de Malestroit*. In it, Bodin takes a contrary position. "I find that the dearness which we see today has some four or five causes. The main and almost the only cause (which no one has mentioned until now) is the abundance of gold and silver, which is greater in this kingdom today than it has been during the past 400 years. I go no further back because the court registers and those of the Chambre des Comptes do not extend back beyond 400 years. The rest has to be gleaned from old histories with little reliability. The second cause of the rise in prices is, in part, monopolies. The third is scarcity, caused partly by the export trade and partly by waste. The fourth is the pleasure of kings and great lords who raise the prices of thc things of which they are fond. The fifth is the price of money, debased from its ancient value." (Bodin 1568, 59). Bodin writes that Malestroit fails to take into account the influence of American silver and does not know how to interpret the existing data, resulting in an inadequate explanation (O'Brien 2000, 277).

According to Bodin, the Price Revolution resulted from:

1. an increase in the supply of money and silver,
2. monopolies' pricing power,
3. supply shortages due to exports and waste,
4. the luxury expenditure of kings and princes, and,
5. coin deterioration.

However, the most important reason was the increase in the supply of precious metals. "The chief cause of the rise in prices of all things in all places is the abundance of what gives things their value and price" (Bodin 1568, 59).

The coins' precious metal content had fallen by less than the prices had risen. "If Monsieur de Malestroit consults the records of the Chambre des Comptes, he will agree with me that more gold and silver has been found in France to meet the needs of the king and the commonwealth between 1515 and 1568 than could be found in the previous 200 years" (Bodin 1568, 63). Therefore, Bodin attributed the Price Revolution to this imported increase in the money supply.

In 1568, Bodin provided an explicit and theoretically sound explanation for the Price Revolution that had spread across Europe (O'Brien 2007, 29–30; O'Brien 2000, 277–9; critically Arestis and Howells 2002, 201). Schumpeter wrote: "The reader will observe that this analysis needs [...] generosity of interpretation to be a correct diagnosis of the historical case as it presented itself in 1568. Even as regards general theoretical content, it is superior to much later work" (Schumpeter 1954, 312). However, according to Schumpeter's definition, Bodin's version of the Quantity Theory of Money is clearly the naive or metallistic form.

Despite this seemingly modern, secular analysis of money being based on numerical and historical evidence, it comes from a man who argued for the persecution of witches and rejected the concept of autonomous natural law. Consequently, his ideas were still connected to those of older theorists, who understood money from a moral and communitarian perspective, such as Oresme (Parsons 2024, 772).

Taxonomic Classification

Although Boding is often considered the "inventor" of the *Quantity Theory of Money*, he is a proponent of the metallistic version. This version is based on the function of currency as a medium of exchange, and raises the question of the value of money.

8.2 Bernardo Davanzati (1529–1606): The View from Heaven

8.2.1 Biography[2]

Bernardo Davanzati Bostichi (1529–1606) was a Florentine scholar, writer, and translator from an old patrician family, deeply rooted in the humanist milieu of his city. A serious and laconic man, he worked as a merchant and wrote on a variety of topics, including Tuscan agriculture (1579), money (first presented in 1588 to the Florentine Academy as *Lezione delle monete*), and the English Reformation (1600). His most notable achievement was his Italian translation of Tacitus's works, which was partially published in 1600 and completed posthumously in 1637.

8.2.2 Selected Text

Davanzati, Bernardo. 1588. *A Discourse upon Coins*. Translated by John Toland. London: John Churchil. 1696.

8.2.3 Historical Background

His 1588 treatise *Lezione delle monete* deals with issues of monetary theory in light of gold imports from America. In 1696, this treatise was translated by the Irish philosopher and freethinker John Toland, who saw it as reinforcing John Locke's arguments in the debate about the Great Recoinage that same year (preface as a letter of the translator to his friend, Davanzati 1588, iii–vi). In terms of editions sold, Davanzati's writing is one of the "economic bestsellers" from the period before 1850 (Reinert et al. 2017, 26–27).

8.2.4 Discussion

According to Davanzati, money is created from precious metals by means of convention. "Money therefore is Gold, Silver, or Copper coin'd by publick Authority at pleasure, and by the Consent of Nations made the Price and Measure of things, to contract them the more easily" (Davanzati 1588, 12). Other forms, including paper, would be possible, but only domestically accepted. Central is the character of money as a convention: "men have agreed to fix that Value upon those Metals" (Davanzati 1588, 14).

[2] This biography follows Stackelberg (1960).

How is the value of money determined? "All Men labour to become happy, and they think to find this Happiness in the Satisfaction of all their Wants and Desires, to answer which all Earthly Things were created very good. Now all these by the Consent of Nations are worth all the Gold (comprehending also the Silver and Copper) that is wrought in the World. All Men then do passionately covet all the Gold, to buy all things for the Satisfaction of all their Wants and Desires, and so to become happy" (Davanzati 1588, 15).

Davanzati contrasts gold and goods. In order to satisfy their needs, people must acquire money, which they desire as a medium of exchange rather than for its use value. The scarcity of money compared to goods determines its value. "To be always acquainted with the Rule and Arithmetical Proportion which things bear among themselves and with Gold, it were necessary to look down from Heaven [...]. Then we might cast up the Sum and say, there is on Earth just so much Gold, so many Things, so many Men, so many Desires: As many of those Desires as any thing can satisfy, so much it is worth of another thing, so much Gold it is worth" (Davanzati 1588, 15–16). From heaven, seen as aggregates, the quantities of money and goods can be determined, and it is their ratio that determines the value of money.

Davanzati also compares, earlier than William Petty, money to blood in a body. "Every State must have a quantity of Money, as every Body a quantity of Blood to circulate therein. But as the Blood stopping in the Head or the larger Vessels puts the Body naturally into a Consumption, Dropsy, or Apoplexy, etc. so should all the Money be only in a few Hands, as in those of the rich for Example, the State falls unavoidably into Convulsions, and other dangerous Distempers" (Davanzati 1588, 18). Using the analogy of circulating blood, he warns that there is too little money in circulation, and that inequality in its distribution could cause this shortage.

According to Schumpeter, Davanzati's version of the *Quantity Theory of Money* is the developed, quasi-nominalist version; for Schumpeter, he has "to be credited with superior formulation of the quantity theorem" (Schumpeter 1954, 314).

Taxonomic Classification
Davanzati was the first proponent of a clear, quasi-nominalist version of the Quantity Theory of Money. He describes money as a convention and understands it as a means of payment.

8.3 Summary: The Emergence of the Quantity Theory

The *Quantity Theory of Money* is considered to be the oldest economic theory. However, since its introduction, it has manifested itself in many different ways. In its naive form, based on metallism, an increase in the amount of coin metal in circulation leads to a loss of metal value, resulting in rising prices (as measured in this metal). This can be seen in Bodin, for example. Davanzati clearly formulated the pure juxtaposition of money and goods for the first time, which required a solution to strict metallism and acceptance of money as a quasi-nominalistic entity.

However, these approaches to the *Quantity Theory* have some shortcomings in common: central questions have not yet been considered. The implicit causalities from the exogenous money supply to the price level are often not clearly worked out. The velocity of money circulation is more or less overlooked. Similarly, only the supply of money is considered; the demand for money is not investigated. The diversity of quantity theories continues among the authors who will be discussed later (especially Locke, Hume, Ricardo, Wicksell, and Fisher).

References

Arestis, Philip, and Peter Howells. 2002. The 1520-1640 'great inflation': an early case of controversy on the nature of money. *Journal of Post Keynesian Economics* 24 (2): 181–203.

Bodin, Jean. 1568. *Response to the paradoxes of Malestroit*. Translated and edited by Henry Tudor and R.W. Dyson. Bristol: Thoemmes Press. 1997.

Davanzati, Bernardo. 1588. *A Discourse upon Coins*. Translated by John Toland. London: John Churchil. 1696.

O'Brien, Denis P. 1997. Introduction. In *Response to the Paradoxes of Malestroit*, ed. Jean Bodin (1568), 11–34. Translated and edited by Henry Tudor and R. W. Dyson. Bristol: Thoemmes Press.

O'Brien, Denis P. 2000. Bodin's analysis of inflation. *History of Political Economy* 32 (2): 267–292.

O'Brien, Denis P. 2007. The Development of Monetary Economics: A Modern Perspective on Monetary Controversies. https://www.e-elgar.com/shop/gbp/the-development-of-monetary-economics-9781847202604.html?srsltid=AfmBOoojumqk-_OdOLlRLpGIrm3eXKMSSJXGVVywiIf7m_WbyLRORQKz

Parsons, J. 2024. Philosophy of money in Renaissance France. In *The Palgrave Handbook of Philosophy and Money*, 755–775. Cham: Palgrave Macmillan.

Reinert, Erik S et al. 2017. *80 Economic Bestsellers Before 1850: A Fresh Look at the History of Economic Thought*. Working Papers in Technology Governance and Economic Dynamics No. 74. Tallin.

Schumpeter, Joseph. 1954. *History of Economic Analysis*. Edited from manuscript by Elizabeth Boody Schumpeter. New York: Oxford University Press.

Stackelberg, Jürgen von. 1960. Bernardo Davanzatis Florentiner Tacitus. *Romanische Forschungen* 72:1–13.

Chapter 9
John Law (1671–1729): Money and Economic Growth

9.1 Biography[1]

John Law was born in Edinburgh in April 1671, the son of the wealthy Goldsmith and Wardein William Law. As Goldsmiths also acted as lenders, he was introduced to the world of money and finance at an early age. After his father's death in 1688, he lived a carefree life and moved to London in 1691, but by 1692 he had squandered his inheritance and had accumulated debts.

In order to support himself, Law turned to gambling, at which he excelled. However, in 1694 he became involved in a duel, was sentenced to death, and escaped with the help of friends.

Over the next few years, he travelled across Europe as a merchant and gambler, visiting major financial centers such as Amsterdam, Paris, and Genoa, where he studied the latest banking and credit practices. It was in Paris that he met the future regent, Philippe d'Orléans, at the gambling table. He began to engage seriously with economics during this period.

By 1704 he had returned to Scotland. In 1705 he published *Money and Trade*. He also produced several memoranda in French on the idea of land-backed money. After his petition for pardon was rejected in 1707, he left again, living first in Genoa and then settling in Paris in 1713.

The death of Louis XIV in 1715 opened up new opportunities. The regent of the young Louis XV, Philippe d'Orléans, was receptive to Law's proposals. Law established a system that included a state bank issuing paper money and the Mississippi Company, which consolidated government debt and attracted investors. Between 1716 and 1721 France experienced a dramatic boom under his system, before it collapsed in the infamous Mississippi Bubble.

[1] This biography follows Murphy (1997) and Quaas (2023).

J. Greitens, *Currency and Credit Money*, Springer Studies in the History of Economic Thought, https://doi.org/10.1007/978-3-032-24113-9_9

Law fled the country. In the following years, he attempted to rehabilitate his reputation through numerous letters, but without success. He died lonely, impoverished, and embittered in Venice in 1729.

9.2 Selected Text

Law, John. 1705. *Money and Trade Considered: With a Proposal for Supplying the Nation with Money*. Glasgow: R. & A. Foulis. 1750.

9.3 Historical Background

The establishment of state-chartered banks had been the subject of intensive discussion in Europe for several years. The founding of the Bank of England in 1694 prompted the Scottish Parliament to launch the Bank of Scotland in 1695. The scarcity of silver also led to the idea of establishing banks that used land as collateral for paper money. Law joined the discussion in 1705 with his book *Money and Trade Considered* (Wennerlind 2011, 114–116; Murphy 1997, 67–76).

In 1705, the Scottish Parliament was debating entering into union with England. However, this was overshadowed by the insolvency of the Bank of Scotland. Founded as a public bank by Parliament in 1695, from the outset the bank had insufficient silver reserves and a severe cash shortage. Although an audit of the bank's books in 1704 revealed that it was probably solvent, following the *Great Coinage* of 1696 in England, coinage was still scarce. Scotland was virtually bankrupt, not least because of the failed Darién colony project in Panama. William Paterson, the co-founder of the Bank of England, had launched the colony, known as New Caledonia. The project severely weakened Scotland's finances, and was one cause of the 1707 decision to enter into Union with England.

The idea of land banks and land-backed money had already been introduced into debate by William Potter in 1650 and was later taken up intensively in Scotland, where Hugh Chamberlen repeatedly advocated for it. Against this backdrop, the Scottish Parliament not only discussed John Law's currency proposals, but also those of his rival Chamberlen. Law had first presented his plan for a land bank to the English government in 1704, then to the Scottish Parliament in 1705, and finally to the French authorities in 1706/07, always with the aim of overcoming the chronic shortage of money. In preparation for the parliamentary negotiations of 1705, he hastily expanded an earlier essay on a land bank into his major work *Money and Trade Considered: With a Proposal for Supplying the Nation with Money*, which was printed anonymously by his aunt's publishing house to draw the attention of Scottish legislators. It soon became known who was behind the book. Despite the urgency of Scotland's financial difficulties, Parliament rejected Law's proposal, fearing that such a land bank would ultimately bring all landed property under its control (Murphy 1997, 74; Quaas 2023)

9.4 Discussion

9.4.1 Supply and Demand

Law begins *Money and Trade Considered* by discussing the basic concepts of supply and demand: "Goods have a value from the uses they are applied to; and their value is greater or lesser, not so much from their more or less valuable, or necessary uses, as from the greater or lesser quantity of them in proportion to the demand for them, example; water is of great use, yet of little value; because the quantity of water is much greater than the demand for it. Diamonds are of little use, yet of great value, because the demand for diamonds is much greater, than the quantity of them" (Law 1705, 4). Law begins with an early depiction of the diamond/water paradox, known from Davanzati, which later inspired neoclassical economists.

Law advocates a commodity theory of money, arguing that the exchange value of goods is based on their use value, with their price being determined by supply and demand (Murphy 1997, 82). Law sees his approach as a further development of Locke's (Murphy 1997, 51, 85). The value of silver is higher and more volatile than that of the pure metal due to the additional demand for it as a form of currency. This additional demand does not exist for land (Law 1705, 15–16; Murphy 1997, 87).

9.4.2 Problems with Silver Money

Law wants to offer a solution to the problem of Scotland's shortage of silver money, which limits the number of people who can be employed (Law 1705, 3, 28). To achieve this, he reviews the approaches that other countries have tried, drawing on his experience of travelling through Europe: "Some countries have raised money in the denomination, when others have lowered it; some have alloyed it, when others who had alloyed it have rectified it; some have prohibited the export of money under severest penalties, when others have by law allowed it to be exported; some thinking to add to the money, have obliged traders to bring home bullion, in proportion to the goods they imported, most countries have tried some or all of these measures, and others of the same nature, and have tried contrary measures at one time, from what they used immediately before, from the opinion, that since the method used had not the effect designed, a contrary would: yet it has not been found, that any of them have preserved or increased money; but on the contrary. The use of banks has been the best method yet practised for the increase of money" (Law 1705, 63–64).

Prohibiting the export of coins has not been successful, Law observes. Currency devaluation, which is intended to increase nominal circulation, only leads to redistribution and hinders trade. By contrast, the establishment of banks—whether in Sweden, Amsterdam, or England—has been successful. Accordingly, the founding of the Bank of Scotland was a suitable approach for solving the shortage of money (Law 1705, 65–71, 79–80).

Law argues that credit could have the same stimulating effect as money: "they may be brought to work on credit, and that is not practicable, unless the credit have a circulation, so as to supply the workman with necessaries; if that's supposed, then that credit is money, and will have the same effects, on home, and foreign trade" (Law 1705, 21).

However, the amount of credit money is tied to the amount of currency—namely, silver coins—and therefore cannot be expanded sufficiently due to the small amount of silver available in Scotland: "Credit that promises a payment of money, cannot well be extended beyond a certain proportion it ought to have with the money, and we have so little money, that any credit could be given upon it, would be inconsiderable" (Law 1705, 111).

9.4.3 Proposal for Land Money

Therefore, Law's goal is to introduce a new currency that can function as a base money for credit money. "It remains to be considered, whether any other goods than silver, can be made money with the same safety and convenience" (Law 1705, 112). For Law, this new currency must be stable in value but also ensure the necessary quantitative elasticity (Law 1705, 120).

The value of silver money fluctuates according to supply and demand: "Silver in bullion or money changes its value, from any change in its quantity, or in the demand for it" (Law 1705, 116). "If last year a 100 sheep were sold for a 100 crowns, and the person sold them desires this year to buy the same number of sheep; tho' the quantity of the sheep, and the demand for them be the same as last year: yet if the money is increased in quantity, and the demand for it not increased in proportion, the 100 sheep will be equal in value to more money than the year before, so the money is cheaper" (Law 1705, 118). Law cites the *Price Revolution* of the last 200 years as evidence in this regard.

Currency based on precious metals benefits the countries that mine this metal. "Considering the present state of Europe, France and Spain being masters of the mines, the other nations seem to be under a necessity of setting up another money, the only reason can be given why it has not yet been done, is, that the nature of money has not been rightly understood" (Law 1705, 145).

Chamberlen's alternative proposal to Parliament would not sever the link between credit money and silver. This is why Law suggests establishing a Parliament-controlled bank that issues paper money in exchange for land. Although he acknowledges that land is not an ideal measure of value, as its value is subject to change, Law favors it over precious metals because the value of land is more stable than the value of silver. "Land has a more certain value than other goods, for it does not increase in quantity, all other goods may" (Law 1705, 170). "Land cannot lose any of its uses, so will not be less valuable" (Law 1705, 189).

Law outlines the possible charter of the bank, describing how the new land-backed currency should be issued through a kind of open-market transaction managed by a designated committee accountable to Parliament. Law provides detailed regulations governing the issuance of notes and the bank's commercial operations for three proposed variants. These rules are designed to prevent the paper money from being subject to the same value fluctuations as metallic silver currency.

9.4.4 *Money and Trade*

In the spirit of mercantilism, Law's proposal aims to increase the power of the state through economic means. Money is a key prerequisite for achieving this. "National power and wealth consists in numbers of people, and magazines of home and foreign goods, these depend on trade, and trade depends on money, so to be powerful and wealthy in proportion to other nations, we should have money in proportion with them" (Law 1705, 110). John Law understood the word *trade* more broadly, in line with contemporary usage, to encompass production. This depends on the amount of money in circulation: "Domestic trade depends on the money, a greater quantity employs more people than a lesser quantity" (Law 1705, 20).

An increase in trade also results in a larger population, which is important for military purposes. "As trade depends on money, so the increase or decrease of the people depends on trade" (Law 1705, 33). When money is based on land, economic growth and population growth become indirectly related to land. The aim of land-backed money is to ensure steady economic development without inflation (Murphy 1997, 89).

9.4.5 *The Island Model*

Law integrates these ideas into a macroeconomic model that describes an island economy (Murphy 1997, 90–94). At the outset, the island has an underemployed economy and no money, with trade performed by barter. "Suppose an island belonging to one man, the number of tenants [serfs] a 100, each tenant 10 in family, in all a 1000; by these the island is laboured, part to the product of corns, the rest for pasturage: besides the tenants and their families, there are 300 poor or idle, who live by charity, there is no money, but rents are paid in kind, and if one tenant has more of one product, and less of another than his family has occasion for, he barters with his neighbour" (Law 1705, 182–183)."

In this initial situation, the economy is static and has unused capacity. "The people of this Land know nothing of manufacture; the island being plentiful, furnishes enough for their consumption, and an overplus which they exchange on the continent for clothes, and what other goods they want: but as that overplus is only sufficient to make a return of such a quantity of goods as they consume yearly, so they have no magazines of their own or foreign goods to serve them in bad years, nor no magazines of arms, ammunition, & for their defence" (Law 1705, 183).

Law now introduces paper money to this island. According to Law, trade depends on money, and there is a direct correlation between the amount of money in circulation and the number of people employed. Consequently, production increases. "Tis propos'd to the proprietor, that if a money were establish'd to pay the wages of labour, the 300 poor might be imployed in manufacturing such goods as before were exported in product; and as the 1000 that labour the ground were idle one half of their time, they might be imployed so as their additional labour would be equal to that of 500 more, which would lessen their import by providing them with a part of such goods as before they brought from the continent, and raise their export to 3 or 4 times the value it had the return of which would furnish them with greater quantities of foreign goods than they wanted for consumption, which might be laid up in magazines" (Law 1705, 183–184).

The situation changes when landowners start paying workers in the newly created manufacturing sector with paper money. These workers then buy grain and other agricultural products from farmers, who now pay rent. Thus, money circulates between these three groups, financing the purchase of goods and land rents. The money flows back to the landowner, who can then initiate a new round of economic activity (Murphy 1997, 91).

Law assumes that production could react so quickly to an increase in the money supply that it would be possible to transform an agricultural society into a manufacturing one by eliminating the need for cash, funded from real savings, and offering paper money instead. Another highly restrictive assumption of the model is that, despite the increased money supply, domestic consumption would not increase, and surplus products could be exported (Murphy 1997, 92): "more money, by imploying more people, will make an overplus to export" (Law 1705, 23).

9.5 Evaluation

Law wanted to change the currency from metal-based to land-based because the supply would be more stable and elastic. However, he overlooked the potential impact on prices of an increasing money supply, believing that the link to land provided a sufficient brake on inflation. Law failed to recognize that land prices will not remain stable if the supply of land is fixed. When demand increases, land prices will rise significantly, making land unsuitable as a basis for currency.

Law then introduced a *Development Theory of Credit* based on the widely held view at the time that economic development is based on the expansion of the money supply (Wagner 1937, 271).

Due to his activities in France from 1716 to 1720, Law's reputation varies greatly. He has been described as an unscrupulous criminal and imaginative dreamer, but also as a brilliant pioneer of modern money theory who simply misjudged the irrational nature of financial markets.

During Law's lifetime, a number of ideas about land banking emerged, but only his is still discussed today. This is not so much due to the originality of his theory, but rather to his role in France from 1716 to 1720 and his literary achievements, which have a somewhat populist aspect.

Taxonomic Classification

Law wants to replace silver with land as the basis for the currency. For Law, it is not the commodity itself that makes it usable as money, but its scarcity, whose value is determined by supply and demand. Therefore, sufficient medium of exchange to allow the economy to develop is necessary.

(*continued*)

Although Law is concerned with the currency, as land cannot be exchanged directly, he is seeking to introduce a form of covered credit money. Moreover, he sees private loans as being tied to this currency.

9.6 The French Paper Money Experiment of 1720

The reforms initiated by Colbert in 1662 to rebuild the French state was not successful over the long term. Between 1689 and 1715, the coin standard changed 43 times. France had not fully transitioned from a barter to a money economy. In terms of both form and quantity, financial markets were underdeveloped, and the hoarding of money remained common. This made it difficult to raise credit for setting up and running businesses. State finances suffered due to an ineffective and corrupt tax system, as well as massive debt, both of which significantly hindered the country's economic development (Murphy 1997, 121–122).

After 1705, Law connected his ideas about paper money with state debts, as France was experiencing severe financial difficulties. He adapted his concept of a land bank to address the issue of governmental debt management. Invited by the regent, the Duke of Orléans, who was overseeing state affairs on behalf of the young Louis XV, Law established the Banque Générale in 1716 (Murphy 1997, 154).

The Compagnie d'Occident was founded in 1717 as a trade company for the French colonies in America. In exchange for its trade monopoly and property rights in the French colony of Louisiana, the company assumed a share of the French national debt. The owners of government bonds could exchange these bonds for shares in the company, and many took this opportunity, enticed by the riches promised by Law in the Mississippi region.

In 1718, the Banque Générale was converted into the Banque Royale, which was authorized to issue state-guaranteed banknotes. The Compagnie d'Occident absorbed competing French companies, resulting in the formation of the Compagnie des Indes in 1719, which was a merger of the bank and the company. This new company held a monopoly on overseas trade and was granted the right to collect indirect taxes in France.

The prospect of dividends and rising share prices triggered a speculative mania, resulting in share price increases by 400% between August and December 1719. Even at the start of 1720, there was a massive influx of foreign capital. However, shareholders engaged in profit taking following the company's failures in overseas trade. Law could only maintain the share price through his own purchases. However, when the sell-off began in August 1720, a crash ensued. In London, a similar speculative bubble in the South Sea Company took place in 1720, taking advantage of Law's failure (Quaas 2023, 255–371).

In view of Law's spectacular failure, the question arises as to whether the theory or its implementation was flawed. While it is not possible to answer this question definitively, it is worth pointing out that the plan from 1705 and its implementation from 1716 to 1720 differed significantly. While Law originally intended to

Fig. 9.1 Satirical engraving of the Mississippi Bubble (frontispiece from Johannes Oosterwyk, Arlequin actionist, 1720): The buffoon opens the curtain to reveal the grand John Law Theatre. On a stack of Compagnie des Indes shares resembling a wall, coins (good money) are funneled into a man. Below, he gives them back as a flood of paper money, for which the crowd fights. In the foreground on the right, Mercury, who is trapped in a cage, is supplied with air via bellows. At the very front, the monkey holds a banknote bearing the inscription "Null"

introduce a land-backed currency, he instead caused a credit-based asset price bubble in France. Consequently, France returned to a metal currency, and banknotes and state-issued paper money were discredited in many countries for a long time. Law's system became an archetypal negative example (Fig. 9.1).

References

Law, John. 1705. *Money and Trade Considered: With a Proposal for Supplying the Nation with Money*. Glasgow: R. & A. Foulis. 1750.

Murphy, Antoin E. 1997. *John Law: Economic theorist and policy-maker*. Oxford: Oxford University Press.

Quaas, Friedrun. 2023. *John law (1671-1729). Pionier der Geldtheorie*. Marburg: Metropolis.

Wagner, Valentin F. 1937. *Geschichte der Kredittheorien. Eine dogmen-kritische Darstellung*. Vienna: Springer.

Wennerlind, Carl. 2011. *Casualties of credit: The English financial revolution*. Cambridge: Harvard University Press.

References

Chapter 10
John Locke (1632–1704): The Wheels of Trade Are Turned by Silver

10.1 Biography[1]

John Locke, the son of a Somerset lawyer, received a modest inheritance that allowed him to pursue an academic career at Oxford. He distinguished himself as a lecturer in Greek from 1660 and in rhetoric from 1662, before being elected to a permanent fellowship at Christ Church. Although he was deeply interested in the natural sciences and medicine and had close ties to the chemist Robert Boyle, Oxford prevented him from pursuing a formal doctoral degree in medicine.

Locke's intellectual and political career was transformed through his association with Anthony Ashley Cooper, who would later become the Earl of Shaftesbury and Lord Chancellor. Employed as a tutor to Shaftesbury's son, Locke quickly became an invaluable member of the family, notably by overseeing a life-saving surgical operation on the Earl of Shaftesbury for a severe liver abscess. Locke then entered public service, taking on various administrative and advisory roles, and produced his first significant economic writings, including a treatise on the consequences of lowering interest rates and his draft of the *Fundamental Constitution of Carolina* (1669).

Shaftesbury's political downfall and dismissal from government in 1674 led Locke into exile, first in France and later in the Netherlands. During this time abroad, he wrote his most notable works, including *An Essay Concerning Human Understanding* (1690) and *Two Treatises of Government* (1689). The latter advanced a theory of political authority based on a contractual relationship between the ruler and ruled, and argued that the people had the right to depose any sovereign who violated their liberties and property rights. These ideas provided the philosophical basis for the *Glorious Revolution* of 1688, which saw James II replaced by William of Orange.

[1] This biography follows Eltis (2000, 209–212).

J. Greitens, *Currency and Credit Money*, Springer Studies in the History of Economic Thought, https://doi.org/10.1007/978-3-032-24113-9_10

Upon returning to England in 1689, Locke established himself as a leading figure in the Whig movement. He turned down several ambassadorial appointments in favor of devoting his energies to philosophy, economics, and the controversies that his writings had provoked. Alongside the *Two Treatises* and the *Essay*, he published *A Letter Concerning Toleration*, further reinforcing his reputation as a defender of religious liberty and constitutional government.

Locke spent his later years at Otes Hall, the Essex country estate of Lady Masham, where despite his fragile health he remained active in philosophical discussion and maintained intellectual friendships with contemporaries such as Isaac Newton and John Dryden. He died there on 28 October 1704.

Alongside Isaac Newton and David Hume, John Locke is regarded as one of the leading figures of British empiricism. He held the view that all knowledge is derived solely from experience. In addition to being recognized for his contributions to epistemology, he is considered one of the most influential contract theorists of the early Enlightenment. By challenging absolutism, supporting the separation of powers, and advocating for government based on individual rights and political consent, Locke had a significant historical impact that continued long after his death, influencing the development of modern liberal thought while also helping to inspire the American Declaration of Independence.

10.2 Selected Text

Locke, John. 1692. *Some Considerations of the Consequences of the Lowering of Interest and Raising the Value of Money*. In a Letter to a Member of Parliament. London: Printed for Awnsham and John Churchill.

10.3 Historical Background

Rather than ushering in a new age of stability, the *Glorious Revolution* produced a state of near-permanent crisis. For much of the 1690s, England was engaged in an intense war against France that encompassed the Rhineland and Low Countries in Europe while ranging from the Hudson Bay to Madras in the colonies: the *Nine Years' War*. In this conflict, the expansionist plans of Louis XIV were opposed by a broad European coalition consisting of England, Austria, the Holy Roman Empire, the Dutch Republic, and Spain. However, for England, the war had an even more existential political dimension, and quickly became a perilous undertaking. Not only was it the country's first major military involvement on the continent since the Hundred Years' War, but it was also a war of succession concerning the future of the new political order in England, given France's active support of Jacobite forces and its preference for James's return to the throne.

This political situation was mirrored by a deeply entrenched monetary crisis. The volume and quality of circulating silver coins had been deteriorating for years, but during the *Nine Years' War*, the shortage of silver reached unprecedented levels, affecting both everyday transactions and the public purse. Coin clipping intensified dramatically and became the most visible sign of the crisis. Much of seventeenth-century English coinage had been clipped, but by the end of 1695, coins in circulation lacked more than half of their original silver content. Moreover, the coins with milled edges that could not be clipped rapidly disappeared from circulation, either being hoarded or sold abroad as bullion. While clipping was perhaps an understandable response to the shortage of silver, it had become so extreme that confusion ensued, due to the significant difference between the nominal and metal values of clipped coins (Eich 2020, 6–9).

Locke's most famous work on economics, *Some Considerations of the Consequences of the Lowering of Interest and Raising the Value of Money*, was originally written in 1668 for Lord Ashley, who was then Chancellor of the Exchequer. It was published in response to the contemporary debate on legal interest rate ceilings, which was reignited by Sir Josiah Child's influential book of the same year, in which he argued for reducing the maximum permissible rate from 6 to 4 percent. At the urging of Sir John Somers, Locke made his earlier response to Child, rewritten in 1692, available to a wider public. However, the work failed to achieve its immediate objective, for in 1692 Parliament passed a bill reducing the legal interest rate from 6% to just 5%, where it remained until the nineteenth century (Eltis 2000, 212–213, 222).

10.4 Discussion

Locke opposed any attempt to restrict interest rates by law. In his view, the interaction between supply and demand for loans would determine the natural market rate of interest. If legislation were to impose a lower rate, some potential lenders would withdraw their funds from the market, thereby reducing the amount of money in circulation. Lending always carries risks; the interest rate must be high enough to compensate for possible default. Insofar as 4% interest was viewed as insufficient, no money would be lent out. "The first thing to be consider'd, is, Whether the Price of the Hire of Money can be regulated by Law. And to that I think, generally speaking, one may say, 'tis manifest it cannot. For since it is impossible to make a Law that shall hinder a Man from giving away his Money or Estate to whom he pleases, it will be impossible, by any Contrivance of Law, to hinder Men, skill'd in the Power they have over their own Goods, and the ways of Conveying them to others, to purchase Money to be lent them at what Rate soever their Occasions shall make it necessary for them to have it" (Locke 1692, 1–2).

Consequently, the goal of reducing the cost of credit to support industry and commerce would not be achieved, as fewer loans would be available. "And so the reducing of Money to 4%, which will discourage men from lending, will be a Loss to the Kingdom, in stopping so much of the Current of Money, which turns the Wheels of Trade" (Locke 1692, 17). Locke describes money as the component of the economic system that "keeps the wheels turning." David Hume, among others, later invoked this metaphor of money as a commodity.

The money would either remain unproductive or go abroad, and fewer foreign investments would be made in England if interest rates were lower. Therefore, reducing the legal maximum interest rate would cut the amount of money in active circulation (Eltis 2000, 216).

Locke observes that in countries lacking domestic silver mines, such as England, the amount of silver in national reserves depends on foreign trade. "For we having no Mines, nor any other way of getting or keeping of Riches amongst us but by Trade, so much of our Trade as is lost, so much of our Riches must necessarily go with it; and the over-ballancing of Trade between us and our Neighbours, must inevitably carry away our Money, and quickly leave us Poor and exposed" (Locke 1692, 14). Locke therefore describes the outflow of silver as a loss in trade: "Whenever we, by a losing Trade, contract Debts with our Neighbours; they will put a great Value on our Silver, and more Money will be got by transporting Silver than any thing can be sent" (Locke 1692, 179).

Locke, in line with his *Second Treatise of Government* (1689), defines money as a stable medium of exchange and as a pledge for transactions that antedates civil government. It is a convention in which silver, valued for its own intrinsic worth, is used as currency, while the denomination is only an official confirmation of the value med by the state. "Now Money is necessary to all these sorts of Men, as serving both for Counters and for Pledges, and so carrying with it even Reckoning and Security that he that receives it shall have the same Value for it again, of other things that he wants, whenever he pleases. The one of these it does by its Stamp and Denomination; the other by its intrinsick Value, which is nothing else but its Durableness, Scarcity, and not being apt to be counterfeited. Which intrinsick Value, though it be not natural, but is only in the Opinion of men consenting to it, yet being universal, has generally, but not always, […] the same effect as if it were natural" (Locke 1692, 30). The convention, a social contract, concerns the status of pledges made regarding precious metal, not money itself. The purpose of accumulating silver is to have a fixed value in exchange, i.e., a store of value (Carey 2024, 48).

Locke explained that money has two functions: it is a convenient medium of exchange and it acts as pledge or security for transactions. The former is achieved through its denomination, while the latter is achieved through the intrinsic value of money. The state cannot enforce or ensure this convention, "because a Law cannot give to Bills that intrinsick Value, which the universal Consent of mankind has annexed to Silver and Gold" (Locke 1692, 31).

Locke presents a thought experiment. On an island cut off from trade with the rest of the world, the government could declare any durable material object as money, even if the rest of the world did not value it. However, for any nation that trades with the rest of the world, money must consist of precious metals. "That therefore in any Country that hath Commerce with the rest of the World, it is almost impossible now to be without the use of Silver Coin, and having Money of that, and

Accounts kept in such Money, it is impossible to have any standing, unalterable measure of the value of things" (Locke 1692, 75).

Locke explicitly defines money as a commodity. "Money has a Value, as it is capable by Exchange to procure us the Necessaries or Conveniencies of Life; and in this it has the Nature of a Commodity, only with this difference, That it serves us commonly by its Exchange" (Locke 1692, 51). "Money therefore in buying and selling being perfectly in the same Condition with other Commodities, and subject to all the same Laws of Value" (Locke 1692, 53).

Locke argues that, as with other goods, the value of money is determined by scarcity and the relationship between supply and demand. "The mistake of this plausible way of Reasoning will be easily discovered, when we consider that the measure of the value of Money, in proportion to any thing purchasable by it, is the quantity of the ready Money we have in Comparison with the quantity of that thing and its Vent; […] or which amounts to the same thing, the price of any Commodity rises or falls by the proportion of the number of Buyers and Sellers" (Locke 1692, 44). This value cannot be altered by the state. "That the Value of Money in respect of those depends only on the Plenty or Scarcity of Money in proportion to the Plenty and Scarcity of those things, and not on what Interest shall be by Necessity, Law or Contract at that time laid on the borrowing of Money" (Locke 1692, 45).

In a world where there is trade, and silver is the established monetary metal, it no longer follows that any quantity of money will suffice to finance any level of transactions. In a country that trades openly with the rest of the world and uses the same currency as its trading partners, any quantity of money will not facilitate any level of trade; there must be a certain proportionality between money and trade. Drawing on this insight, Locke explains the interrelationship between the quantity of silver, economic output, and price levels. "Supposing then, that we had now in England but half as much Money as we had seven Years ago, and yet had still as much yearly Product of Commodities, as many Hands to work them, and as many Brokers to disperse them, as before; and that the rest of the World we Trade, with had as much money as they had before, [...]'tis certain that either half our Rents should not be paid, half our Commodities not vented, and half our Labourers not imployed, and so half the Trade be clearly lost; or else, that every one of These must receive but half the Money for their Commodities and Labour they did before, and but half so much as our Neighbours do receive, for the same Labour, and the same natural Product, at the same time" (Locke 1692, 76–77).

Locke's version of the *Quantity Theory of Money* is a specific application of the law of supply and demand that he assumes to be applicable to all commodity markets. In the case of money, demand is determined by payment habits, and remains relatively constant. Locke calculates the amount of money a country will require for trade by identifying the factors that determine demand for money. For Locke, changes in price can be attributed solely to changes in the money supply, i.e., an increase or decrease in the availability of silver.

Locke supplements these quantitative reflections with an analysis of the velocity of money: "This shews the necessity of some Proportion of Money to Trade; but what Proportion that is, is hard to determine, because it depends not barely on the quantity of Money, but the quickness of its Circulation; which since it cannot be easily traced" (Locke 1692, 32).

Regarding the bimetallism debate, Locke is also opposed to a fixed exchange rate between silver and gold coins, as their value should fluctuate in line with the precious metals market. "You will as fruitlesly endeavour to keep two different Things steadily at the same price one with another, as to keep two Things in an Aequilibrium, where their varying weights depend on different Causes" (Locke 1692, 168–169).

In anticipation of the Bank of England's founding in 1694, Locke warned in 1692 that a legal monopoly over the money market must be accompanied by corresponding regulation. "If Money were to be hired, as Land is, or to be had as Corn, or Wooll, from the Owner himself, and known good security be given for it, it might then probably be had at the Market (which is the true) Rate, and would be a constant gauge of your Trade and Wealth; But when a kind of Monopoly, by consent, has put this general Commodity into a few hands, it may need Regulation (Locke 1692, 102)."

In the final quarter of the book, Locke addresses debates surrounding the adjustment of coin denominations. This section, titled *Of Raising our Coin*, was not included in the 1668 version of the text. He emphasizes his strictly metallistic position—namely, that the denomination of coins by the state must be based on their intrinsic value as a precious metal, as determined by supply and demand. "But thus nothing can raise or fall the value of your Money, but the proportion of its Plenty or Scarcity, in proportion to the Plenty, Scarcity, or Vent of any other Commodity, with which you compare it, or for which you would exchange it. And thus Silver, which makes the Intrinsick Value of Money, compar'd with it self, under any Stamp or Denomination of the same or different Countries, cannot be raised" (Locke 1692, 134). Accordingly, for Locke, the government is unable to raise the value of the coinage.

Locke asserts that the state is committing fraud if it alters the denomination of a coin, insofar as this denomination does not correspond to the underlying silver content. "The Stamp was a Warranty of the publick, that under such a denomination they should receive a piece of such a weight and such a fineness; that is, they should receive so much silver. And this is the reason why the counterfeiting the Stamp is made the highest Crime, and has the weight of Treason laid upon is; because the Stamp is the publick voucher of the instrinsick value. The Royal Authority gives the stamp: the Law allows and confirms the denomination and both together gibe as it were the publick faith, as a security, that sum of Money contracted for under such denomination shall be of such a value" (Locke 1692, 145). While Locke calls this robbing the people, the king also receives less silver in taxes. Therefore, reducing the amount of silver in the pound sterling would result in both creditors and the government being defrauded. This was similar to the points made by Oresme in the fourteenth century.

Locke was aware of the problems associated with his goal of allowing only full-value coins to circulate: "The melting down of our Coin; the other, The carrying away of our Bullion. These are both Inconveniencies I fear we lie under, but neither of them will be in the least removed or prevented by the proposed alteration of our

Money" (Locke 1692, 147). In order to achieve the goal of sound money, both problems had to be accepted.

In an effort to combat the large number of counterfeit coins in circulation, Locke advocated the adoption of the latest coin production techniques, including machine striking instead of hammering and the introduction of milled edges. "Mill'd-money is therefore certainly best for the Publique" (Locke 1692, 151).

The problem of counterfeiting provides the context for another of Locke's arguments. For Locke, it was not just money that had been corrupted; the language used to describe money had been corrupted as well. Locke accused experts in monetary affairs of acting out of self-interest, an argument similar to that waged earlier by Oresme and later by Justi. "This business of Money and Coinage is by some Men, and amongst them some very Ingenious Persons, thought a great Mystery, and very hard to be understood. Not that truly in it self it is so: but because interessed People that treat of it, wrap up the Secret they make advantage of in mystical, obscure, and unintelligible ways of Talking [...]. Whereas, would they look into those Discourses, enquire what meaning their Words have, they would find, for the most part, either their Positions to be false; their Deductions to be wrong; or (which often happens) their words to have no distinct meaning at all. Where none of these be; there, their plain, true honest Sense, would prove very easie and intelligible, if express'd in ordinary and direct Language" (Locke 1692, 171).

10.5 Evaluation

Locke's writings on the debasement of money became required reading for enlightened politicians in the United Kingdom (Sartori 2021, 501). In the debates between metallists and nominalists, John Locke was considered by many to be the ultimate metallist. For Locke, "the telos of money is to serve as a store of value" (Dick 2020, 301).

Locke's metallism appears very traditional. However, his arguments exhibit various points of divergence from standard metallist positions. His influential description of money as the wheels of trade is striking. His consistent emphasis that the value of goods are determined by supply and demand differs from that of later classical economists. Furthermore, he extends the Quantity Theory of Money to consider the velocity of circulation.

Many critics have attacked Locke's simplistic reduction of money to its bullion content. Sargent and Velde regarded Locke's monetary theory as a regression to medieval norms (Sargent and Velde 2003, 239–244). Nevertheless, Locke's monetary theory was not his most important contribution, but rather his role as the "patron saint of sound money" (Eich 2020, 3). Eich (2020) highlights Locke's role in the political depoliticization of money, whereas Caffentzis (2022) interprets Locke's metallism as a class-bound strategy that removes monetary authority from the sphere of political debate.

Taxonomic Classification
Locke follows in the footsteps of various traditional thinkers by focusing on the function of currency as a store of value. For Locke, the essence of currency was silver. In this respect, his theory of monetary value is straightforward.

10.6 The Great Recoinage of 1696

By the late seventeenth century, England's silver coins had become severely worn and clipped, undermining public confidence in the currency. William Lowndes proposed raising the denominations of coins as part of a new minting program. However, Locke considered this to be a dangerous breach of a public trust. Sir John Somers, Lord Chancellor of England and a supporter of Locke's belief in metallism, had previously encouraged Locke to publicly state his position in 1692. He now called on Locke again to contribute to the political debate and convince Parliament. The result was Locke's essay, *Further Considerations Concerning Raising the Value of Money*, written in December 1695.

To the surprise of many, his proposal won out against competing plans to devalue the currency. Parliament passed the Act in January 1696, initially setting the date for the enormous undertaking of recoinage for May, before moving it to June. A wholesale recoinage—the first since 1299—was carried out in the summer of 1696 at the existing Elizabethan rate. The new coins had milled edges that made clipping them impossible without detection. Worn and clipped coins were removed from circulation during the summer of 1696 and replaced with newly minted coins. To enforce the new emphasis on the intrinsic value of coins, anyone found with counterfeit coins faced severe punishment. While the Great Recoinage largely stopped the clipping of coins, it did not prevent the new coins from quickly disappearing abroad for profit as soon as they left the mint. In fact, the amount of money in circulation decreased sharply as a result of the recoinage.

In assessing Locke's legacy, it is important to recognize that the implementation of the new coinage diverged from his recommendations in several significant procedural respects. Most notably, while Locke had recommended immediate demonetization, the implemented plan provided for a gradual process over several months. This compensated the owners of clipped coins and encouraged further clipping at the state's expense in the interim period (Eich 2020, 20–22).

References

Caffentzis, George. 2022. *Clipped coins, abused words, and civil government: John Locke's philosophy of money*. London: Pluto Press.

Carey, Daniel. 2024. Locke, money, and America. In *The Palgrave handbook of philosophy and money. Volume 2: Modern thought*, 39–65. Cham: Palgrave Macmillan.

Dick, David G. 2020. What money is and ought to be. *Journal of Social Ontology* 6 (2): 293–313.
Eich, Stefan. 2020. John Locke and the politics of monetary depoliticization. *Modern Intellectual History* 17 (1): 1–28.
Eltis, Walter. 2000. John Locke and the establishment of a sound currency. In *Britain, Europe and EMU*, 209–233. London: Palgrave Macmillan.
Locke, John. 1692. *Some Considerations of the Consequences of the Lowering of Interest and Raising the Value of Money*. In a Letter to a Member of Parliament. London: Printed for Awnsham and John Churchill.
Sargent, Thomas J., and François R. Velde. 2003. *The big problem of small change*. Princeton: Princeton University Press.
Sartori, Andrew. 2021. Silver and the social in Locke's monetary thought. *The Journal of Modern History* 93:501–532.

Chapter 11
Ferdinando Galiani (1728–1787): Money as a Public Ledger

11.1 Biography[1]

Ferdinando Galiani was born on 2 December 1728, in Chieti, in the Kingdom of Naples. At the age of seven, he was sent to Naples to live with his uncle, Archbishop Celestino Galiani (1681–1753), an influential churchman and university reformer who also oversaw his nephew's education. Galiani's teachers included the philosopher Giambattista Vico (1668–1744) and the economist Antonio Genovesi (1712–1769), both of whom left a profound mark on his intellectual development.

In 1745, Galiani entered the clergy and received the minor orders. Only a few years later, in 1751, at the age of 22, he published his major work *Della Moneta*. In recognition of this achievement, he was granted several ecclesiastical benefices.

In 1759, Galiani was appointed secretary to the Neapolitan embassy in Paris, where he remained for the next decade. Within the city's literary and philosophical salons, he quickly gained a reputation as a brilliant conversationalist, renowned for his wit and biting satire. His sharp intellect and playful irony made him a celebrated figure of Enlightenment society, despite his small stature, rotund physique, and hunchbacked posture.

After returning to Naples, he held prominent administrative posts and continued to contribute to economic and political debates until his death in 1787.

11.2 Selected Text

Galiani, Ferdinando. 1751. *On Money*: A Translation of Della Moneta by Ferdinando Galiani. By Peter R. Toscano. Ann Arbor: University Microfilms Monographs. 1977.

[1] This biography follows Tabarelli (1999).

J. Greitens, *Currency and Credit Money*, Springer Studies in the History of Economic Thought, https://doi.org/10.1007/978-3-032-24113-9_11

11.3 Historical Background

The public banks of Naples, founded in the sixteenth century as the Monte di Pietà (a type of savings bank), played a central role in the city's economic and political history. They issued paper certificates in exchange for coins. These certificates could be passed on with a signature and were held by private banks as a reserve. The main benefit of this system was that it reduced the negative effects of scarcity in coin metals. However, since not all notes would be redeemed for coins at any time, the banks only held coins in a certain reserve share to the value of notes in circulation. This paper money was not just accepted by state authorities; it was also regulated. In the event of liquidity problems, the banks were required to exchange the notes for government bonds (Avallone 2013, 97–98).

In 1744, Galiani translated John Locke's *Some Considerations of the Consequences of the Lowering of Interest and the Raising the Value of Money* (1692) into Italian, marking the beginning of his engagement with questions of monetary theory. The translation remained unpublished (Tabarelli 1999, 30).

In his anonymously published work of 1751, *Della Moneta*, Galiani mentions Locke several times. Despite the anonymous publication, Galiani's authorship was widely known, and was revealed in the second edition of 1780. Contrary to the title, the book covers not only monetary theory, but also value theory, public finances, and other subjects.

Throughout the work, Galiani explicitly attempts to argue scientifically, repeatedly deploying phrasing such as "this seems to me to be demonstrable on the evidence" (Galiani 1751, 48). Galiani's aim is to distill general economic principles (Patalano 2020, 362).

11.4 Discussion

Like many of his contemporaries, Galiani distinguishes between two types of money according to their use: *ideal* money (moneta ideale), which as a unit of account expresses the price of goods, and *real* money (moneta reale), which serves as a medium of exchange (Cesarano 1976, 384): "Money is of two sorts: ideal and real. It is adopted for two different uses: to evaluate things and to purchase them. […] Whenever money is used to express the value of anything, ideal money is considered" (Galiani Galiani, 49).

- Galiani defines *ideal* money: "Money is a common measure used to denote the price of each thing. This application of the concept is useful beyond all belief, because without a common measure the proportions between things would be poorly understood" (Galiani 1751, 49).
- Galiani defines *real* money: "Money consists of pieces of metal which have been divided, by public authority, into either equal or proportional parts. These parts are given or taken without hesitation by all, as a pawn and a pledge of perpetual

assurance that they will always be accepted by others, as an equivalent of that which was given originally in order to acquire the pieces of metal" (Galiani 1751, 49–50).

For Galiani, there are thus two central functions of money—namely, to serve as a unit of account and as a medium of exchange (Cesarano 1976, 385). This distinction has provoked extensive discussions as to whether Galiani was a metallist or a nominalist and whether he developed a hierarchy between these two types of money (Costabile 2016, 401–402). However, this distinction is not unique to Galiani; a similar description of the contemporary situation can be found in the works of other mercantilists, such as Justi. Furthermore, simply distinguishing between *ideal* and *real* money based on discrete functions is not sufficient to answer this question.

Both types of money are interconnected. "One must think of prices and contracts as valued in ideal money and executed in real money" (Galiani 1751, 49). Therefore, fluctuations between these types of money lead to problems: "If the coins of all well governed states were of equal goodness, and if a just ratio were adopted among the three metals, it would not matter how and with what thing counting were performed. On the other hand, if coins were not equal but all circulated freely, then good coins would be used for expressing values but everyone would try to pay with bad ones. Hence, good coins would leave the state" (Galiani 1751, 171)." Here we find Galiani's description of Gresham's Law.

Even though Galiani explains the advantages of nominalistic money, he cannot imagine a monetary system without precious metals: "If imaginary money were the absolute name of a number explaining an idea of price, and if this idea were fixed in our minds and separated from other things to such a degree that it was not disturbed by the movement of anything else, it would certainly be invariant and constant. But this will never be" (Galiani 1751, 76).

A link to a commodity such as precious metals remains necessary because "men are not able to accustom themselves to compute, from the outset, on the basis of abstract numbers which do not correspond to any specific material. Only when removed, by sensible degrees, from the scene of actual events, do people become very comfortable with the abstract" (Galiani 1751, 60).

Nevertheless, the most interesting part of Galiani's book is his thought experiment in which he proposes a monetary system that does not rely on precious metals. In this model, he addresses the issue of the double coincidence of wants in barter trade, as described, among others, by Carl Menger (Cesarano 1976, 387): "The necessity of trade for sustaining life and achieving happiness on earth is well known, for trade is related to the mutual needs of men. [...] The inconvenience of ancient and primitive methods of trading, which consists of people bartering one thing for another, obviously arises from the fact that it would be too difficult for a person to know to whom a thing which he has in excess is lacking, or to know who possesses precisely what he himself is lacking" (Galiani 1751, 67).

Because of these problems in barter, Galiani is looking for simpler ways to allocate goods. He draws comparisons with communities in which direct exchange is not necessary. "I have wondered whether this inconvenience might not be eliminated by communal living. For example, we know from experience, that small communal societies, such as religious orders, live better communally and generally more happily than others. Why wouldn't even large bodies, such as cities, or even whole kingdoms, also live blissfully communally?" (Galiani 1751, 67).

Galiani proposes that produced goods could be stored in public warehouses, which would be accessible to all members of this community: "I have found, that it is not possible for such communities—which are not made up of carefully selected men of common virtue—to compel each person to labor until he is exhausted and to require him to place the results of his labor into a common, open warehouse in which he would find all things he might need for his own pleasure, deposited by others. But, unfortunately, with such an arrangement, a lazy man could easily defraud the public and live unjustly on the labor of others" (Galiani 1751, 67).

To avoid such free-rider problems, tokens (*bullettini*) could be handed out to the depositors; these tokens would record the quantity of goods they have deposited and their right to withdraw goods of the same value. "We could keep an accounting of how much each person labors. He would then share in the contributions of others only insofar as the results of his industry are of use to society, and no more. Moreover, the system should be so constituted that anyone who brings the results of his labors to a warehouse designated for the purpose would be given a note which would say, in effect: 'This person has deposited such a quantity of such-and-such goods in the public warehouse—for example, 100 pairs of shoes—for the value of which he remains a creditor to society.' Such an arrangement should be made that no one would be allowed to remove anything from the warehouse without first presenting notes indicating how much he had to his credit; thus, he would not be allowed to withdraw more value than that of the goods which had been credited to his account. Once he had withdrawn merchandise equivalent to that value, he would then either leave at the warehouse the note he had originally received, or he would destroy it" (Galiani 1751, 68). For Galiani, these tokens are a certificate of the claim one has to societal resources, measured by a simple value theory of labor (Costabile 2016, 405–407).

Another prerequisite for successful implementation would be the fungibility of the tokens: "Notes should be accepted freely at the doors of all warehouses, so that everyone would be able to provide himself with whatever he might need" (Galiani 1751, 68).

The state would be responsible for the organization and supervision of the system, which would be paid for by taxes. "The prince would have to be allotted a certain number of notes which he could distribute to persons who serve the entire body of people so that they might live according to a standard determined by the importance and merit of their respective functions. Because this system obviously requires that the warehouse have no greater debt, in bills, than the quantity of goods it actually contains, it would be necessary that all citizens be obliged to contribute some goods to the warehouse gratis, that is, without receiving any notes for them. The quantity of these goods would be equal to the total amount given to the prince for distribution to the ministers of the society" (Galiani 1751, 67).

If the tokens were issued based on the goods delivered to the warehouse, the quantity of tokens in circulation would be determined by production levels, i.e., endogenously. In this way, money is merely a representation of the real economy (Cesarano 1976, 398).

Galiani sees fraud as the main problem for implementation: "The unique disadvantage of this arrangement is the possibility of fraudulent notes. [...] Such fraud would soon empty the warehouses of the goods in their care [...] But this could be avoided in many ways, the best of which would seem to be for the prince to sign only a fixed quantity of notes, all of the same denomination [...] printed on either paper or leather" (Galiani 1751, 69).

However, the system can also function without governmental warehouses: "In reality, there are no common warehouses among us, there are only private stores which correspond to them. [...] With much greater wisdom, each person cares for his own labor and tries to fill his own store, giving up money which he receives by trading, or acquires by selling, merchandise" (Galiani 1751, 70).

Although Galiani develops this form of nominalism, he rejects the convention theory of money while directly referencing Locke: "Men are truly laughable when they say that all men agreed, at the same time, to use those metals which were of themselves of no use as money, thus bestowing value upon them. Where are these meetings, these conventions of all the human race? In what century did they occur – at what place?" (Galiani 1751, 48).

Galiani also addresses the *Price Specie Flow Mechanism* associated with David Hume: "They should be saying, instead, that the better value of things is the most secure concomitant for understanding where the greatest riches are" (Galiani 1751, 85). "In periods of prosperity (...) the greater industry of a country causes money to enter it. In this case, higher prices are useful, because they bring more money into the country. For example, the manufactures of England, which are so perfect, are bought competitively by all and draw money into England. If people could live there at a lower cost, things would be valued less. But then less money would be attracted to them. Therefore, it is an advantage for prices to be high in England" (Galiani 1751, 86).

11.5 Evaluation

Although money has two functions for Galiani—that is, as a medium of exchange and as a unit of account—he presents a model of a nominalistic currency system as an ideal. In this system, the quantity of money is derived from production; accordingly, the tokens used to acquire goods are endogenously determined. This system requires a public ledger for tracking inputs and outputs, and this ledger must be managed and monitored by the state. Galiani describes a system of social bookkeeping.

Karl Marx mentions Galiani several times in a positive light. However, Marx rejects the idea of establishing a "labor money" that directly accounts for the labor inputs required to produce goods, their concrete labor value: "The question—Why does not money directly represent labour-time, so that a piece of paper may represent, for instance, x hours' labour, is at bottom the same as the question why, given the production of commodities, must products take the form of commodities? This is evident, since their taking the form of commodities implies their differentiation into commodities and money. Or, why cannot private labour—labour for the account of private individuals—be treated as its opposite, immediate social labour? [...] On this point I will only say further, that Owen's *labour-money*, for instance, is no more "money" than a ticket for the theatre. Owen presupposes directly associated labour, a form of production that is entirely inconsistent with the production of commodities. The certificate of labour is merely evidence of the part taken by the individual in the common labour, and of his right to a certain portion of the common produce destined for consumption. But it never enters into Owen's head to presuppose the production of commodities, and at the same time, by juggling with money, to try to evade the necessary conditions of that production" (Marx 1867, 188–189, footnote).

Joseph Schumpeter repeatedly praised Galiani in his writings. This is not surprising, given that Schumpeter's monetary theory draws heavily on the token theory pioneered by Galiani. Although Galiani's writing has had little direct influence, largely because it was only published in Italian, the concept of money as a token has been taken up repeatedly.

There is a paradox when comparing Galiani with John Law. In *Money and Trade*, Law can be described as a theoretical metallist, as his currency is based on land. However, Law's practical activities in France, he is a practical nominalist. Galiani, by contrast, is a theoretical nominalist but a practical metallist. Galiani's assessment of Law is thus highly critical, due to Law's violation of the metallist principle (Cesarano 1990, 336).

Taxonomic Classification

Emphasizing the role of money as a unit of account, Galiani derives an endogenous, token-based currency that serves as a claim on goods. Galiani does not write about the value of money or credit money.

References

Avallone, Paola. 2013. Bankruptcy in the Kingdom of Naples: the case of public banks (17th to 18th centuries). In *The history of bankruptcy*, 97–107. London: Routledge.

Cesarano, Filippo. 1976. Monetary theory in Ferdinando Galiani's Della Moneta. *History of Political Economy* 8 (3): 380–399.

Cesarano, Filippo. 1990. Law and Galiani on money and monetary systems. *History of Political Economy* 22 (2): 18–27.

Costabile, Lilia. 2016. The value and security of money. Metallic and fiduciary media in Ferdinando Galiani's Della Moneta. *European Journal for the History of Economic Thought* 23 (3): 400–424.

Galiani, Ferdinando. 1751. *On Money* A Translation of Della Moneta by Ferdinando Galiani. By Peter R. Toscano. Ann Arbor: University Microfilms Monographs. 1977.

Patalano, Rosario. 2020. Ferdinando Galiani's Newtonian social mathematics. *Journal of the History of Economic Thought* 42 (3): 357–383.

Marx, Karl. 1867. *Capital: A critique of political economy*. Volume One. Translated by Ben Fowkes. London: Penguin Books.

Tabarelli, Werner. 1999. Della Moneta: Die Zeit und der Autor. In *Ferdinando Galiani "Über das Geld"*, 21–48. Düsseldorf: Verlag Wirtschaft und Finanzen.

Chapter 12
Alexander Hamilton (1757–1804): Disciple of John Law and Founder of Wall Street

12.1 Biography[1]

Alexander Hamilton was born in 1757 on the West Indian island of Nevis, where slaves made up a large share of the population. He was the illegitimate son of a Huguenot mother and a Scottish nobleman, who abandoned the family in 1766 and died 3 years later. When Hamilton's mother passed away in 1771, he and his brother, left destitute, were taken in by a local merchant.

Hamilton quickly proved himself in business and by 1771 he was already managing affairs for his employer. In 1772, a patron recognized his talent and enabled him to leave for North America to pursue an education. He attended a preparatory school near New York and then enrolled at King's College (now Columbia University), where he studied until 1776.

During the American Revolution, Hamilton joined the New York militia. Known for his political essays, he soon became an artillery captain and, in 1777, was appointed George Washington's aide-de-camp. During the quieter periods between 1778 and 1781, Hamilton devoted himself to studying economics and politics, as well as to writing.

In 1780, Hamilton married Elizabeth Schuyler, the daughter of a wealthy New York general. Two years later he qualified as a lawyer and began representing New York in Congress. In 1784, he helped establish a private bank.

In debates over the US Constitution, Hamilton championed a strong central government. As a principle author of the Federalist Papers and one of the Founding Fathers, he played a decisive role in securing its ratification.

As the first Secretary of the Treasury (1789–1795), he presented three landmark reports to Congress: the *Report on Public Credit* (1790), the *Report on a National Bank* (1790), and the *Report on Manufactures* (1791). These outlined his

[1] This biography follows Sylla (2016).

J. Greitens, *Currency and Credit Money*, Springer Studies in the History of Economic Thought, https://doi.org/10.1007/978-3-032-24113-9_12

mercantilist-inspired program for the new republic. Hamilton died in a duel with Vice President Aaron Burr in 1804.

He led an extraordinary life and was a staunch advocate of conservative values and the consolidation of central authority in the newly formed USA. He had many enemies and was often criticized as being untrustworthy.

12.2 Selected Text

Hamilton, Alexander. 1790. "Report on a National Bank." *Reports of the Secretary of the Treasury of the United States*. Vol. 1. Washington: Duff Green. 1828. 54–77.

12.3 Historical Background

The war against Great Britain left the federal government heavily in debt. At that time, there were no significant sources of precious metals in North America, and money had already been scarce during the colonial period. The persistent shortage of reliable currency and bank credit hampered commercial growth, as the government and financial institutions were unable to provide businesses with a stable medium of exchange or sufficient credit money.

As early as 1781, Alexander Hamilton began promoting the idea of establishing a national bank. In a letter to Robert Morris, the superintendent of finance for Congress, he set out his vision for such an institution. Funded by capital from wealthy Americans and supported by credit from abroad, the bank was intended to strengthen public finances and support the young nation's economic development. It would issue pound notes partially backed by real estate, redeem the government's outstanding paper money obligations, and provide loans to the government and private businesses. Hamilton believed that this institution would stabilize the state's finances and stimulate American commerce by ensuring a reliable currency and providing credit to individuals and enterprises: "The tendency of a national bank is to increase public and private credit. The former gives power to the state for the protection of its rights and interests, and the latter facilitates and extends the operations of commerce among individuals. Industry is increased, commodities are multiplied, agriculture and manufactures flourish, and herein consist the true wealth and prosperity of a state. Most commercial nations have found it necessary to institute banks and they have proved to be the happiest engines that ever were invented for advancing trade" (letter quoted from Sylla 2016, 67–68). Founded in 1781, the Bank of North America fell short of this goal and became a normal commercial bank in 1784. Also in 1784, the Continental Currency, established in 1775, collapsed due to excessive issuance.

In 1789, Washington appointed Hamilton as Secretary of the Treasury. This finally put Hamilton in a position to implement his long-standing plans for a national bank. In his *Report on a National Bank* of 14 December 1790—officially, the *Second Report on the Further Provision Necessary for Establishing Public Credit*—Hamilton again focused on improving the young nation's creditworthiness. This had already been a central concern of his *Report on Public Credit* of January 1790. At the outset, he makes his mission clear: "A National Bank is an institution of primary importance to the prosperous administration of the Finances, and would be of the greatest utility in the operations connected with the support of the Public Credit" (Hamilton 1790, 54).

In line with his earlier proposals, Hamilton emphasized the need for a quasi-public structure for the Bank of the United States. He envisaged an institution that would serve the national interest yet remain under the control of private individuals rather than government officials. This proposal immediately provoked controversy, with opponents arguing that it represented another attempt to consolidate the power of the federal government at the expense of the states. Despite these objections, President George Washington signed the law establishing the bank in February 1791. It was formed as a private company with a government charter and minority government participation, but without direct congressional control.

Congress authorized the new Bank of the United States to hold $10 million in capital—an unprecedented sum at the time—and to operate across state boundaries. This announcement sparked great anticipation among businessmen and investors. When the bank's shares were offered to the public in July 1791, it triggered a wave of speculation. The bank's success inspired many states to establish their own financial institutions, contributing to the rapid development of a financial sector in the young republic. Government bonds and bank shares soon formed the basis of a growing securities market, with prices being published in newspapers as early as the 1790s.

12.4 Discussion

Hamilton believes that a state's creditworthiness is essential for avoiding revolutionary upheavals, increasing tax revenues, and gaining an advantage in international competition. Hamilton wants to follow the example of other European countries. "It is a fact, well understood, that public banks have found admission and patronage among the principal and most enlightened commercial nations. [...] Theorists and men of business unite in the acknowledgment of it" (Hamilton 1790, 54). For Hamilton, promoting national creditworthiness and banking were complementary measures. In 1790, for example, there were only three banks in the young USA (Sylla and Cowen 2018, 118).

Hamilton begins this report by providing some theoretical explanations of monetary policy, based on the ideas of John Law. First, he warns against the hoarding of money: "Gold and silver, when they are employed merely as the instruments of exchange and alienation, have not been improperly denominated dead stock; but when deposited in banks, to become the basis of a paper circulation, which takes their character and place, as the signs or representatives of value, they then acquire life, or, in other words, an active and productive quality. [...] the money which a merchant keeps in his chest, waiting for a favorable opportunity to employ it, produces nothing until that opportunity arrives. But if, instead of locking it up in this manner, he either deposits it in a bank, or invests it in the stock of a bank, it yields a profit during the interval" (Hamilton 1790, 55). Hamilton shares the idea of a *Development Theory of Credit* as defined by Wagner (1937, 227–342).

However, Hamilton is not focused on the currency itself, which could remain precious metal-based, but on credit money based on it: "His money, thus deposited or invested, is a fund upon which himself and others can borrow to a much larger amount. It is a well-established fact, that banks in good credit can circulate a far greater sum than the actual quantum of their capital in gold and silver. The extent of the possible excess seems indeterminate; though it has been conjecturally stated at the proportions of two and three to one" (Hamilton 1790, 55).

Hamilton assumes there is a money multiplier between currency and credit money: "Every loan which a bank makes, is, in its first shape, a credit given to the borrower on its books, the amount of which it stands ready to pay, either in its own notes, or in gold or silver, at his option. But, in a great number of cases, no actual payment is made in either. The borrower, frequently, by a check or order transfers his credit to some other person, to whom he has a payment to make [...] Thus large sums are lent and paid, frequently through a variety of hands, without the intervention of a single piece of coin" (Hamilton 1790, 55).

To grant this credit, the banks must hold gold and silver as a reserve: "There is always a large quantity of gold and silver in the repositories of the bank, besides its own stock, which is placed there with a view partly to its safe keeping, and partly to the accommodation of an institution which is itself a source of general accommodation. These deposits are of immense consequence in the operations of a bank. Though liable to be redrawn at any moment, experience proves, that the money so much oftener changes proprietors than place, and that what is drawn out is generally so speedily replaced, as to authorize the counting upon the sums deposited, as an effective fund; which, concurring with the stock of the bank, enables it to extend its loans, and to answer all the demands for coins, whether in consequence of those loans, or arising from the occasional return of its notes" (Hamilton 1790, 55–56). The quantity of money is determined by the demand for credit money and the elasticity of credit.

Money people doubted that a purely public institution could resist the temptation to issue unlimited banknotes without covering them. In order to build trust in the proposed bank, Hamilton wants to introduce certain capital requirements. This would enable the bank to offer large loans to the state and promote foreign trade. Hamilton recognizes the dangers of adventurism and fraud—a concern clearly drawn from Law—but believes that the risks are overestimated. Furthermore, he envisages oversight of the bank by the Ministry of Finance (Hamilton 1790, 56–61).

12.5 Evaluation

Hamilton is a mercantilist in the tradition of Law and the *Development Theory of Credit*. Despite the misfortunes caused by Law's ideas and other paper money experiments in North America, Hamilton remains convinced that paper money has highly positive effects. While Hamilton's proposal is partially inspired by the Bank of England, in comparison to the English model, the power to create credit money of Hamilton's bank is limited though partial state ownership and capital requirements for lending. He describes credit money creation in terms of a money multiplier, as can still be found in textbooks to this day.

Hamilton's plan served numerous aims in the area of nation-building: it sought to solve the state's debt problems, promote economic activity, and augment the strength of the federal government. His report significantly influenced further developments; indeed, his promotion of the banking sector helped to shape the modern US financial system (Sylla and Cowen 2018, 119–21).

Hamilton was familiar with the works of European authors, having studied the likes of Adam Smith. However, his primary focus was on the promoting the development of the young nation through protectionism and targeted industrial policy. Although he shows liberal tendencies in his writing, his specific conclusions are mercantilist (Harlen 1999).

Taxonomic Classification

Hamilton's foundational concern is to enhance the borrowing capacities of the state. This leads him to focus on the function of money as a medium of exchange. Hamilton wants to promote institutional development, and thus lending by banks. He is concerned with credit money rather than currency. He therefore has a broad understanding of the money supply, including active credit money creation by banks.

References

Hamilton, Alexander. 1790. "Report on a National Bank." *Reports of the Secretary of the Treasury of the United States*. Vol. 1. Washington: Duff Green. 1828. 54–77.

Harlen, Christine Margerum. 1999. A reappraisal of classical economic nationalism and economic liberalism. *International Studies Quarterly* 43 (4): 733–744.

Sylla, Richard. 2016. *Hamilton*. New York: Sterling.

Sylla, Richard, and David J. Cowen. 2018. *Alexander Hamilton on finance, credit and debt*. New York: Columbia University Press.

Wagner, Valentin F. 1937. *Geschichte der Kredittheorien. Eine dogmen-kritische Darstellung*. Vienna: Springer.

Chapter 13
Richard Cantillon (1680–1734): Money Flows Like a River—Fluctuating and Uneven

13.1 Biography[1]

Richard Cantillon was born in County Kerry, Ireland, between 1680 and 1690, the second son of Philip Cantillon. He moved to Paris as a young man, and was granted French citizenship in 1708. From 1711 to 1713, he lived in Spain, where he organized payments to British *Prisoners of War* during the War of the Spanish Succession. In 1714, he joined his uncle's banking business in Paris. His uncle died in 1717, leaving him with heavy debts. Thanks to his extensive network of contacts in London and Paris—including to Isaac Newton, the Master of the Royal Mint—Cantillon's banking business quickly flourished again.

Cantillon's life was strongly influenced by John Law and his infamous Mississippi Company, which managed French colonial trade. Cantillon arranged a meeting with Law in 1718; in the following year, Cantillon's brother Bernard founded a colonial settlement in Louisiana. Cantillon capitalized on the speculative interest in the Mississippi Company by betting on rising prices until early 1720. However, as the Mississippi Bubble began to burst, he profited once again by betting on falling prices—possibly acting on information supplied by his brother.

In the autumn of 1720, Law tried to persuade Cantillon over to help him save his project, but Cantillon declined. For the rest of his life, Cantillon was embroiled in lawsuits with investors who had lost their shirts, and was also briefly jailed. He liquidated his banking business in 1723, after the death of his partner, and moved to London in 1733. In 1734, he was likely the victim of murder as he died in a fire that burnt his home to the ground.

[1] This biography follows Murphy (1986, 2014) and Niehans (1987).

J. Greitens, *Currency and Credit Money*, Springer Studies in the History of Economic Thought, https://doi.org/10.1007/978-3-032-24113-9_13

13.2 Selected Text

Cantillon, Richard. 1755. *Essay on Economic Theory*. An English translation of Richard Cantillon's Essai sur la Nature du Commerce en Général. Translated by Chantal Saucier. Edited by Mark Thornton. 2010.

13.3 Historical Background

Cantillon's seminal work, the *Essai sur la Nature du Commerce en Général*, was probably written around 1730. It circulated for many years solely in manuscript form. The oldest known printed version appeared in 1755, about 20 years after Cantillon's death. While this French edition was published anonymously, Cantillon was widely recognized as the author. Immediately respected as an important work, it was reprinted numerous times in the following years (van den Berg 2015, 4–25).

13.4 Discussion

The *Essai* is divided into three sections. The first develops a theory of land value, the second explores monetary theory, and the third examines balance of payments.

13.4.1 Theory of Land Value

Cantillon traces the value of all goods back to land: "Land is the source or matter from which all wealth is drawn; man's labor provides the form for its production, and wealth in itself is nothing but the food, conveniences, and pleasures of life" (Cantillon 1755, 21). The market price of a commodity fluctuates around this intrinsic value, which is "the measurement of the quantity of land and of labor entering into its production, having regard to the fertility or productivity of the land, and to the quality of the labor" (Cantillon 1755, 54). The intrinsic value of precious metal used for money, like the intrinsic value of all goods, is therefore determined by its production costs, i.e., how much land is used for its production.

13.4.2 Mercantilism

Cantillon would appear to be a Physiocrat, given this focus on land; alternatively, he appears to be a classicist, given his stringent value theory. Yet he is actually a mercantilist in terms of his goals: "The point that seems to determine the comparative greatness of states is their reserve stock above the yearly consumption, [i.e. savings] like reserves of doth, linen, grain, etc., to be used in times of need, or war. And as gold and silver can always buy these things, even from the enemies of the state, gold and silver are the true reserve stock of a state, and the larger or smaller the actual quantity of this stock necessarily determines the comparative greatness of kingdoms and states" (Cantillon 1755, 98–99).

Like many mercantilists, Cantillon views precious metals as an important security reserve, as they can be traded for other goods in the future.

For Cantillon, money represents power and, in a silver-based monetary system, the state should therefore aim to achieve export surpluses. "When a state has arrived at the highest point of wealth, and I always assume that the comparative wealth of states consists mainly in their respective quantities of money, it will inevitably fall back into poverty by the ordinary course of things" (Cantillon 1755, 160).

13.4.3 The Monetary System

For Cantillon, silver is a commodity like any other, and its value is determined in the long run by land. However, Cantillon is less of a metallist than many of his contemporaries. He sees the market value of all goods determined by scarcity in the short term. "The market value of metals, as with other commodities and merchandise, is sometimes above, sometimes below, the intrinsic value, and varies with their abundance or scarcity, according to demand" (Cantillon 1755, 104).

Credit money simplifies exchange, reduces the need for currency, and accelerates circulation: It "does seem to reduce the cash in circulation, or at least to accelerate its movement by making it unnecessary when people have confidence in each other and can use this method of exchange by valuation. It is not without reason, as is commonly said, that trust in commerce makes money less scarce" (Cantillon 1755, 134). Nevertheless, Cantillon assigns to credit money a subordinate role: "In the regular course of the circulation, the help of banks and credit of this kind is much smaller and less solid than is generally assumed" (Cantillon 1755, 238).

13.4.4 Quantity Theory of Money

While Cantillon generally agrees with the Quantity Theory of Money, he contributes to contemporary thought: "Mr. Locke lays it down as a fundamental maxim that the quantity of goods in proportion to the quantity of money is a regulator of market prices. I have tried to elucidate his idea in the preceding chapters: he has clearly seen that the abundance of money makes everything more expensive, but he has not considered how this happens. The great difficulty of this question consists in knowing in what way and in what proportion the increase of money raises the price of things" (Cantillon 1755, 148).

First, Cantillon points out that money and prices vary in space. He develops a thought experiment that differentiates between the provinces, where goods are produced, and the capital, where they are sold. "The difference between the prices in the capital and the provinces must pay for the costs and risks of transport, otherwise cash will be sent to the capital to pay the balance and this will continue until the differences in prices between the capital and the provinces cover the costs and risks of transport. Then the merchants and entrepreneurs of the market towns will buy the products of the villages at a low price and will have them transported to the capital to be sold at a higher price" (Cantillon 1755, 140).

Cantillon also clarifies that the entire stock of available money is not the relevant factor, but rather only the share of that stock in circulation: "Let us assume that there are butchers on one side, and buyers on the other. The price of meat will be determined after some bargaining, and a pound of beef will be valued in silver [i.e., money] approximately the same as all beef offered for sale in the market [i.e., supply], is to all the silver brought there to buy beef [i.e., demand]. This proportion [or price] is settled by bargaining. The butcher sets his price according to the number of buyers he sees, while the buyers, on their side, offer less if they think the butcher will make fewer sales" (Cantillon 1755, 119).

Cantillon fundamentally rejects the existence of strict proportionality between money and prices: "I conclude from all this that by doubling the quantity of money in a state, the prices of products and merchandise are not always doubled. The river, which runs and winds about in its bed, will not flow with double the speed when the amount of water is doubled" (Cantillon 1755, 156).

The metaphor of water in a river leads Cantillon to posit that money in circulation has a specific *velocity*. Again, similar to other mercantilist writers like Davanzati, the circulation of money is described by him as the "lifeblood of circulation" (Cantillon 1755, 238). Cantillon views the velocity of money circulation as a decisive factor for the Quantity Theory of Money. Depending on the demand for money, the velocity of circulation changes: "However, if the owners stipulate that their farmers make payments every six months instead of once a year, and if the other debtors also make their payments every six months, this will alter the pace of circulation. While 10,000 ounces were needed to make the annual payments, only 5,000 will now be required because 5000 ounces paid twice over will have the same effect as 10,000 ounces paid once" (Cantillon 1755, 126).

The demand for money is determined by payment behavior and by the share of revenues that are held as currency. Thus, the demand for money has an impact on price levels. Accordingly, Cantillon views the velocity of circulation and overall money supply as closely related substitutes: "In states where money is scarcer, there usually is more barter by valuation, than in those where money is plentiful, and circulation is more prompt and less sluggish than in those where money is not so scarce. Thus it is always necessary, when estimating the amount of money in circulation, to take into account the speed of its circulation" (Cantillon 1755, 127).

13.4.5 The Transmission Mechanism

Cantillon was the first author to systematically address the process by which changes in the money supply affect price levels—that is, the transmission mechanism. Cantillon describes how consumption acts as a transmission channel:

> If the increase of hard money comes from gold and silver mines within the state, the owner of these mines, the entrepreneurs, the smelters, refiners, and all the other workers will increase their expenses in proportion to their profits. Their households will consume more meat, wine, or beer than before. They will become accustomed to wearing better clothes, having finer linens, and to having more ornate houses and other desirable goods. Consequently, they will give employment to several artisans who did not have that much work before and who, for the same reason, will increase their expenditures. All this increased expenditure on meat, wine, wool, etc. necessarily reduces the share of the other inhabitants in the state who do not participate at first in the wealth of the mines in question. The bargaining process of the market, with the demand for meat, wine, wool, etc. being stronger than usual, will not fail to increase their prices. These high prices will encourage farmers to employ more land to produce the following year, and these same farmers will profit from the increased prices and will increase their expenditure on their families like the others. Those who will suffer from these higher prices and increased consumption will be, first of all, the property owners, during the term of their leases, then their domestic servants and all the workmen or fixed wage earners who support their families on a salary. They all must diminish their expenditures in proportion to the new consumption, which will compel a large number of them to emigrate and to seek a living elsewhere. The property owners will dismiss many of them, and the rest will demand a wage increase in order to live as before. It is in this manner that a considerable increase of money from mines increases consumption and, by diminishing the number of inhabitants, greater expenditures result by those who remain (Cantillon 1755, 148–9).

Hayek referred to this passage—which discloses how an increase in the money supply does not evenly affect all areas of an economy—as “brilliant” and recognized him as the first author to spotlight the uneven impact of monetary expansion, a phenomenon called the “Cantillon effect” (Hayek 1931, 8). When the money supply increases, specific incomes rise, and only later, in the longer run, do general price levels increase. Since contracts extend over a certain period of time, price adjustments in individual markets only adjust with a time delay. Cantillon provides a microeconomic explanation for the associated distributional effects. Cantillon argues explicitly against John Locke (Cantillon 1755, 148) and implicitly against John Law by neglecting long-term positive effects that result from the expansion of the money supply (Kopp 1995, 216).

13.4.6 Foreign Trade

An increase in the money supply due to a positive balance of trade leads to higher prices: “Currently, if a state or kingdom supplies foreign countries with goods from its own factories and does enough of this commerce to draw in a constant balance of money from abroad every year, money will be more plentiful and the circulation will become more substantial than in foreign countries, and consequently, land and labor will gradually command a higher price. It therefore follows that in all the branches of commerce, this state will exchange a smaller amount of land and labor with the foreigner for a larger amount, so long as these circumstances continue" (Cantillon 1755, 143).

Cantillon was very aware of what Mark Blaug later called the "mercantilist dilemma": the desired trade surplus leads to an increase in the money supply and thus to rising prices, which makes exports more expensive (Blaug 1985, 18).

Cantillon examines different scenarios in which the money supply increases. If the additional money comes from domestic mines, he considers this to be the worst form, since only domestic products become more expensive and net imports increase. By contrast, when the increase comes from trade surpluses, this creates domestic employment. But for Cantillon, this surplus should not be sustained. Rather, it should be used to increase imports and reach a price neutral trade balance (Cantillon 1755, 148–164). David Hume later developed this idea further when positing his Price–Specie Flow Mechanism (Schumpeter 1954, 289)

13.4.7 Banks

Although—or perhaps because—he was a banker, Cantillon has a mixed perspective on banks. "In the regular course of the circulation, the help of banks and credit of this kind is much smaller and less solid than is generally assumed. Silver alone is the true lifeblood of circulation" (Cantillon 1755, 238). For him, banks are helpful instruments for financing public debt, but are less beneficial for the financing of private companies: "In a city where there are public debts for considerable amounts, the presence of a bank enables one to buy and sell capital stock in an instant, and for enormous sums, without causing any disturbance in the circulation" (Cantillon 1755, 237). Cantillon was writing during the Financial Revolution, when the stormy development of the financial system created large and liquid markets for government debt. "This means that when a state is not in debt, and has no need of purchases and sales of stock, the assistance of a bank will be less necessary and less important" (Cantillon 1755, 238).

Against this backdrop, Cantillon assess the actions of his old business partner Law, without naming him explicitly:

> If the bank alone makes the price of public stock rise by buying it, it will make it fall when it sells it in order to cancel its extraordinary notes. However, many individuals usually follow the agents of the bank in then operations and contribute in keeping the price high. Some of them get caught because they do not understand these operations, in which are found infinite refinements or rather trickery, which lie outside my subject. It is then evident that a bank, with the complicity of a public administrator, is able to raise and support the price of public stock, and to lower the rate of interest in the state at the pleasure of this administrator. When the steps are taken discreetly, it can pay off the state's debt. But these refinements, which open the door to making large fortunes, are rarely carried out for the sole advantage of the state, and those who take part in them are generally corrupted. The excess banknotes,

made and issued on these occasions, do not upset the circulation because they are used for the buying and selling of stock. They are not used for household expenses and are not exchanged into silver. But if some panic or unforeseen crisis drove note holders to demand silver from the bank, the bomb would burst and it would be seen that these are dangerous operations (Cantillon 1755, 242–243).

In this way, with the benefit of hindsight, Cantillon acknowledges that the Mississippi Bubble was a fraudulent enterprise that had been orchestrated with the help of corrupt government officials.

13.5 Evaluation

Richard Cantillon marks an important step from mercantilism and simple versions of the Quantity Theory of Money to later developments, especially in English monetary thought. He was the first to systematically analyze the transmission mechanism and the velocity of circulation, even if not necessarily discovering them.

The mercantilist dilemma is an important problem, and Cantillon suggested solutions for its effects. In some respect, e.g., in his metallistic understanding of money, Cantillon stands closer to the classical economists who argued based on value theory than to the mercantilists (Murphy 2014, 1933).

Taxonomic Classification
For Cantillon, money is a commodity whose value is determined by land. Its main function is to serve as a medium of exchange. However, he acknowledges that scarcity and abundance determine the short-term value of money, and that credit money is important. He thus shifts slightly toward an understanding of money as a nominalistic means of payment, which is the beginning of an approach that David Hume would later adopt. Although Cantillon also considered credit money and banks, he nevertheless focused on the currency of his time, which was based on silver.

13.6 Summary of Mercantilist Monetary Theory

The rise of financial systems paralleled the development of the nation state. During this period, money was often seen as representative and measure of the wealth and power of the nation state.

A central question was whether the lack of money frequently lamented at this time (after the sixteenth-century Price Revolution) acted as a drag on economic development (Wennerlind 2005, 226). On account of this view, many mercantilists advocated for the increased circulation of money, and hoarding was condemned, because land and resources were considered underutilized. Export surpluses paid for by foreign countries in a precious metal-based currency were seen as a substitute for expansionary monetary policy.

The large amounts of precious metal flowing in from the New World in the sixteenth century led to the development of the oldest monetary theory of all—the Quantity Theory of Money. The need to correct trade imbalances through precious metals meant that most mercantilists were also metallists. This leads Schumpeter to describe the first quantity theories as naïve, for they were bound to the non-monetary value of money as a commodity. However, during this period, we also find tentative formulations of a nominalistic Quantity Theory of Money, such as proposed by Davanzati and not least by Cantillon in his discussion of how credit money impacts the velocity of circulation.

Cantillon only touched upon the problem referred to by Mark Blaug as the mercantilist dilemma (Blaug 1985, p. 18), whereby more money leads to higher domestic prices, thus counteracting the desired trade surplus. The predominant view was that a growth effect resulted from the increasing circulation of money, i.e., in line with the Development Theory of Money posited by Law for an underemployed economy.

Some early thinkers thus had a broader understanding of money, not viewing it merely as a precious metal; in addition to Davanzati and Cantillon, Copernicus presented concepts pointing in this direction.

References

Blaug, Mark. 1985. *Economic Theory in Retrospect*. 4th ed. Cambridge: Cambridge University Press.

Cantillon, Richard. 1755. *Essay on Economic Theory*. An English translation of Richard Cantillon's Essai sur la Nature du Commerce en Général. Translated by Chantal Saucier. Edited by Mark Thornton. 2010.

Hayek, Friedrich A. 1931. *Prices and Production*. London: George Routledge & Sons.

Kopp, Torsten. 1995. *Die Entdeckung der Nationalökonomie in der schottischen Aufklärung*. Dissertation No. 1746., Hochschule St. Gallen.

Murphy, Antoin. 1986. *Richard Cantillon: Entrepreneur and economist*. Oxford: Clarendon Press.

Murphy, Antoin. 2014. Richard Cantillon and John Law. *Économies et Sociétés*. 51 (11-12): 1905–1937.

Niehans, Jürg. 1987. Richard Cantillon und sein Essai. In *Vademecum zu einem frühen Klassiker der ökonomischen Wissenschaft*, 11–38. Düsseldorf: Verlag Wirtschaft und Finanzen.

Schumpeter, Joseph. 1954. *History of economic analysis*. Edited from manuscript by Elizabeth Boody Schumpeter. Oxford University Press.

van den Berg, Richard. 2015. *Richard Cantillon's essay on the nature of trade in general: A variorum edition*. London: Routledge.

Wennerlind, Carl. 2005. David Hume's monetary theory revisited: Was he really a quantity theorist and an inflationist? *Journal of Political Economy* 113 (1): 223–237.

Part IV
Authors of the Classical Period

Chapter 14
David Hume (1711–1776): The Natural Allocation of Money

14.1 Biography[1]

David Hume was born in Edinburgh in 1711. He first studied law but soon turned to philosophy. After an unsuccessful attempt to start a career in business, he went to France in 1734, where he began writing his *Treatise of Human Nature*, published between 1738 and 1740. Returning to England in 1738, he worked for a time as a private tutor. In 1744 he unsuccessfully applied for a chair of philosophy at the University of Edinburgh.

Two years later, in 1746, Hume served as a secretary to General James St. Clair (1688–1762), accompanying him on a naval expedition to the French coast. In 1747/48 he followed St. Clair as an adjutant to Vienna and Turin, where the general had been sent as an envoy. Hume returned to Scotland in 1748, publishing his *Political Discourses* in 1752. That same year, after another unsuccessful application for a professorship in Glasgow, he accepted the post of librarian at the Advocates Library in Edinburgh. Between 1754 and 1761 his monumental *History of England* appeared.

In 1763 Hume went to Paris, serving as a secretary to the British embassy, where he met various prominent figures, including Jean-Jacques Rousseau. From 1767 to 1769 he held the office of Under-Secretary of State before finally returning to Edinburgh. Shortly before his death, he wrote his autobiography, *The Life of David Hume*, which was published posthumously by his close friend and literary executor Adam Smith.

Hume died in Edinburgh in 1776. He is regarded as the most important representative of the Scottish Enlightenment.

[1] This biography follows Murphy (2008, 95–99) and Peacock (1987, 25–35).

J. Greitens, *Currency and Credit Money*, Springer Studies in the History of Economic Thought, https://doi.org/10.1007/978-3-032-24113-9_14

14.2 Selected Text

Hume, David. 1752. *Political Discourses*. Edinburgh: R. Fleming. Sections "Of Money," "Of Interest," and "Of the Balance of Trade."

14.3 Historical Background

Hume's early writings, including *A Treatise on Human Nature*, were not very successful commercially. However, as he depended on income from book sales, he turned to writing on economic issues, for which there was greater demand (Murphy 2008, 99).

Hume only devoted a short period of his life to economic research. Influenced by the financial revolution during his youth, he primarily wrote the *Political Discourses* in 1752. Some of these discourses had already been published as supplements to the *Essays, Moral and Political* of 1741, and they were revised several times up to his death. In these writings, Hume classified economics as a sub-discipline of politics within his moral-philosophical system (Schabas and Wennerlind 2011, 223–227).

At this time, a conflict was taking place within the fast-developing Scottish banking system. A number of smaller banks had broken away from the influence of the two major joint-stock banks, the Bank of Scotland and the Royal Bank of Scotland, and were no longer using their banknotes. Instead, they were issuing their own paper money without having sufficient liquidity (Boyer des Roches 2013, 554).

In addition, Hume's *Political Discourses* also made him a key figure in the "Rich Country–Poor Country" debate. This debate centered on the relationship between rich countries that are technologically superior and have an industrial sector and poor countries that are technologically inferior and focus on agriculture. Hume argues that initially rich countries are superior, but they gradually lose this advantage because of the Price–Specie Flow Mechanism, which causes rising domestic price levels. This leads poor countries to catch up technologically (Schumacher 2016, 765–71).

14.4 Discussion

The *Political Discourses* contain a series of economic essays. The sections "Of Money," "Of Interest," and "Of the Balance of Trade" are particularly relevant to monetary theory.

14.4.1 *The Real and Monetary Spheres*

An important contributor to the development of classical economics, Hume holds the view that there is a dichotomy between the real and monetary spheres. At the outset he writes: "Money is not, properly speaking, one of the subjects of commerce; but only the instrument which men have agreed upon to facilitate the exchange of one commodity for another. It is none of the wheels of trade: It is the oil which renders the motion of the wheels more smooth and easy" (Hume 1752, 41).

Hume thus opposes a metallistic conception of money. His understanding of money is directly opposed to that of John Locke, who believes that money "turns the Wheels of Trade" and thus as a part of trade, so he considers money to be a commodity itself (Murphy 2008, 102). For Hume, by contrast, money has no intrinsic worth; rather, it has "chiefly a fictitious value" (Hume 1752, 63).

He therefore advocates nominalism, which emphasizes money's function as a unit of account: "that gold and silver seemed [...] of no use [...], but to assist them in numeration and arithmetic. It is indeed evident, that money is nothing but the representation of labour and commodities, and serves only as a method of rating or estimating them" (Hume 1752, 46). Money could thus be anything—paper, silver, or salt—if it can be standardized and be the generally accepted means of payment by convention.

For Hume, money is thus economically neutral: "From the whole of this reasoning we may conclude, that it is of no manner of consequence, with regard to the domestic happiness of a state, whether money be in a greater or less quantity" (Hume 1752, 50). This was a position that took direct aim at mercantilism.

14.4.2 *The Quantity Theory of Money*

If the amount of money does not matter, then a change in the money supply can only affect prices. "All augmentation has no other effect than to heighten the price of labour and commodities; and even this variation is little more than that of a name" (Hume 1752, 62). The causes of price increases are therefore to be found in the monetary arena.

However, Hume clarifies his assumptions with important caveats:

- "If we consider any one *kingdom by itself*, it is evident, that the greater or less plenty of money is of no consequence; since the prices of commodities are always proportioned to the plenty of money" (Hume 1752, 41, my emphasis).
- "Where coin is in greater plenty; as a greater quantity of it is required to represent the same quantity of goods; it can have no effect, either good or bad, *taking a nation within itself*" (Hume 1752, 46, my emphasis).
- "But money, however plentiful, has no other effect, *if fixed*, than to raise the price of labour" (Hume 1752, 61, my emphasis).

The italicized portions of the first two quotes restrict applicability to a closed economy. And in the third quote, "if fixed" imposes the condition of stationarity, which limits the applicability of the assertion to long-term equilibria. Accordingly, Hume is conducting a thought experiment, identifying characteristics that only apply over the long term to a closed economy.

He then specifies his quantity theory by discussing other relevant variables: "It is also evident, that the prices do not so much depend on the absolute quantity of commodities and that of money, which are in a nation, as on that of the commodities, which come or may come to market, and of the money which circulates. If the coin be locked up in chests, it is the same thing with regard to prices, as if it were annihilated; if the commodities be hoarded in magazines and granaries, a like effect follows. As the money and commodities, in these cases, never meet, they cannot affect each other" (Hume 1752, 80). The value of money is determined by the money in circulation, not the total money supply. Hoarded money is irrelevant. Thus, for Hume, not the total amount of goods in the economy, but the volume of goods actually exchanged in the market is relevant for his Quantity Theory of Money.

Hume diverges from Locke in asserting that the amount of money required in a country is indeterminate. "If gold and silver have increased in the state together with the industry, it will require a great quantity of these metals to represent a great quantity of commodities and labour; if industry alone has increased, the prices of everything must sink, and a very small quantity of specie will serve as a representation" (Hume 1752, 69).

Invoking Cantillon's analogy of a river that flows and winds about in its bed, Hume writes: "This seems to me, almost in every case, a groundless apprehension; and I should as soon dread, that all our springs and rivers should be exhausted, as that money should abandon a kingdom where there are people and industry" (Hume 1752, 80). On the one hand, the volume of money in circulation only influences prices, and on the other hand, the Price–Specie Flow Mechanism prevents the total outflow of money from a country.

14.4.3 Hume's Transmission Mechanism

Similar to Cantillon, Hume also describes a monetary transmission mechanism: "To account, then, for this phenomenon, we must consider, that though the high price of commodities be a necessary consequence of the increase of gold and silver, yet it follows not immediately upon that increase; but some time is required before the money circulates through the whole state, and makes its effect be felt on all ranks of people. At first, no alteration is perceived; by degrees the price rises, first of one commodity, then of another; till the whole at last reaches a just proportion with the new quantity of specie which is in the kingdom. In my opinion, it is only in this interval or intermediate situation, between the acquisition of money and rise of prices, that the increasing quantity of gold and silver is favourable to industry. When any quantity of money is imported into a nation, it is not at first dispersed into many hands; but is confined to the coffers of a few persons, who immediately seek to employ it to advantage. Here are a set of manufacturers or merchants, we shall suppose, who have received returns of gold and silver for goods which they sent to Cadiz. They are thereby enabled to employ more workmen than formerly, who never dream of demanding higher wages, but are glad of employment from such good paymasters. If workmen become scarce, the manufacturer gives higher wages, but at first requires an increase of labour; and this is willingly submitted to by the artisan, who can now eat and drink better, to compensate his additional toil and fatigue. He carries his money to market, where he finds everything at the same price as formerly, but returns with greater quantity and of better kinds, for the use of his family. The farmer and gardener, finding, that all their commodities are taken off, apply themselves with alacrity to the raising more; and at the same time can afford to take better and more cloths from their tradesmen, whose price is the same as formerly, and their industry only whetted by so much new gain. It is easy to trace the money in its progress through the whole commonwealth; where we shall find, that it must first quicken the diligence of every individual, before it increase the price of labour" (Hume 1752, 70–71). The short-term non-neutrality of money is thus explained by the fact that increases in the money supply are transmitted through the economy gradually and unevenly.

"Accordingly we find, that, in every kingdom, into which money begins to flow in greater abundance than formerly, everything takes a new face: labour and industry gain life; the merchant becomes more enterprising, the manufacturer more diligent and skilful, and even the farmer follows his plough with greater alacrity and attention. This is not easily to be accounted for, if we consider only the influence which a greater abundance of coin has in the kingdom itself, by heightening the price of commodities, and obliging everyone to pay a greater number of these little yellow or white pieces for everything he purchases" (Hume 1752, 70–71). While money is neutral in the long run, over the short term, an increase in its supply stimulates the economy: "In the progress towards these changes, the augmentation may have some influence, by exciting industry; but after the prices are settled, suitably to the new abundance of gold and silver, it has no manner of influence" (Hume 1752, 62).

In this sense, the following statement by Hume is traditionally interpreted as advocating inflationary policies: "The good policy of the magistrate consists only in keeping it, if possible, still increasing; because, by that means, he keeps alive a spirit of industry in the nation, and increases the stock of labour, in which consists all real power and riches. A nation, whose money decreases, is actually, at that time, weaker and more miserable than another nation, which possesses no more money, but is on the increasing hand. This will be easily accounted for, if we consider, that the alterations in the quantity of money, either on one side or the other, are not immediately attended with proportionable alterations in the price of commodities. There is always an interval before matters be adjusted to their new situation; and this interval is as pernicious to industry, when gold and silver are diminishing, as it is advantageous when these metals are increasing" (Hume 1752, 50). In this way, as the monetary supply begins to increase, but before generally higher price levels are achieved, the transmission mechanism has a positive effect on the economy; indeed, (slight) inflation is better than a deflation. From this it is concluded that good monetary policy should aim for a low but steady inflation rate (Blaug 2001, 155).

14.4.4 The Price–Specie Flow Mechanism

Among Hume's contributions to monetary theory, he is best known for his Price–Specie Flow Mechanism. Moving away from the concept of a closed economy, he describes the international effects of a precious metal standard, which, from a modern perspective, can be generalized to any fixed exchange rate system. In response to the mercantilist demand to increase the money supply through export surpluses, Hume argues that the benefits of an increased money supply are small and short-term, and that the resulting price increase weakens foreign trade. "But the greater plenty of money is very limited in its use, and may even sometimes be a loss to a nation in its commerce with foreigners" (Hume 1752, 42).

In relation to the "rich country–poor country" debate, Hume notes that poorer countries have lower price levels, which can offset their disadvantage in trade. "But these advantages are compensated, in some measure, by the low price of labour in every nation which has not an extensive commerce, and does not much abound in gold and silver. Manufactures, therefore gradually shift their places, leaving those countries and provinces which they have already enriched, and flying to others, whither they are allured by the cheapness of provisions and labour; till they have enriched these also, and are again banished by the same causes. And, in general, we may observe, that the dearness of everything, from plenty of money, is a disadvantage, which attends an established commerce, and sets bounds to it in every country, by enabling the poorer states to undersell the richer in all foreign markets" (Hume 1752, 43).

In a thought experiment, Hume considers the consequences of a sudden and massive change in the money supply under a precious metal standard: "Suppose four-fifths of all the money in Great Britain to be annihilated in one night, and the nation reduced to the same condition, with regard to specie [...] what would be the consequence? Must not the price of all labour and commodities sink in proportion, and everything be sold as cheap as they were in those ages? What nation could then dispute with us in any foreign market, or pretend to navigate or to sell manufactures at the same price, which to us would afford sufficient profit? In how little time, therefore, must this bring back the money which we had lost, and raise us to the level of all the neighbouring nations? Where, after we have arrived, we immediately lose the advantage of the cheapness of labour and commodities; and the further inflow of money is stopped by our fullness and saturation. Again, suppose, that all the money of Great Britain were multiplied fivefold in a night, must not the contrary effect follow? Must not all labour and commodities rise to such an exorbitant height, that no neighbouring nations could afford to buy from us; while their commodities, on the other hand, became comparatively so cheap, that, in spite of all the laws which could be formed, they would be run in upon us, and our money flow out; until we fall to a level with foreigners, and lose that great superiority of riches, which had laid us under such disadvantages? Now, it is evident, that the same causes, which would correct these exorbitant inequalities [...] must prevent their happening in the common course of nature, and must forever, in all neighbouring nations, preserve money nearly proportional to the art and industry of each nation. All water, wherever it communicates, remains always at a level. Ask naturalists the reason; they tell you, that, were it to be raised in any one place, the superior gravity of that part not being balanced, must depress it, until it meets a counterpoise; and that the same cause, which redresses the inequality when it happens, must forever prevent it, without some violent external operation" (Hume 1752, 82–84).

A current account surplus results in an influx of precious metals, or specie. This automatically reduces the foreign money supply while increasing the domestic money supply. The result is that foreign prices fall and domestic prices rise. Consequently, there is a reduction in foreign demand for domestic goods and an increase in domestic demand for foreign goods. These shifts in demand reduce the domestic current account surplus while also lowering the foreign current account deficit. Over time, this brings the movement of money and goods into parity, resulting in a balance of payments equilibrium for both countries. Ultimately, it does not matter which country is in surplus or deficit; disturbances to the international balance of trade activate forces that counteract the disturbance, leading to an equilibrium. It is the current account that determines the monetary reaction, with the adjustment mechanism occurring via the price level.

Hume reasons that over the long term, the money supply will be naturally distributed in relation to the population and productivity of each place. "How is the balance kept in the provinces of every kingdom among themselves, but by the force of this principle, which makes it impossible for money to lose its level, and either to rise or sink beyond the proportion of the labour and commodities which are in each province?" (Hume 1752, 86).

Hume draws an analogy with hydraulic dynamics: "But as any body of water may be raised above the level of the surrounding element, if the former has no communication with the latter; so in money, if the communication be cut off, by any material or physical impediment, (for all laws alone are ineffective) there may, in such a case, be a very great inequality of money (Hume 1752, 83–84)."

In international trade, any excess money in the domestic market always flows back into the foreign market, where it is distributed in the natural ratio. Like water levels, the price level is determined by general forces. In the long run, international competition balances the supply of money between countries. This means that all national price level adjustments and imbalances are temporary, as there is a general long-term tendency toward uniform price levels and for the money supply to be naturally distributed based on countries' productivity (Cesarano 1998; Dimand 2013, 294–296).

The price of precious metals adjusts quickly, while the price of other goods only adjusts over the long term. Thus, the flow of precious metals accelerates general price equalization and balances current accounts internationally.

The central point of Hume's work is to criticize mercantilist bans on the export of precious metals. For Hume, it is misguided to assume that a country can ensure an influx of precious metals (and thus become wealthy) by promoting exports and restricting imports. The Price–Specie Flow Mechanism automatically corrects current account imbalances. Accordingly, the productivity and competitiveness of domestic industries are the sole source of wealth. "But are there not frequent instances, you will say, of states and kingdoms, which were formerly rich and opulent, and are now poor and beggarly? Has not the money left them, with which they formerly abounded? I answer, If they lose their trade, industry, and people, they cannot expect to keep their gold and silver: For these precious metals will hold proportion to the former advantages" (Hume 1752, 99).

14.4.5 Hume's Rejection of Credit Money

When the volume of money in circulation is increased, and this increase is not attributable to an expanded supply of precious metals, but rather to an increase in credit money, this leads domestic precious metals to flow abroad, and credit money to replace coins domestically. This is because it is not possible to adjust exchange rates under a gold or silver standard, which provides for fixed exchange rates. Hume was against the establishment of banks due to the price pressures that result from an increased money supply, and the resulting outflow of precious metals. "This has made me entertain a doubt concerning the benefit of banks and paper-credit, which are so generally esteemed advantageous to every nation" (Hume 1752, 43–4). "I scarcely know any method of sinking money below its level, but those institutions of banks, funds, and paper-credit, which are so much practised in this kingdom. These render paper equivalent to money, circulate it throughout the whole state, make it supply the place of gold and silver, raise proportionally the price of labour and commodities, and by that means either banish a great part of those precious metals, or prevent their further increase. What can be more shortsighted than our reasonings on this head?" (Hume 1752, 89–90).

In Hume's opinion, a public bank that exclusively issues paper money fully backed by precious metals seems to be the only advantageous option. "And therefore it is better, it may be thought, that a public company should enjoy the benefit of that paper-credit, which always will have place in every opulent kingdom. But to endeavour artificially to increase such a credit, can never be the interest of any trading nation; but must lay them under disadvantages, by increasing money beyond its natural proportion to labour and commodities, and thereby heightening their price to the merchant and manufacturer. And in this view, it must be allowed, that no bank could be more advantageous, than such a one as locked up all the money it received, and never augmented the circulating coin, as is usual, by returning part of its treasure into commerce. A public bank, by this expedient, might cut off much of the dealings of private bankers and money-jobbers; and though the state bore the charge of salaries to the directors and tellers of this bank […], the national advantage, resulting from the low price of labour and the destruction of paper-credit, would be a sufficient compensation" (Hume 1752, 44–45).

Although Hume acknowledges the practical advantages of paper money and does not subscribe to a metallistic monetary conception of money, he still rejects paper money. Having studied John Law, Hume's remarks on banks are in part a criticism and rejection of Law's project. Due to the practical experience gained in France, Hume does not believe that monetary scarcity can be maintained. Consequently, Hume can be described as a "practical" but not a "theoretical" metallist (Murphy 2008, 111; Wennerlind 2008, 105–106).

14.5 Evaluation

The success of Hume's monetary theory is attributable in no small part to his linguistic style and method. While his ideas were not necessarily new, he presented them in a simple, clear, and elegant fashion, making even difficult concepts accessible. In his thought experiments (e.g., "Suppose four-fifths of all the money in Great Britain were annihilated over night"), he presented models of action based on clear assumptions (e.g., "if fixed" or "by its own") and consistent reasoning.

His work was directed against mercantilist policies, which were still widespread in Europe at the time. Not being known for the novelty of his thought, he was renowned for his clear and explicit formulations of existing abstract concepts. This strength is showcased by his quantity theory, which describes the money supply's causal effect on the prices of goods. However, when it comes to the sophistication of his theory on the velocity of circulation or distributional effects of the transmission mechanism, Hume lags behind other thinkers such as Cantillon.

With his Price–Specie Flow Mechanism, Hume described a fundamental principle of fixed exchange rate systems. However, even in Hume's day, this mechanism did not work perfectly, leading to a mismatch between the model and historical reality; countries running a deficit were subject to much greater pressures than those running a surplus.

The idea that money is neutral over the long term but not over the short term, which is accepted as a core premise of today's monetary policy, is generally attributed to Hume. Due to this attribution, Hume is believed to be an advocate of a slow but steady increase in the (exogenous) money supply. Consequently, he is often considered an inflationist. As such, Hume is a key figure in neoclassical monetary theory, and has greatly influenced monetarism. Evidence of his influence on neoclassicists can be seen in Robert Lucas' Nobel Prize speech of 1996, which uses Hume as a starting point to elaborate on the importance of Lucas' distinction between expected and unexpected monetary policy (Wennerlind 2005, 224–225).

In *A Treatise of Human Nature*, Hume examines the role of habit in human behavior and uses this to explain the emergence of money as a social institution, as well as the phenomenon of a gradual, steady rise in prices. The influence of this philosophical work on other aspects of his monetary theory has been emphasized by various authors (Wennerlind 2001; Cazenave 2020).

In contrast to this traditional understanding of Hume's theory, Wennerlind argues that Hume draws a distinction between endogenous and exogenous increases in the money supply. Here, *exogenous* refers to an acatallactic increase in the money supply through the emission of paper money, trade restrictions, or the discovery of new gold or silver mines. Such an increase in the money supply only serves to raise prices and ultimately makes a country less competitive internationally.

However, if the money supply is increased *endogenously* (i.e., catallactically)—for example, through the expansion of domestic production—the effect of this increase is positive. Initially, industry becomes more productive, causing prices to fall and exports to increase, which attracts money from abroad. In an open economy with fixed exchange rates, competitiveness in trade thus determines the money supply.

Wennerlind emphasizes that for Hume, it is not an increasing money supply that "quickens the diligence" in industry, but rather increasing exports. Therefore, government should not seek to directly increase the money supply but rather promote a trade surplus through stimulative economic policies. Trade is not a zero-sum game. According to Hume, the state should ignore money and conduct active economic policy rather than active monetary policy (Wennerlind 2005; Wennerlind 2008).

Paganelli takes this argument further by arguing that if the "good policy of the magistrate" is to keep the money supply increasing, then the only way to achieve this is to remove it from circulation and store it in the country's treasury. Hume tells us that a country should accumulate precious metals to increase its military might, which it can do by hoarding them. According to Hume, growth comes from maintaining low domestic prices by hoarding money, while trade takes care of the rest (Paganelli 2025).

Taxonomic Classification

For Hume, money has fictitious value and is a convention; he is not a metallist. Therefore, he focuses on money's function as a means of payment, using the Quantity Theory of Money to determine its value. By rejecting credit money, he focuses on a narrow conception of the money supply.

References

Blaug, Mark. 2001. No history of ideas, please, we're economists. *Journal of Economic Perspectives* 15 (1): 145–164.

Boyer des Roches, Jerome. 2013. Bank liquidity risk: From John Law (1705) to Walter Bagehot (1873). *European Journal of the History of Economic Thought* 20 (4): 547–571.

Cazenave, Ariadna. 2020. Reason and experience in David Hume's specie-flow mechanism. *Enfoques* 32 (2): 71–85.

Cesarano, Filippo. 1998. Hume's specie-flow mechanism and classical monetary theory: An alternative interpretation. *Journal of International Economics* 45:173–186.

Dimand, Robert W. 2013. David Hume and Irving Fisher on the quantity theory of money in the long run and the short run. *European Journal for the History of Economic Thought* 20 (2): 284–304.

Hume, David. 1752. *Political Discourses*. Edinburgh: R. Fleming. Sections "Of Money," "Of Interest," and "Of the Balance of Trade."

Murphy, Antoin. 2008. *The genesis of macroeconomics*. Oxford: Oxford University Press.

Paganelli, Maria Pia. 2025. Was Hume a mercantilist? For Smith, yes: The friendly disagreement of Adam Smith and Davis Hume on money. *Journal of the History of Economic Thought* 47 (1): 1–10.

Peacock, Alan. 1987. Über Humes political discourses. In *Vademecum zu einem frühen Klassiker der ökonomischen Wissenschaft*, 21–61. Düsseldorf: Verlag Wirtschaft und Finanzen.

Schabas, Margaret, and Carl Wennerlind. 2011. Hume on money, commerce, and the science of economics. *Journal of Economic Perspectives* 25 (3): 217–230.

Schumacher, Reinhard. 2016. Adam Smith and the 'rich country – poor country' debate: Eighteenth-century views on economic progress and international trade. *European Journal of the History of Economic Thought* 23 (5): 764–793.

Wennerlind, Carl. 2001. The link between David Hume's treatise of human nature and his fiduciary theory of money. *History of Political Economy* 33 (1): 139–160.

Wennerlind, Carl. 2005. David Hume's monetary theory revisited: Was he really a quantity theorist and an inflationist? *Journal of Political Economy* 113 (1): 223–237.

Wennerlind, Carl. 2008. An artificial virtue and the oil of commerce: A synthetic view of Hume's theory of money. In *David Hume's political economy*, 105–126. London: Routledge.

Chapter 15
Henry Thornton (1760–1815): Paper Money in Times of Crises

15.1 Biography[1]

Henry Thornton was born in Clapham as the youngest son of John Thornton, a wealthy merchant and noted evangelical philanthropist. Henry grew up in an environment that combined commercial wealth with deep religious conviction. His cousin, the future abolitionist William Wilberforce, was partly raised in the Thornton household. Together, they formed the core of the Clapham Sect: a group of evangelical reformers who campaigned against the slave trade and promoted missionary, educational, and philanthropic initiatives.

After receiving his education, Thornton joined a relative's counting house in 1778 and later his father's firm. Disillusioned with speculative trading practices, he moved into banking, becoming a partner at Down, Thornton & Free in 1784, a position he would hold for life. Meanwhile, he embarked on a political career, and was elected Member of Parliament for Southwark in 1782. He retained this seat until his death, pursuing an independent liberal course that combined support for peace, parliamentary reform, Catholic emancipation, and fiscal innovation.

Thornton's reputation as an economist is primarily based on his *Enquiry into the Nature and Effects of the Paper Credit of Great Britain* (1802). He had been a partner at his London banking firm for over a decade when he wrote the book, and he understood the business well. He was regarded by his peers as the firm's most talented banker. In addition, his brother was a director of the Bank of England, which provided him with intimate knowledge of the bank's operations.

Thornton later served on the 1810 Bullion Committee, where he recommended resuming gold convertibility at a depreciated rate in order to mitigate the effects of deflation. His combination of intellectual independence and practical banking experience made him one of the most respected monetary thinkers of his

[1] This biography follows Hayek (1965).

J. Greitens, *Currency and Credit Money*, Springer Studies in the History of Economic Thought, https://doi.org/10.1007/978-3-032-24113-9_15

generation. Upon his death in 1815, he was remembered as a man of exceptional integrity, combining public service, intellectual originality, and Christian benevolence.

15.2 Selected Text

Thornton, Henry. 1802. *An Enquiry into the Nature and Effects of the Paper Credit of Great Britain.* Edited with an introduction by F. A. von Hayek. Augustus M. Kelley, Bookseller, New York 1965.

15.3 Historical Background

An intense controversy over monetary theory took place in the first half of the nineteenth century in Great Britain. The country's involvement in the First Coalition War against France in 1793 marked the beginning of a period of more than 20 years of wars and war financing. State expenditures and deficit financing increased significantly.

The resulting uncertainty led to the hoarding of gold and Bank of England notes, tightening the money supply. At the same time, demand for these paper currencies increased significantly, not least because numerous Country Banks held Bank of England notes as reserves. In the following years, many Country Banks were forced to close their counters, and the large-scale financing of canals during this period, known as *Canal Mania*, collapsed under the deteriorating conditions.

The government tried to combat the crisis by issuing additional treasury bills that were convertible into cash, with the intention of increasing the money supply and restoring confidence in the general solvency. This led to an expansion of the money supply through the growth of government spending.

When rumors arose in 1797 that Napoleon would attack the British Isles and a French frigate landed 1200 men in Fishguard, Wales, in February of that year, panic led to a run on some country banks. Due to its pivotal role in the two-tier structure of the English banking system, the Bank of England experienced a heavy drain of its reserves, threatening its existence. The Restriction Act of 1797 suspended the Bank of England's and the Country Banks' obligation to redeem banknotes in gold. This effectively turned redeemable pound notes into irredeemable paper money. Thus, the Bank of England's banknotes effectively became England's paper currency.

These events triggered the so-called Bullion Controversy. The nature of banknotes and their relationship to precious metal currencies was discussed. The issue was whether the increased issuance of irredeemable banknotes posed a threat to the value of money, not only internally (via inflation) but also externally (via exchange rates). The bullionists saw the expansion of the money supply as the reason for high prices, whereas the anti-bullionists blamed real factors (e.g., poor harvests, war expenditures, and trade problems due to the Continental Blockade) (Fig. 15.1).

The first round of the Bullion Controversy (1800–1803): Following the increase in the price of gold in 1800, vibrant debate was triggered by Walter Boyd's pamphlet letter to William Pitt, which discussed the impact of the Bank of England's suspension of specie payments. According to Boyd, the overissuance of banknotes permitted by the suspension of convertibility caused the prices of commodities, including gold and silver, to rise and exchange rates to fall. Sir Francis Baring responded that the circulation of Bank of England notes had increased by 30% in four years, but argued that this alone could not have caused the general price increase, which was the result of war, not excessive issuance of Bank of England notes (Boyer des Roches and Solis Rosales 2018, 168–169).

The second round of the Bullion Controversy (1809–1811) and the Bullion Report: This time, the debate was initiated by a newcomer who had made a name for himself in the City as a successful jobber and loan contractor of government funds: David Ricardo. In 1810, the British Parliament set up the Bullion Committee to investigate the causes of the crisis with the help of experts. The commission concluded in their report that the poor exchange rate, high gold price, and rise in consumer goods prices were due to the Bank of England's excessive issuance of paper money: "This excess is to be ascribed to the want of a sufficient check and control in the issues of paper from the Bank of England; and originally, to the suspension of cash payments, which removed the natural and true control" (House of Commons 1810, 30). Therefore, it would be best to return to the gold convertibility of banknotes as soon as possible, regardless of the further course of the war.

From 1813 onward, the Bank of England was increasingly willing to redeem notes. The first Peel Bank Act of 1819 (named after the chairman of the Commons' Committee and later Prime Minister Robert Peel) was the Resumption Act, which decided on the complete return to cash redemption of notes by 1823. This was intended to prevent the redistribution of wealth. A decline in the price level ensued from 1815 onward (Deleplace 2024).

Thornton's *Enquiry* is his contribution to the first round of the controversy. It is packed with banking details and draws on his practical experience, while also providing a theoretical framework. Yet the work "is not, in form, a theoretical book" (Hicks 1967, 174). It is difficult to read and has a hard-to-follow structure. At first, Thornton warns against deflation, and then, in the second part, against inflation. He thus seeks a middle ground in the Bullion Controversy. On the one hand, Thornton is looking for an appropriate response from the Bank of England to the internal drain following 1797, which caused a financial panic. On the other hand, the recent experience with French revolutionary money ("assignats"), which became worthless due to inflation, stood as a warning.

Fig. 15.1 Midas, transmuting all into gold paper (Gillray, 1797, ©Trustees of the British Museum): William Pitt (Prime Minister) depicted as legendary King Midas, who turns everything he touches not into gold, but paper money, while he collects gold in his belly. The rotunda invokes the Bank of England. The dark clouds allude to invasion from France

15.4 Discussion

Thornton begins by stating that he intends to correct the mistakes of other authors. "The first intention of the Writer of the following pages was merely to expose some popular errors" (Thornton 1802, 67). He is particularly focused on Adam Smith, whom he references throughout the book. "In the course of this enquiry, several passages in the work of Dr. A. Smith on the Wealth of Nations are animadverted on, as are also some observations made by Mr. Hume in his Essays on Money and on the Balance of Trade, and by Sir James Stewart in his book on Political Economy, as well as some remarks in the writings of Locke and Montesquieu" (Thornton 1802, 68).

Thornton starts by discussing the risks associated with crisis and deflation. He then addresses the overissuance of currency and rising prices: "The earlier parts of the work having tended to shew the evil of a too great and sudden diminution of our circulating medium, some of the latter Chapters are employed in pointing out the consequences of a too great augmentation of it" (Thornton 1802, 68).

Thornton begins by discussing bills of exchange, a form of commercial credit granted by merchants to one another: "Letters ordering the transfer of the debt, are termed, in the language of the present day, bills of exchange" (Thornton 1802, 82). Bills reduce the need for coins in circulation; this "spares the use of the expensive article of gold" (Thornton 1802, 76). For Thornton, bank notes are essentially a generalized bill of exchange. "The circulation of a bank note is owing rather to the circumstance of the name of the issuer being so well known as to give to it an universal credit" (Thornton 1802, 92).

"This commercial credit is the foundation of paper credit" (Thornton 1802, 76). And this paper money increases the money supply: "A multitude of bills pass between trader and trader in the country in the manner which has been described; and they evidently form, in the strictest sense, a part of the circulating medium of the kingdom" (Thornton 1802, 92).

But paper money is different from coins. "Paper constitutes [...] an article on the credit side of the books of some men; but it forms an exactly equal item on the debit side of the books of others. It constitutes, therefore, on the whole, neither a debit nor a credit" (Thornton 1802, 79). By contrast: "The case of gold [...] differs from that of paper inasmuch as the possessor of gold takes credit for that for which no man debits himself" (Thornton 1802, 80).

Thornton criticizes Smith's "real bills doctrine," which states that real bills—bills backed by goods—are clearly defined and their quantity is restricted. According to Smith, banks' self-interest would force them to discount only such bills. However, Thornton argues that banks cannot differentiate between "real" and "fictitious" bills (Arnon 2009, 551). "The supposition that real bills represent property, and that fictitious bills do not, seems, therefore, to be one by which more than justice is done to one of these species of bills, and something less than justice to the other" (Thornton 1802, 86–87). Furthermore: "To determine what bills are fictitious, or bills of accommodation, and what are real, is often a point of difficulty (Thornton 1802, 89)."

Contrary to the real bills doctrine, Thornton believes that credit risk is linked to the solvency of the debtor rather than the goods being traded. He introduces the concept of the circulating medium (which includes different kinds of currency and credit money, the notes of different banks, Bank of England notes, and legal tender coins). He also draws attention to the solvency hierarchy existing between the different issuers of debt, with the Bank of England at the top. He then shows that the various components of the circulating medium have different velocities of circulation according to particular interest rates and degrees of confidence (Boyer des Roches and Solis Rosales 2018, 173–174).

According to Thornton, if the supply of bills of exchange does not depend on the quantity of goods in circulation, then it is the difference between the expected return on borrowed money and the actual discount rate at which the Bank of England monetizes bills of exchange. This makes interest rates the key instrument of the developing central banks. Wicksell emphasized this point almost a century later (Deleplace 2024, 108).

Thornton also addresses the issue of financial crises. "Mercantile confidence, however, is not always dealt out in that proportion in which there is reasonable ground for it. At some periods it has risen to a most unwarrantable height, and has given occasion to the most extravagant and hurtful speculations. Of these the cases of the Ayr bank, and of the South Sea scheme, are instances. Evils of this kind, however, have a tendency to correct themselves. In a country possessed of commercial knowledge and experience, confidence, in most instances, will not be misplaced" (Thornton 1802, 78).

Drawing on his experience of the banking crisis of 1797, he focuses on analyzing the consequences of deflation caused by monetary contraction. Even in normal times, the velocity of circulation varies between different types of circulating medium such as bills and banknotes. However, in times of low confidence, everyone seeks to hoard guineas (Thornton 1802, 96).

Thornton considers deflation to be extremely dangerous. It triggers waves of bankruptcies, a general loss of confidence, and economic stagnation: "a diminution [of Bank of England notes], for instance, of one-third or two-fifths, might, perhaps, be sufficient to produce a very general insolvency in London, of which the effect would be the suspension of confidence, the derangement of commerce, and the stagnation of manufactures throughout the country" (Thornton 1802, 114).

In this context, Thornton defends the decision to suspend Bank of England's cash payments in 1797, arguing that it was necessary to prevent a contraction of the money supply and the adverse consequences this would have had for real economic activity (Hetzel 1987, 5). Thornton does not blame the Bank of England for taking advantage of the currency's inconvertibility and issuing excessively. Instead, he attributes the poor state of the currency to external factors that have caused an unfavorable balance of trade. This is the opposite of Ricardo's explanation from 1810, and is an explicit criticism of Hume's Price–Specie Flow Mechanism (Thornton 1802, 246–247).

Based on the foregoing, Thornton deduces the Bank of England's responsibilities: "In order to secure that this interchange shall at all times take place, it is important that, generally speaking, a considerable fund of gold should be kept in the country, and there is in this kingdom no other depository for it but the Bank of England. This fund should be a provision not only against the common and more trifling fluctuations in the demand for coin, but also against the two following contingencies. First, it should serve to counteract the effects of an unfavourable balance of trade [...] secondly, that the reserve of gold should be sufficient to meet any extraordinary demand at home" (Thornton 1802, 111–112).

Thus, for Thornton, the Bank of England must act as the lender of last resort; it should "maintain the amount of their paper circulation. How, then, is the bank to issue it? The only means which the bank, on its part, is able to take for the extension of its paper circulation, is to enlarge its loans" (Thornton 1802, 125).

In a two-tier banking system, the Bank of England must intervene to stabilize the monetary situation and expand the paper money supply. Gold cannot play a role in such a system, as gold is only imported through export surpluses. "The bank paper serves, it is true, to regulate, in a great degree, that other paper; but not with exactness" (Thornton 1802, 152). In this system, Bank of England notes are considered as secure as gold, forming the foundation of the monetary system as safe assets (Thornton 1802, 182). In this way, paper credit is much more than just a placeholder for gold and silver.

The second part of Thornton's discussion begins in chapter 8, as he turns to the dangers of excessive paper-money issuance. He begins by stating that price levels depend on the amount of the circulating medium, "that the price at which the exchange (or sale) takes place depends on two facts; on the proportion between the supply of the particular commodity and the demand for it, which is one question; and on the proportion, also, between the state of the general supply of the circulating medium and that of the demand for it, which is another" (Thornton 1802, 194)." Thornton makes it clear that this effect stems in part from paper money, and not just from currency (Thornton 1802, 195). He thus extends the Quantity Theory of Money to include not only outside money (currency), but also inside money (credit money) (Hetzel 1987, 6).

Prices depend on the quantity of money, but not in a strict, proportional way. "I shall, for the present, consider the doctrine which has been laid down, as being sufficiently established, namely, that paper fluctuates in price on the same principles as any other article, its value rising as its quantity sinks, and vice versa, or, in other words, that an augmentation of it has a general tendency to raise, and a diminished issue to lower, the nominal cost of commodities [...], an exact correspondence between the quantity of paper and the price of commodities can by no means be expected always to subsist" (Thornton 1802, 197).

Thornton asks whether the issuance of paper money and bills of exchange is endogenous or exogenous. Again, he adopts a middle position. He views rising price levels as being partly an effect and partly a cause of increased issuance. "The reader possibly may think that, in treating of this subject, I have been mistaking the effect for the cause, an encreased issue of paper being, in his estimation, merely a consequence which follows a rise in the price of goods, and not the circumstance which produces it. That an enlarged emission of paper may often fairly be considered as only, or chiefly, an effect of high prices, is not meant to be denied. It is, however, intended to insist, that, unquestionably, in some cases at least, the greater quantity of paper is, more properly speaking, the cause" (Thornton 1802, 197–198).

Excessive issuance of Bank of England notes can cause the exchange rate to fall as paper takes the place of coins as the circulating medium. And then the issuance of paper money becomes a cause of rising prices. "In saying […] that war enhances the price of goods, and thus causes an encrease of payments, we ought here to bear in mind that it ought only to be allowed to lift them up to that point to which they can be raised consistently with the general maintenance of our exchanges; and that, so far as they permanently stand above that point, it is the enlarged and too great quantity of notes of the Bank of England which is to be considered as the cause of the high price of goods, rather than the high price of goods which is to be taken to be the cause of the enlarged quantity of notes of the Bank of England" (Thornton 1802, 221).

Another reason for Thornton's nuanced position is the complicated relationship between country banks, London private banks, and the Bank of England. Thornton firmly defends the British banking structure. For Thorton, the Bank of England used its monopoly power to steer the system between dangerous alternatives (Arnon 2009, 559–561). "We have been lately placed between two dangers; between that of a depreciated paper currency on the one hand, and that of an interruption to our paper credit, and a consequent stagnation of our commerce and manufactures, on the other" (Thornton 1802, 226).

Thornton developed the idea of a central bank that could control the monetary base formed by the Bank of England's notes. By controlling the base, the central bank could control the money supply of the entire country. Ultimately, by controlling the money supply, the central bank could influence the price level. A key theme of the *Enquiry* is the importance of the central bank explicitly accepting responsibility for determining the price level (Hetzel 1987, 3).

In a paper money system, the money supply does not depend entirely on the current account surplus, as Locke believed. With a redeemable note, "banks, if they pay in gold, or if, while not paying in gold, they maintain the value of their notes, must observe some limit in respect to their emission of them" (Thornton 1802, 248). Without any obligation to redeem, the Bank of England can act as lender of last resort. This raises the question of "whether those bounds within which Bank of England paper must be confined, in order to guard against a dangerous depreciation of it, are likely to be observed, in consequence of some natural tendency which it has to limit itself, so that it is unnecessary that the bank should restrain it" (Thornton 1802, 251).

Like Hume, whom he quotes, Thornton believes that the impact of an increased money supply will be short-lived. It does not alter the fundamental features of the economy or generate additional capital or trade, except perhaps during a brief period when those with extra money try to spend it, causing prices to rise (Arnon 2009, 562). Thornton believes that the negative consequences of price increases are sufficient reason for the bank to be "compelled to restrict its issues" (Thornton 1802, 263).

15.5 Evaluation

Thornton's stance on the Bullion Controversy was unique. He did not support either bullionism or anti-bullionism. In his *Enquiry*, he criticized Smith's real bills doctrine and contributed to the Quantity Theory of Money by offering views on the motives for holding money and effects of changes in the velocity of circulation.

Unlike the bullionists, Thornton did not oppose the 1797 Restriction Act. Through his theory, he defended a system based on inconvertibility. He recognized that credit money was endogenous, and probably due to his private connections, he had a good understanding of banking and the money-creation mechanism in a two-tier system. Thornton insisted on the need to implement discretionary monetary policy measures. In times of crisis, a central bank is necessary to stabilize the system. Thornton innovated the idea of a modern central bank exercising control over commercial bank liabilities (Hetzel 1987, p. 15).

While Thornton's ideas were often not attributed to him, they remained influential for their impact on other major thinkers, especially those from the banking school (Arnon 2009, 547). Hicks emphasizes Thorton's importance for later Keynesian ideas (Hicks 1967, 174).

The consistency of Thornton's ideas has been a frequent topic of debate. Thornton appears to advocate an inflationary policy in the first part of the book and a deflationary policy in the second. Hayek focused primarily on the second part (Hayek 1965, 45–48), while Hicks viewed Thornton's analysis as covering short-term policy in the first part and long-term policy in the second (Hicks 1967, 186). However, one could also argue that this inconsistency reflects a distinction between periods of crisis and periods of normalcy.

Interestingly, by 1810, Thornton had changed his position based on events in the real world, having learned that the Bank of England was not exercising what he considered to be adequate discretionary policy. He lost confidence in the Bank of England's directors, given their enthusiastic embrace of the real bills doctrine. Accordingly, as a co-author of the Bullion Report, he advocated urgent reimposition of convertibility as a constraint on the Bank of England's activities (Arnon 2009, 550).

Taxonomic Classification

Thornton addresses a wide range of topics. He reflects on the essence of currency, and whether paper money can be part of it. He has a mixed view on the value of money and on the causes and effects of increasing in the quantity of money in circulation. He also discusses the endogenous reaction of credit money. However, the unit of account function of money always takes center stage.

References

Arnon, Arie. 2009. Reexamination of Thornton's innovative monetary analysis: The bullion debate during the restriction once again. *History of Political Economy* 41 (3): 545–574.

Boyer des Roches, Jérôme, and Ricardo Solis Rosales. 2018. Bullionist and anti-bullionist schools. In *Handbook on the history of economic analysis. Volume II. Schools of thought in economics*, 167–179. Cheltenham: Edward Elgar Publishing.

Deleplace, Gishlain. 2024. Storm in a teacup? The impact of war on the English monetary system and thought (1797–1821). In *Money in times of crisis. Pre-classical, classical and contemporary theories*, 91–126. Roma: Accademia Nazionale dei Lincei Proceedings.

Hayek, Friedrich August. 1965. Introduction. In *An enquiry into the nature and effects of the paper credit of Great Britain*, 11–63. New York: Augustus M. Kelley.

Hetzel, Robert L. 1987. Henry Thornton: Seminal monetary theorist and father of the modern central bank. *Economic Review* 73:3–16.

Hicks, John. 1967. Thornton's paper credit (1802). In *Critical essays on monetary theory*, 174–188. Oxford: Clarendon.

House of Commons. 1810. *Report, together with minutes of evidence, and accounts, from the select committee on the high price of gold bullion*. London: House of Commons.

Thornton, Henry. 1802. *An Enquiry into the Nature and Effects of the Paper Credit of Great Britain*. Edited with an introduction by F. A. von Hayek. Augustus M. Kelley, Bookseller, New York 1965.

Chapter 16
David Ricardo (1772–1823): Monetary Policy Orthodoxy

16.1 Biography[1]

David Ricardo was born in London in 1772 as the third of seventeen children of a wealthy Jewish stockbroker of Portuguese descent who had emigrated from the Netherlands. From 1783 to 1785, he is believed to have attended the high school of the Portuguese–Jewish community in Amsterdam. Back in England, he was educated by private tutors; he was introduced to the stock market at an early age, beginning work in 1786 at just fourteen. In 1793, his marriage to a Quaker, against the wishes of his parents, led to a break with his family and his disinheritance. Nevertheless, Ricardo continued his career as a stockbroker and, through skillful trading—particularly in highly volatile government bonds during the wartime period—amassed a considerable fortune. He acted as a loan contractor, raising loans for the British government in return for a commission.

From 1798 onward, Ricardo devoted himself to the study of mathematics, chemistry, mineralogy, and geology, and he became a founding member of the Geological Society. In 1799, by chance, he encountered Adam Smith's *The Wealth of Nations*, which sparked his interest in economics. Following his active role in the Bullion Controversy of 1810–1811, he published his major work, On the *Principles of Political Economy and Taxation*, in 1817. Two years later, in 1819, he entered Parliament, where he remained active until his sudden death in 1823 from a middle-ear infection.

Ricardo was a self-taught thinker who, after acquiring immense wealth in practical business, went on to transform economic theory with his rigorously deductive and abstract method. His friend Thomas Robert Malthus sought to defend the Smithian tradition against Ricardo's approach with his own *Principles of Political Economy*, published in 1820.

[1] This biography follows Pierenkemper (2012, 76–8).

J. Greitens, *Currency and Credit Money*, Springer Studies in the History of Economic Thought, https://doi.org/10.1007/978-3-032-24113-9_16

16.2 Selected Text

Ricardo, David. 1810. *The High Price of Bullion*. A Proof of the Depreciation of Bank Notes. 3rd edition. London: Murray.

16.3 Historical Background

The second round of the Bullion Controversy (1809–1811) was initiated by David Ricardo's newspaper article "The Price of Gold," which appeared in the *Morning Chronicle* in 1809. Two additional articles followed due to the interest aroused by this polemic. In January 1810, a first-edition summary of the newspaper articles called *The High Price of Bullion* was published; second and third editions followed the very next month.

Parliament established the Bullion Committee in February 1810 with Henry Thornton as a member and Ricardo as a contributor. The Bullion Report, which was presented in June and published in August of 1810, largely endorsed the Bullionist diagnosis: overissuance of banknotes had driven down the value of the paper pound and had raised the price of gold. It recommended resumption of convertibility within two years and, in the interim, the adoption of a strict rule tying note issuance to the price of bullion.

The report provoked an intense pamphlet war. In April 1811, a fourth edition of *The High Price of Bullion* appeared, which was revised and expanded with an appendix. In May 1811, the House of Commons debated the Bullion Report (Marcuzzo and Roselli 1994, 9–12; Deleplace 2024).

The Bullionists' victory was profound. They received an implicit acknowledgement of their victory from Parliament in 1819 with the first Peel Bank Act, followed shortly afterward by an explicit acknowledgement from the Bank that its principles would henceforth be derived from "theory" rather than "practice." This approach was later identified by others as a threat to the social order (Walter 2019, 468).

16.4 Discussion

Ricardo's key concern was the institutional safeguarding of a stable currency, which he considered essential for economic development. Increases in paper money and devaluation caused uncertainty among consumers and investors. Ricardo aimed to identify the reasons for the devaluation, which he attributed to an abundance of paper money (Ricardo 1810, iii–iv)

16.4.1 Production Costs and Quantity Theory

At the beginning, Ricardo adopts a number of central assumptions from other authors (i.e., "the most approved writers on political economy" (Ricardo 1810, 1); Adam Smith is the most frequently cited in the further course of the book.

First, referencing Smith (and implicitly Locke), he defines money as a commodity. The intrinsic value of precious metals is determined by rarity, labor inputs, and capital costs. This concept predates the introduction of coins. "Gold and silver, like other commodities, have an intrinsic value, which is not arbitrary, but is dependent on their scarcity, the quantity of labour bestowed in procuring them, and the value of the capital employed in the mines which produce them (Ricardo 1810, 1)." This means that Ricardo is a metallist and a representative of the production cost theory of money.

Ricardo then assumes a quantitative relationship between prices and the money supply, again referencing Smith, and implicitly Hume and Locke. "If the quantity of gold and silver in the world employed as money were exceedingly small, or abundantly great, it would not in the least affect the proportions in which they would be divided among the different nations—the variation in their quantity—would have produced no other effect than to make the commodities for which they were exchanged comparatively dear or cheap" (Ricardo 1810, 2). The quantities of precious metals used as money are in quantitative proportion to the goods traded and are therefore more expensive or cheaper. In this way, he describes a barter economy with precious metals as a general medium of exchange.

He then addresses the statement that the absolute amount of money is irrelevant when it comes to fulfilling the function of a medium of exchange: "The smaller quantity of money would perform the functions of a circulating medium, as well as the larger" (Ricardo 1810, 2). This also relates to a quote from Smith, but the work of Hume can also be found here.

This leads to a contradiction: either the value of money is determined by the value of the commodity used as money—that is, the intrinsic value of precious metals—or it is determined by the Quantity Theory of Money—that is, according to the money supply and executed volume of trade. Ricardo seems to juxtapose both explanations here.

This contradiction relates to Schumpeter's distinction between the metallistic and naïve versions of the Quantity Theory of Money: in the first case, money derives its value from the commodity underlying it; in the second case, the value of money is directly proportional to the money supply (Schumpeter 1954, 312–313).

16.4.2 The Price–Specie Flow Mechanism

Ricardo notes that the existing supply of precious metals is distributed among countries in proportion to their level of economic development. "The precious metals employed for circulating the commodities of the world [...] have been divided into certain proportions among the different civilized nations of the earth, according to the state of their commerce and wealth, and therefore according to the number and frequency of the payments which they had to perform. While so divided they preserved every where the same value, and as each country had an equal necessity for the quantity actually in use, there could be no temptation offered to either for their importation or exportation" (Ricardo 1810, 1). If the value of money is the same everywhere, current accounts will also be balanced. Furthermore, current accounts do not need to be balanced with each individual country bilaterally, only in total (Ricardo 1810, 3).

Ricardo now introduces an exogenous shock to this equilibrium by asking us to consider the effects of a new gold mine. "If a mine of gold were discovered in either of these countries, the currency of that country would be lowered in value in consequence of the increased quantity of the precious metals brought into circulation, and would therefore no longer be of the same value as that of other countries. Gold and silver, whether in coin or in bullion, obeying the law which regulates all other commodities, would immediately become articles of exportation; they would leave the country where they were cheap, for those countries where they were dear, and would continue to do so, as long as the mine should prove productive, and till the proportion existing between capital and money in each country before the discovery of the mine, were again established, and gold and silver restored every where to one value. In return for the gold exported, commodities would be imported; and though what is usually termed the balance of trade would be against the country exporting money or bullion, it would be evident that she was carrying on a most advantageous trade, exporting that which was no way useful to her, for commodities which might be employed in the extension of her manufactures, and the increase of her wealth" (Ricardo 1810, 3–4).

The new gold mine increases the domestic gold money supply and decreases the production costs of the precious metal, making gold cheaper domestically. Since, in Ricardo's view, money is a commodity, this cheaper medium of exchange is transported abroad in exchange for other goods, where the price of gold is higher. The balance of payments remains negative until a new equilibrium is reached and a uniform gold price is achieved again. If all goods are priced in gold, the flow of gold between countries will lead to balanced international prices. In useful trade, importing investment goods expands industry and increases wealth.

As an alternative, Ricardo asks us to consider the establishment of a bank. "If instead of a mine being discovered in any country, a bank were established, such as the Bank of England, with the power of issuing its notes for a circulating medium; after a large amount had been issued either by way of loan to merchants, or by advances to government, thereby adding considerably to the sum of the currency, the same effect would follow as in the case of the mine. The circulating medium would be lowered in value, and goods would experience a proportionate rise. The equilibrium between that and other nations would only be restored by the exportation of part of the coin" (Ricardo 1810, 4).

In this way, similar developments occur when a bank is established. An increase in the currency supply through the issuance of paper money reduces its value.

Precious metals that are accepted abroad are exported in exchange for goods. Meanwhile, domestically, paper currency is increasingly used. "The establishment of the bank and the consequent issue of its notes therefore, as well as the discovery of the mine, operate as an inducement to the exportation either of bullion or of coin, and are beneficial only in as far as that object may be accomplished. The bank substitutes a currency of no value for one most costly, and enables us to turn the precious metals (which, though a very necessary part of our capital, yield no revenue) into a capital which will yield one" (Ricardo 1810, 4–5). The banknotes replace the precious metal, which can then be used to import useful goods.

Ricardo explicitly refers to Hume's Price–Specie Flow Mechanism and notion of a natural distribution, that is, of an international balance in the supply of money between countries: "Mr. Hume has supported the same opinion. The value of the circulating medium of every country bears some proportion to the value of the commodities which it circulates. [...] No increase or decrease of its quantity, whether consisting of gold, silver, or paper-money, can increase or decrease its value above or below this proportion" (Ricardo 1810, 44). The focus is therefore on balancing the value of currencies, which creates an international balance in the supply of money.

"Thus then it appears that the currency of one country can never for any length of time be much more valuable, as far as equal quantities of the precious metals are concerned, than that of another; that excess of currency is but a relative term; that if the circulation of England were ten millions, that of France five millions, that of Holland four millions, &c. &c. whilst they kept their proportions, though the currency of each country were doubled or trebled, neither country would be conscious of an excess of currency. The prices of commodities would everywhere rise, on account of the increase of currency, but there would be no exportation of money from either. But if these proportions be destroyed by England alone doubling her currency, while that of France, Holland, &c. &c. continued as before, we should then be conscious of an excess in our currency, and for the same reason the other countries would feel a deficiency in theirs, and part of our excess would be exported till the proportions of ten, five, four, &c. were again established" (Ricardo 1810, 61).

If the amount of currency in England increases, gold is exported because it is the cheapest commodity that can be exchanged: "Thus then specie will be sent abroad to discharge a debt only when it is superabundant; only when it is the cheapest exportable commodity" (Ricardo 1810, 14).

Although Ricardo refers to Hume and his Price–Specie Flow Mechanism, he reverses his argument (Glasner 2017, 18–20): For Ricardo, the starting point, rather than the long-term conclusion, is the uniform price of all tradable goods, including precious metals, due to arbitrage. If the prices of precious metals deviate from each other—for example, due to the discovery of a new gold mine—this leads to the import or export of gold and silver. Therefore, the resulting imbalances in the balance of payments are a monetarily triggered phenomenon and only temporary. "The exportation of the coin is caused by its cheapness, and is not the effect, but the cause of an unfavorable balance" (Ricardo 1810, 12). Adjustments to the money supply resulting from the export or import of precious metals lead to a new equilibrium in the balance of payments.

Ricardo goes on to assert that gold movements between countries do not respond to imbalances in the balance of payments, but to imbalances in the money market. Gold flows in and out until its purchasing power in relation to currencies is the same everywhere. This is indicated by the difference between the market value and the official value of gold. "The error of this reasoning proceeds from not distinguishing between an increase in the value of gold, and an increase in its money price" (Ricardo 1810, 11). This was a phenomenon that could be observed in Ricardo's time.

Ricardo argues that the balance of payments is monetarily determined by the exchange rate. "If I pay him in paper-money; as he cannot send it abroad, he will consider whether it will purchase as much gold or silver bullion as is contained in the coin for which it is a substitute if it will do this, paper will be as acceptable to him as coin; but if it will not, he will expect a further premium for his bill, equal to the depreciation of the paper. While the circulating medium consists, therefore, of coin undebased, or of paper-money immediately exchangeable for undebased coin, the exchange can never be more above, or more below par, than the expenses attending the transportation of the precious metals. But when it consists of a depreciated paper-money, it necessarily will fall according to the degree of the depreciation. The exchange will, therefore, be a tolerably accurate criterion by which we may judge of the debasement of the currency, proceeding either from a clipped coinage, or a depreciated paper-money" (Ricardo 1810, 24–25). Furthermore: "No person ever exports or imports bullion without first considering the rate of exchange. It is by the rate of exchange that he discovers the relative value of bullion in the two countries between which it is estimated" (Ricardo 1810, 26).

Under a gold standard or fixed/exogenous exchange rate, the money supply is endogenous and determined in relation to a country. Conversely, with an exogenously determined money supply—for example, based on the amount of paper money issued by the Bank of England—the exchange rate adjusts endogenously. "The circulation can never be over-full. If it be one of gold and silver, any increase in its quantity will be spread over the world. If it be one of paper, it will diffuse itself only in the country where it is issued. Its effects on prices will then be only local and nominal, as a compensation by means of the exchange will be made to foreign purchasers" (Ricardo 1810, 47). An excess of paper currency is counterbalanced by its depreciation.

Ricardo defined the gold standard as a self-regulating system with an unfixed money supply. Equilibrium is achieved through the precious metal market, whereby gold has the same value and purchasing power in all countries. This is linked to his rejection of mercantilist legal regulations against the export of precious metals (Marcuzzo & Rosselli 1994, 51).

In summary, this means:

- With Hume, an increase in the domestic money supply leads to an increase in the prices of all goods. As a result, fewer goods are exported, leading to a balance of payments deficit. The outflow of gold reduces the domestic money supply and

leads to a lower price level and higher exports until a new equilibrium is reached. The current account adjusts accordingly.
- In Ricardo's view, an increase in the domestic money supply depreciates the value of the currency against foreign currencies. As a result, gold is exported because it is worth more abroad. This leads to balance of payment deficits until a new equilibrium is reached. The capital account adjusts accordingly.

The difference between Hume and Ricardo is not surprising, as Ricardo is a metallist and sees money as a commodity, while for Hume money has a fictitious value.

16.4.3 Paper Money and Monetary Standards

An increase in the amount of paper money may be advantageous if the gold that is then exported is used to import investment goods. "The Bank might continue to issue their notes, and the specie be exported with advantage to the country, while their notes were payable in specie on demand, because they could never issue more notes than the value of the coin which would have circulated had there been no bank" (Ricardo 1810, 7).

The obligation to redeem paper money in gold provides a tool to limit the issuance of paper money, which also stabilizes the exchange rate. "These are the means [...] by which our currency endeavours to equalize itself with the currencies of other countries" (Ricardo 1810, 8).

Only an excess of currency leads to a balance of payments deficit: "In this view of the subject, then, it appears, that the temptation to export money in exchange for goods, or what is termed an unfavourable balance of trade, never arises but from a redundant currency" (Ricardo 1810, 9–10).

"Our circulating medium is almost wholly composed of paper, and it behoves us to guard against the depreciation of the paper currency with at least as much vigilance as against that of the coins. This we have neglected to do. Parliament, by restricting the Bank from paying in specie, have enabled the conductors of that concern to increase or decrease at pleasure the quantity and amount of their notes; and the previously existing checks against an over-issue having been thereby removed, those conductors have acquired the power of increasing or decreasing the value of the paper currency" (Ricardo 1810, 27). The convertibility of paper money prevents banks from issuing too many notes, as they otherwise risk insolvency. However, the abolition of convertibility removes these restrictions. It is not the abolition of the obligation to redeem that leads to depreciation and inflation, but the excessive issuance of paper money. The same effect would occur if not paper money, but inferior coins had been minted to this extent (Ricardo 1810, 32).

Nevertheless, precious metal is still most suitable as a unit of account: "Strictly speaking, there can be no permanent measure of value. A measure of value should itself be invariable; but this is not the case with either gold or silver, they being subject to fluctuations as well as other commodities. Experience has indeed taught us, that though the variations in the value of gold or silver may be considerable, on a comparison of distant periods, yet for short spaces of time their value is tolerably fixed. It is this property [...] which fits them better than any other commodity for the use of money. Either gold or silver may therefore, in the point of view in which we are considering them, be called a measure of value" (Ricardo 1810, footnote 17).

Against this backdrop, the aforementioned contrast between the theory of production costs and the quantity theory must be addressed (Marcuzzo & Rosselli, 1994, 41–43). While the value of money as a commodity is determined by the laws of value, the quantity theory applies to inconvertible paper money, for which there are no production costs. Marcuzzo and Rosselli combine the two approaches in Ricardo using the following equation:

$$\begin{aligned} \textit{Monetary price of commodity A} &= \frac{\textit{Quantity of money}}{\textit{Unit of commodity A}} \\ &= \frac{\textit{Quantity of money}}{\textit{Quantity of standard}} \times \frac{\textit{Quantity of standard}}{\textit{Unit of commodity A}} \end{aligned}$$

The price of a commodity is determined by the ratio of the amount of money and the quantity of goods. Under a gold standard, the amount of money has a fixed ratio to gold. This allows us to identify two reasons for inflation:

- *Monetary reasons for inflation*: These are reasons related to the ratio of money to the standard, which is determined according to the Quantity Theory of Money. The only reason for inflation is excessive issuance, because the purchasing power of the currency strictly depends on the volume of money in circulation.
- *Real economic reasons for inflation*: These are reasons related to the ratio of the standard to the commodity, which is determined by Ricardo according to his value theory (e.g., through labor costs, taxes, etc.).

If the ratio of the currency to the standard remains constant, inflation can only be caused by real factors. The standard serves as a *numéraire* and can theoretically be any commodity (such as, for example, grain). Gold is chosen because its value is relatively stable, thus effectively limiting price fluctuations. The standard is used to regulate the amount of money in circulation.

From this, Ricardo derives his political demands for a reduction in the volume of notes: "The remedy which I propose for all the evils in our currency, is that the Bank should gradually decrease the amount of their notes in circulation until they shall have rendered the remainder of equal value with the coins which they represent, or, in other words, till the prices of gold and silver bullion shall be brought down to their mint price" (Ricardo 1810, 50). Ricardo prefers an open state bankruptcy to further depreciation.

Only the return to convertibility, the reintroduction of a standard, prevents such an outcome: "The only legitimate security which the public can possess against the indiscretion of the Bank is to oblige them to pay their notes on demand in specie" (Ricardo 1810, 56).

16.5 Evaluation

Ricardo is considered a hardliner and a staunch advocate of the Quantity Theory of Money and monetary orthodoxy (Blaug 1996, 31; Stadlin 1954, 84). His goal was the institutional safeguarding of a stable currency. To this end, the circulation of full-value coins is not necessary (as with Locke); rather, convertibility into gold creates the necessary credibility for stability. He is not a deflationist, but, given historical experience, he is very concerned about inflation.

In seeking to determine the value of money, Ricardo only considers the currency while disregarding credit money. Therefore, in his proposal, the money supply is kept very tight, which leads to problems with the elasticity of the money supply. His later monetary theories address this problem, especially his Ingot Plan, which foresees a secure but at the same time elastic currency. Ricardo does not discuss the demand for money (Glasner 2017, 20). Also, he does not describe a monetary transmission mechanism, and the velocity of money is only mentioned in passing in terms of the "rapidity of circulation" (Ricardo 1810, 45).

Taxonomic Classification

Ricardo is concerned with the value of the currency and with money as a store of value. Under a monetary standard such as a gold standard, Ricardo assumes the value of money is ultimately determined by its underlying production costs. By contrast, when paper money is used as a means of payment, the Quantity Theory of Money is decisive. Ricardo does not consider private credit money.

References

Blaug, Mark. 1996. *Economic theory in retrospect*. 5th ed. Cambridge: Cambridge University Press.

Deleplace, Ghislain. 2024. Storm in a teacup? The impact of war on the English monetary system and thought (1797–1821). In *Money in times of crisis: Pre-classical, classical and contemporary theories*, 91–124. Rome: Accademia Nazionale dei Lincei.

Glasner, David. 2017. Monetary disequlibrium and the demand for money in Ricardo and Thornton. In *Ricardo on money and finance: A bicentenary reappraisal*, 15–29. London: Routledge.

Marcuzzo, Maria Cristina, and Annalisa Roselli. 1994. Ricardo's theory of money matters. *Revue économique* 45 (5): 1251–1267.

Pierenkemper, Toni. 2012. *Geschichte des modernen ökonomischen Denkens*. Göttingen: Vandenhoeck & Ruprecht.

Ricardo, David. 1810. *The High Price of Bullion*. A Proof of the Depreciation of Bank Notes. 3rd edition. London: Murray.

Schumpeter, Joseph. 1954. *History of economic analysis*. Edited from manuscript by Elizabeth Boody Schumpeter. New York: Oxford University Press.

Stadlin, Alois E. 1954. *Die Entwicklung der Quantitätstheorie von Cantillon und Hume bis Ricardo*. Winterthur: Keller.

Walter, Ryan. 2019. The Bullion controversy and the history of political thought: experience, innovation and theory. *Intellectual History Review* 29 (3): 467–488.

Chapter 17
Thomas Tooke (1774–1858): Money Follows Prices

17.1 Biography[1]

Thomas Tooke was born on February 29, 1774, in Kronstadt near St. Petersburg, the son of an English clergyman located in Russia at the time. At the age of thirty, he joined a prestigious London firm engaged primarily in trade with Russia and soon established himself as a successful independent merchant. In 1836 he retired from this work, devoting himself instead to entrepreneurial roles for other companies.

Throughout his life, Tooke was an outspoken advocate of free trade. In 1820 he authored the *Merchants' Petition in Favour of Free Trade*, which was introduced in Parliament by Alexander Baring. The following year, he co-founded the Political Economy Club together with Thomas R. Malthus, John Stuart Mill, David Ricardo, and others.

His expertise in monetary and financial matters brought him repeatedly before parliamentary commissions—in 1819, 1820, 1821, 1832, 1840, and again 1848—where he gave evidence on monetary policy and offered proposals for reforming the English banking system.

Tooke's most important scholarly contribution was his monumental six-volume *A History of Prices, and of the State of the Circulation, from 1793 to 1856*, a work that earned him considerable recognition. His 1844 *An Enquiry into the Currency Principle*, a polemic against the Currency School, marked his definitive shift to the Banking School, away from the bullionist tradition.

Thomas Tooke died in London on February 26, 1858.

---

[1] This biography follows Rieter (1971, 108–110).

J. Greitens, *Currency and Credit Money*, Springer Studies in the History of Economic Thought, https://doi.org/10.1007/978-3-032-24113-9_17

17.2 Selected Text

Tooke, Thomas. 1844. *An Enquiry into the Currency Principle*. London, Longman.

17.3 Historical Background[2]

The second phase of controversy over monetary theory in nineteenth-century England is commonly known as the Currency School–Banking School debate. At its core, this dispute centered on the distinction between currency and credit money. While the earlier Bullion Controversy had focused primarily on the role of state-issued paper money as currency, without considering credit instruments such as bills of exchange or cheques, the contours of the debate now expanded, taking credit money into account. Emerging around 1825 and reaching its peak during deliberations over the passage and subsequent implementation of Prime Minister Robert Peel's Second Bank Act of 1844, the controversy involved deeper questions about the regulation of the money supply, the stability of the banking system, and the extent to which the state should intervene in monetary affairs.

In many respects, the Currency School stood in the bullionist tradition, while the Banking School continued the anti-bullionist line of argument. Representatives of the Currency School wanted to ban not only irredeemable state paper money, but also redeemable banknotes that were not fully backed by metallic reserves. For Currency School adherents, the central bank's primary objective should be to ensure the stability of the currency, narrowly defined as banknotes and circulating coins. Furthermore, in the eyes of the Currency School, the prevention of excessive issuance and protection of convertibility were essential for safeguarding monetary stability.

Representatives of the Banking School, by contrast, regarded the redeemability of banknotes as a sufficient limitation on their issuance. Unlike the Currency School proponents, they rejected strict approaches based on quantity theory, emphasizing instead that credit money has a natural limit, as set out in the Real Bills Doctrine and Law of Reflux. In their view, the volume of banknotes is elastic, since their issuance follows actual credit and transaction demand. Consequently, the money supply is endogenous, as it is determined by the needs of trade and price levels, rather than exogenous regulatory constraints.

Discussions about a new law for the Bank of England began in 1837, leading to the establishment of a parliamentary committee in 1840. These discussions were spurred by repeated crises in the financial system, particularly those of 1836–1839. The Currency School gained significant support from politicians, as well as from the directors of the Bank of England. The Currency School prevailed politically.

[2] This description follows Arnon (2011, 217–220), Rieter (1971, 122–152), and Diatkine and de Boyer (2008).

The Bank of England was thus divided into two areas by the Bank Charter Act of 1844. The Issue Department was solely responsible for issuing banknotes as currency; exposure of the Bank of England to liquidity risks was prevented by a close tie to the gold stock. The Bank of England also obtained a legal monopoly over the issue of banknotes. The Banking Department was expected to conduct its business in the same way as a private bank, i.e., by brokering loans and by discounting bills for Bank of England notes acquired from the Issuing Department against gold.

Consequently, the Banking Department's activities were entirely dependent on the quantity of banknotes it obtained from the Issue Department. This reform resulted in the automatic circulation of paper, which behaved exactly like metallic circulation, both in terms of amount and value. In other words, there was no delay in adjusting the issuance of banknotes to gold movements, and the currency could no longer be mismanaged. Stability thus won out over elasticity.

The implementation of the law was associated with deflation. Credit money quickly gained in importance—indeed, to such an extent that cashless payment transactions became a defining feature of the English monetary system. The English economy experienced the inelasticity of this system several times, resulting in the limit on uncovered notes having to be exceeded for the first time in 1847, and then again during the crises of 1857 and 1866.

Tooke's *An Enquiry into the Currency Principle*, published in March 1844—2 months before the final decision on Peel's Bank Act—represented the Banking School's most mature approach. The manuscript was prepared based on notes and was completed in time for the parliamentary debate on the proposed reform. Tooke was already well known to parliament; the third volume of *A History of Prices* had appeared in 1840. However, he departed from his previously held positions in the bullionist tradition. By applying free trade principles to the issuance of notes, Tooke became a proponent of competitive note issue.

17.4 Discussion

17.4.1 The Currency and Banking Principles

Tooke begins his work by presenting the Currency Principle. According to this school of thought, currency should be made of a pure metal; there should be a "purely metallic circulation" (Tooke 1844, 1). Bank notes must be convertible into gold "not only in value, but in amount; that is to say, that the bank notes being supposed to be a substitute, and the only substitute, for so much coin, should vary exactly in amount as the coin would have done if the Currency had been purely metallic" (Tooke 1844, 2). Accordingly, the Currency School argues that the Bank of England should be divided into an Issue Department and a Banking Department. If the Issue Department only "makes paper out of gold," this would increase the stability of the financial system and promote trade.

Tooke quotes George Warde Norman, director of the Bank of England: "I consider a metallic currency to be the most perfect currency, except so far as respects inconvenience in some respects, and cost. [...] bank notes are introduced to supply the place of a certain portion of metallic currency, [...] I do not think it is possible to improve upon a metallic currency, except in the two points of convenience and cheapness" (following Tooke 1844, 4–5).

As a representative of the Currency School, Norman sees the money supply as too elastic under the existing system. This leads to excessive risk-taking, issuance overshoot, and bank failure. The Bank of England's money supply is particularly volatile, which has a destabilizing effect (1844, 5, 55). This position is connected to the Quantity Theory of Money and the Price–Specie Flow Mechanism as described by Ricardo, both of which are rejected by the representatives of the Banking School. They consider the proposed regulations too mechanical and rigid, and existing regulations as sufficient (Tooke 1844, 7–9).

17.4.2 The Nature of Credit Money

Tooke then turns to credit money, arguing that it does not influence the value of the currency. Instead, he argues that these instruments are cheaper to produce, easier to handle, and safer than coins or Bank of England notes (Tooke 1844, 19–22). In order to define the relevant fraction of credit money, he also distinguishes between "dormant" deposits and deposits used for payments: "It sounds oddly, to say the least of it, to speak of deposits or lodgements of money as being active. The activity, if any, is in the payment by cheques founded upon the deposits. It is not the deposits, but the transfers of them; or, in other words, the cheques that constitute the actual instruments of interchange, and effect payments concurrently with bank notes. They perform the functions of money not only as perfectly as bank notes, but in the description of transactions to which they are applicable, they are more convenient than bank notes" (Tooke 1844, 23). Therefore, only deposits upon which checks or bills are drawn are money. However, their relevance and importance increase significantly (Tooke 1844, 26–29).

He supports his assertion that checks perform a monetary function with a quote from the banker William Leatham: "For a great number of years, it had been the custom of merchants to pay the clothiers in small bills of 10*l*, 15*l*, 20*l*, and so up to 100*l*, drawn at two months after date on London bankers. I have always considered this the best part of our paper currency, ranking next to gold; the bills existing only for limited periods, and acquiring increased security as they pass from hand to hand by endorsement" (Tooke 1844, 27). Tooke also quotes Thornton to describe how bills of exchange work. "They not only spare the use of ready money, they also occupy its place in many cases" (Thornton 1802, 91–92 in Tooke 1844, 29).

In contrast to the Currency School, Tooke attributes monetary functions to bills of exchange with short maturities. He believes that these functions can be performed by bills without currency being a prerequisite for settlement. "Active" deposits fulfil a monetary function similar to that of banknotes, but they are not currency and therefore have no influence on prices or the exchange rate: “Sufficient grounds have, as I venture to think, been stated for establishing the claim in behalf of cheques on bankers, and of bills of exchange, to be considered as performing, concurrently with bank notes, the functions of money for the purposes for which they are respectively used” (Tooke 1844, 32).

However, Tooke also has to distinguish from longer-term credit money, which does not serve as a means of circulation: “This applies indeed only to short-dated bills of the most unquestioned credit; longer-dated bills, of more doubtful security, seem to have, been alone in the view of those persons who assert the exclusive title of bank notes to be considered as money. Bills of this description, that is long-dated bills, are sometimes not used for purposes of circulation—they are simply written evidence of a debt which is discharged at maturity, without passing into third hands” (Tooke 1844, 31). In this case, capital is transferred without monetary functions being performed.

17.4.3 The Real Bills Doctrine

While not explicitly mentioned, the Real Bills Doctrine is present in the background of the Banking School. Trust in a bill of exchange is based on trust in the solvency of the “last endorser” (Tooke 1844, 29), while trust in a banknote is based on trust in the solvency of the bank—“an issuer being so well known as to give it universal credit” (Tooke 1844, 30).

“Real” bills of exchange, i.e., bills based on actual transactions of goods and not speculation, adapt elastically to the changing need for money in circulation. According to the Law of Reflux proposed by Banking School representative John Fullarton, the volume of such bills also automatically shrinks again (Fullarton 1844, 66–68). When the loan from the bill is repaid, the means of payment disappears. The Law of Reflux thus stabilizes the Real Bills Doctrine (Arnon 2011, 227–229).

As genuine transactions underlie real bills of exchange, real revenues are not credited multiple times. This is the core insight of the doctrine. However, it is difficult to distinguish between credit that is speculative and credit that is secure. The Law of Reflux is what fundamentally distinguishes banknotes from coins and government paper money.

17.4.4 Behind and Over the Counter

Tooke introduces the distinction between dealer-to-dealer transactions (wholesale) and dealer-to-consumer transactions (retail), quoting Adam Smith (Tooke 1844, 33–34). In the income and consumption spheres (including wage payments), the transaction amounts are smaller, such that currency dominates as money; by contrast, transactions between dealers are handled mainly using credit money. "The reason is obvious why, as far as relates to the interchange between dealers and consumers (including the payment of wages, which constitute the principal means of the consumers), coin, and the smaller denomination of notes serving as coin, are essential to such interchange, and why, consequently, if those smaller notes are withdrawn, their place must be supplied by coin; but not so as regards the interchange between dealers and dealers. Bank notes are not only not essential to that interchange" (Tooke 1844, 34–35). Dealers, in the circulation of capital, use bills of exchange and checks, so only a small amount of currency is necessary.

Accordingly, Tooke also distinguishes between different types of transactions in the banking business: For him, "behind the counter" refers to the credit business between dealers. Ultimately, this is how banks support capital allocation. "Over the counter" refers to currency dealing and pure payment transactions. "One branch of the banker's business is to collect capital from those who have not immediate employment for it, and to distribute or transfer it to those who have. The other branch is to receive deposits of the incomes of their customers, and to pay out the amount, as it is wanted for expenditure, by the latter in the objects of their consumption. The former may be considered as the business behind the counter, and the latter before or over the counter: the former being a circulation of capital, the latter of currency" (Tooke 1844, 36). Tooke's main purpose in introducing the dual circulation framework was to demonstrate that, contrary to the Currency School's position, the majority of monetary transactions in the economy were conducted through checks and bills of exchange, rather than banknotes (Smith 2001, 35).

The amount of currency in circulation cannot be influenced by private banks, as they only react to demands for means of payment. Tooke calls it "the powerlessness of the banks of issue to influence directly the amount of the circulation" (Tooke 1844, 37). Tooke also disputes the Bank of England's ability to influence circulation volumes. "The conclusion from the view here presented is, that neither the country banks nor the Bank of England have a direct power (their advances being on securities, and the paper convertible) of enlarging their circulation" (Tooke 1844, 66). It is only bank notes or assignats where the Bank of England can decide on the supply: "It is only the latter description of circulation of bank notes which admits of being increased in amount at the will of the issuers" (Tooke 1844, 66).

17.4.5 Tooke's Rejection of the Quantity Theory of Money

Tooke rejects the Quantity Theory of Money as it fails to differentiate between the sources and uses of money: "They consider that prices in such cases are under a direct influence from, and affected in the same manner by, variations in the amount of bank notes in circulation, which they designate indiscriminately as paper money. This erroneous impression arises from a neglect of the consideration of the difference in the manner and purpose of the issue" (Tooke 1844, 68).

The issuance of irredeemable state paper money takes place through government expenditure on personnel, construction projects, or the military. These expenditures represent a new and additional source of demand, leading to increasing prices and wages, and a declining exchange rate (Tooke 1844, 69–70).

Tooke believes that prices are determined by the share of income allocated to demand: "In a convertible state of the currency, given the actual and contingent supply of commodities, the greater or less demand will depend, not upon the total quantity of money in circulation, but upon the quantity of money constituting the revenues, valued in gold, of the different orders of the state under the head of rents, profits, salaries, and wages, destined for current expenditure. [...] The cost of production will determine whether and to what extent the supply will be continued, but the extent of the effectual demand, in a given state of the supply, will be measured by the prices which the consumers may be able and willing to pay. Now, the power of purchase by the consumers depends upon their incomes; and the measure of the extent and of the exercise of such power is, as has just been observed, in that portion of their revenues which is destined for expenditure in objects of immediate consumption" (Tooke 1844, 71).

Accordingly, Tooke attributes a change in prices primarily to a change in incomes. "Of the revenues or incomes of the community devoted to immediate expenditure, by far the largest proportion consists of wages [...]. Any increase, accordingly, of incomes, of which wages constitute the largest part, will raise general prices, and a fall of wages will depress them, supposing no alteration in the cost of production, or in the actual and contingent supply" (Tooke 1844, 71–72).

In Tooke's view, prices are determined via demand–pull or cost–push inflation, and the supply of credit money adjusts accordingly. In this way, the Currency School, which relies on quantity theory, "perverts the reasoning, and distorts the view of facts" (Tooke 1844, 76). "The bills of exchange are here supposed to have an effect on price, that is, to be a cause of price; whereas the very reverse is the fact" (Tooke 1844, 73).

17.4.6 The Income Theory of Money

Based on these considerations, Tooke proceeds to reverse the causality of the quantity theory. It is not the money supply that determines prices; rather, prices are determined in advance and the supply of credit money adjusts accordingly. "The bills of exchange are here supposed to have an effect on price, that is, to be a cause of price; whereas the very reverse is the fact. The bills of exchange, so far from being a cause, are the effect of price. The prospect of advantage supplies the motive, and the credit of the buyer constitutes the power of purchase, while the bill of exchange is a mere written evidence or acknowledgement of the debt, accompanied with a promise to pay the amount at some definite period" (Tooke 1844, 73). In accordance with the dual circulation framework, Tooke argued that total consumption expenditure—effective demand for final commodities sold by dealers to consumers—depended on income (Smith 2001, 37).

In the conclusions numbered 12 and 13, Tooke summarizes his Income Theory of Money and this reverse causality. "12. That the prices of commodities do not depend upon the quantity of money indicated by the amount of bank notes, nor upon the amount of the whole of the circulating medium; but that, on the contrary, the amount of the circulating medium is the consequence of prices. 13. That it is the quantity of money, constituting the revenues of the different orders of the State, under the head of rents, profits, salaries, and wages, destined for current expenditure, that alone forms the limiting principle of the aggregate of money prices, the only prices that can properly come under the designation of general prices. As the cost of production is the limiting principle of supply, so the aggregate of money incomes devoted to expenditure for consumption is the determining and limiting principle of demand" (Tooke 1844, 124).

In this way, for Tooke, the money supply is determined endogenously. As it adjusts to demand, a shortage or surplus is not possible. Demand for money is met through the creation or destruction of credit money. Should a shortage of banknotes occur, bills of exchange would be created to the same extent and perform the same function as the banknotes. "The amount of bank notes in the hands of the public is determined by the purpose for which they are required" (Tooke 1844, 122).

Tooke also states that the money supply can fluctuate endogenously without affecting prices or exchange rates. "That the prices of commodities do not depend upon the quantity of money indicated by the amount of bank notes, nor upon the amount of the whole of the circulating medium; but that, on the contrary, the amount of the circulating medium is the consequence of prices" (Tooke 1844, 123–124). Therefore, causation ran from the price level to the quantity of money in circulation, including banknotes (Smith 2001, 46).

17.5 Evaluation

Tooke's *Enquiry into the Currency Principle* remains one of the most significant contributions to banking theory, and is considered the precursor to the theory of endogenous, elastically adapting money. Tooke's ideas have been revisited numerous times since the work's original publication. Assuming a price level determined by real factors, credit money adapts and regulates itself, at least in normal times. The Quantity Theory of Money was thus transformed into an Income Theory of Money, in which credit money adjusts to demand from circulation and is backed by deliverable goods.

The Currency School distinguishes between money issued by the Bank of England or Royal Mint, on the one hand, and ordinary banking transactions involving credit money, such as bills or banknotes issued by private banks, on the other. However, for Tooke, there is no dichotomy between the two. Consequently, for the Banking School, the "circulating medium and all its components are not a multiple of currency, and the latter is not a strategic variable" (Diatkine and de Boyer 2008, 200). In some respects, however, Thornton is clearer than Tooke. This pertains to the endogeneity of credit money, his skepticism of the Real Bills Doctrine, and the concept of the circulating medium.

As credit money circulates in a different sphere to currency, which is used for income and consumption, credit money is essentially used by businesses and merchants. Therefore, they cannot exert a direct influence on prices. Only currency in the form of coins and non-redeemable banknotes can directly influence the prices of consumer goods. These enter the cycle of wage payments and expenditure, but this is not a point of focus for Tooke (Schefold 2019, 133).

Taxonomic Classification

Tooke focuses on credit instruments such as bills of exchange. The demand for these instruments, which is based on incomes, determines the amount of credit money. However, their value of this credit money is derived from the goods for which credit was extended. Thus, the value of money is determined by incomes, while the amount of credit money is based on the Real Bills Doctrine and the Law of Reflux.

References

Arnon, Arie. 2011. *Monetary theory and policy from Hume and Smith to Wicksell.* Cambridge: Cambridge University Press.

Diatkine, Sylvie, and Jérôme de Boyer. 2008. British monetary orthodoxy in the 1870s: A victory for the currency principle. *The European Journal of the History of Economic Thought* 15 (2): 181–209.

Fullarton, John. 1844. *On the regulation of currencies*. London: John Murray.

Rieter, Heinz. 1971. *Die gegenwärtige Inflationstheorie und ihre Ansätze im Werk von Thomas Tooke*. Berlin: Walter de Gruyter.

Schefold, Betram. 2019. Great economic thinkers from the classicals to the moderns. Translations from the series Klassiker der Nationalökonomie. New York: Routledge.

Tooke, Thomas. 1844. *An Enquiry into the Currency Principle*. London, Longman.

Smith, Matthew. 2001. Endogenous money, interest and prices: Tooke's monetary thought revisited. *Contributions to Political Economy* 20 (1): 31–55. https://doi.org/10.1093/cpe/20.1.31.

Thornton, Henry. 1802. An enquiry into the nature and effects of the paper credit of Great Britain. Edited with an introduction by F. A. V. Hayek. New York: Augustus M. Kelley.

Chapter 18
Henry Dunning Macleod (1821–1902): Money as the Highest Form of Credit

18.1 Biography[1]

Henry Dunning Macleod was born in 1821 in Edinburgh into a wealthy landowning family. After being educated at Eton College, the University of Edinburgh, and Trinity College in Cambridge, he quickly gained a reputation as an outstanding economic lawyer.

In 1853, Macleod was appointed director of the Royal British Bank, which collapsed in 1856. Macleod himself was indicted in the ensuing lawsuit, motivating him to engage in intense study of the theory of credit. The trial was a public scandal that permanently tarnished his reputation.

McLeod's subsequent efforts to secure a professorship were unsuccessful. From 1860 onward, he held a variety of teaching appointments at several British universities. Between 1868 and 1870, he also served as an adviser to the government as it contemplated reforming the Bills of Exchange Act. Macleod died in London in 1902.

Throughout his life, he remained something of an outsider within the economics profession, a status owed not only to his unconventional ideas but also to his self-confident and polemical writings.

18.2 Selected Text

Macleod, Henry Dunning. 1892. *The Theory and Practice of Banking*. Vol. 1. 5th edition. London: Longmans, Green and Co.

[1] This biography follows Fryer and Maloney (2004).

J. Greitens, *Currency and Credit Money*, Springer Studies in the History of Economic Thought, https://doi.org/10.1007/978-3-032-24113-9_18

18.3 Historical Background

Over the decades, Macleod wrote numerous extensive works on money and economics, including *Elements of Political Economy*, *The Elements of Economics*, *The Elements of Banking*, and *Economics for Beginners*. As a university lecturer, Macleod sought to reach students, so his works were structured as textbooks. While he continually revised his works over time, many elements reappear with different points of emphases. For example, we find essentially the same ideas in *The Theory of Credit* (1889–1891) and *The Theory and Practice of Banking* (first published in two volumes in 1855–56, with six subsequent editions, the last of which was published posthumously in 1905).

While this chapter draws on the 5th edition of *Theory and Practice of Banking*, which focuses on the role of credit and banks, the first edition, published in 1855, already contains the work's central ideas. Macleod steadily refined his ideas with each subsequent edition. Macleod explicitly takes a legalistic approach: "The purpose of this Work is to exhibit the Juridical and Scientific Principles and mechanism of the great System of Credit" (Macleod 1892, preface). His presentation is repeatedly interrupted by numerous legal cases and historical classifications, so the exposition is often meandering and digressive.

Macleod's focus on the positive effects of credit may have been shaped by his experience growing up in Scotland. However, he does not mention this fact explicitly. Initially a very poor country, Scotland saw strong development thanks to credit extension by banks (Skaggs 2003, 370–372). Macleod was also writing at a time when the gold standard was becoming increasingly common, and this was accompanied by significant fear of deflation (Meyer 1957, 48–49).

18.4 Discussion

18.4.1 Credit

Macleod states that credit is created to simplify barter and that it is used in particular to carry out unequal exchanges. "Now that Promise is only the Right to demand a particular thing from a particular person. […] Hence, such an Order has only particular and precarious Value: but Money has general and permanent Value. […] So, when we buy a Railway Ticket we buy a Right to be carried a certain distance by Rail: hence a Railway Ticket is Credit. So Opera Tickets, and all Tickets to see any dramatic or other performances, are Orders or Promises to see these things and are all forms of Credit" (Macleod 1892, 42–43).

Individual credit then gives birth to general credit, or money: "When persons have sold products or done services to other persons, they are entitled to receive either an equivalent product or service at the same time, or the Right to demand an equivalent at some future time. Now this Right may be in two forms: either that of

Metallic Money which is a General Right to demand any equivalent from the whole mercantile community: or a Right to demand an equivalent from the particular person who has received the product or service. This latter species of Right is what is usually termed a Credit. Hence, in either case, the Creditor is entitled to receive a Right: the only difference is, that in one case the Right is general and permanent, and in the other it is particular and precarious. But, for all that, they are clearly of the same nature. It is, therefore, seen that Money and Credit are homogeneous quantities; and that Money is only the highest and most general form of Credit" (Macleod 1892, 43–44).

In this way, while money is a form of general or societal credit, it is not structurally different from individual credit; indeed, money and individual credit are essentially the same thing (Lindner 1929, 16; Skaggs 1998, 459). The prerequisite for money is debt: "where there is no Debt there can be no Currency" (Macleod 1892, 55). However, Macleod does not have a narrow understanding of currency, e.g., in the sense of legal tender. His use of the term "currency" has aroused critical discussion, as he fails to define it clearly (Schäffle 1864, 550; Lindner 1929, 54).

18.4.2 Banking

For Macleod, tradable credit is money: "Credits, or Debts, are themselves saleable Commodities, Goods and Chattels, or Merchandise, they can be sold or exchanged against each other, just in the same way as material chattels are sold or exchanged for each other. The business of Banking consists exclusively in buying and selling Money" (Macleod 1892, 313).

The traders of this credit are banks. "The essential feature of all these Banks was this: the subscribers advanced the Money as a Loan, or Mutuum: and thus it became the absolute property of the borrowers: and in exchange for their Money they received a Credit: i.e. a Certificate, or Promise to pay interest; and the very essence of 'Banking' is to receive money as a Mutuum: and to give in exchange for it Credits, Debts, Promises to pay, or Rights of action to demand an equal sum back again when they please" (Macleod 1892, 318).

"A Banker, therefore, always buys money with his own Credit: or, by giving in exchange a Right of action to demand back an equal sum at any time: and, moreover, when he buys Commercial Debts, or discounts Commercial Bills of Exchange [...] he does it in exactly a similar way: in exchange for the Bill of Exchange he gives his customer a Credit in his books; or the Right to demand a sum of money from him. Thus, he buys one Debt, or Credit by giving in exchange for it another Debt, or Credit: and experiences show that this Credit may several times exceed the cash in his possession. Thus, the business of a banker is essentially to Create Credit" (Macleod 1892, 320).

But banks do not purchase credit; rather, they create credit themselves. "A Banker is a Trader whose business is to buy Money and Debts by creating other Debts" (Macleod 1892, 321).

According to the Currency Principle, which was enshrined in the Bank Act of 1844, all currency had to be backed by a precious metal. This renders the creation of credit money impossible. This means that banks can only act as intermediaries: "that its sole function should be to exchange Credit for Money and Money for Credit: and thus the quantity of Credit would always be exactly equal to the Money it displaces" (Macleod 1892, 321). Thus, banks are also unable to generate profits: "no Bank constructed on the Currency Principle ever did, or ever could, by any possibility, make profits by business" (Macleod 1892, 322).

18.4.3 Money Creation Instead of Financial Intermediation

Macleod draws a legal distinction between a *mutuum* and *depositum*: "A Depositum, in Roman Law, means anything which is placed in the charge or custody of a person for the mere purpose of safe keeping [...]. It is very often supposed that when a customer pays in money to his account, that money is a Deposit. This is the first error on the subject: because the money so paid in is not a Depositum: it is a Mutuum. The money is in reality sold to the banker: and it has become his actual property to deal with as he pleases. [...] As the error respecting the meaning of the word Deposit is almost universal among writers and speakers on banking" (Macleod 1892, 327).

Under Roman law, depositum refers to custody over a certain thing, such as jewelry. By contrast, mutuum involves a transfer of ownership, and the borrower (in this case the bank) is required to make equivalent repayment. For Macleod, the concept of mutuum is a legal prerequisite for the granting of real credit. In this way, the fungibility of money is highly significant. "Now this money was not placed in their hands to be locked away idle in their cellars, as plate and jewelry are often given to the care of a banker as a Depositum, and to be restored in specie. The money was sold to the banker as a Mutuum: to be restored only *in genere*. And they agreed not only to repay it on demand, but to pay six per cent interest for it: consequently, they were obliged to trade with it in order to make a profit" (Macleod 1892, 324). Macleod then proceeds to describe the creation of credit money in a textbook-like manner, and also addresses the role of liquidity and excess reserves (Macleod 1892, 325).

He summarizes: "A Banker is a Trader who buys Money and Debts by creating other Debts. Thus we see that the essential and distinctive feature of a 'Bank' and a 'Banker' is to Create and Issue Credit payable on Demand: and this Credit is intended to be put into circulation and serve all the purpose of money. A bank, therefore, is not an office for borrowing and lending Money: but it is a Manufactory of Credit" (Macleod 1892, 326).

By comparing banks to "credit factories," Macleod emphasizes the active role they play in this process. They buy with their own payment promises, and extend their balance sheet by making and issuing debt promises in the form of loans. "A banker multiplies his liabilities to pay on demand, and keeps by him a sufficient amount of cash to ensure the immediate payment of all claims which are likely to be demanded at one time" (Macleod 1892, 337).

Banks are free to lend; they do not require prior savings.. "It is commonly supposed that Bankers act only as intermediaries between persons who want to lend and those who want to borrow. The fact is, that a Banker is a Trader, whose business is to buy Money and Debts, by creating other Debts" (Macleod 1892, 337).

The creation of money is initiated by banks and is not a reflection of previous or simultaneous processes in the real economy. Bank loans do not "passively" follow the processes of the real economy. Therefore, deposits are created by the bank and not through the deposit of cash and its reissue. Banks are not intermediaries. Loans are not a consequence of money use; they are its origin. "A Deposit is simply a Credit in a banker's book" (Macleod 1892, 330).

Macleod also asserts that deposits can be used for payment transactions, i.e., they can be used as money, so practically no currency is necessary for this form of circulation: "just as Credits are usually transferred from one account to another in the same bank without a single coin being inquired" (Macleod 1892, 330).

18.4.4 Monetary Effects

Macleod contends that the business activity of banks increases the money supply: "We observe, that the business of banking is to build up a superstructure of Credit several times exceeding the basis of bullion: and this Credit is intended to circulate and produce all the effects of money" (Macleod 1892, 354).

This allows for the financing of productive investment. Loans increase future profits and thus output (Skaggs 2003, 369). Referencing Hamilton, among others, Macleod describes how the prosperity of countries is affected (Macleod 1892, 354–357), noting that "banking augments the Capital of the country" (Macleod 1892, 355). Banks thus promote the economy and are not neutral entities, as they increase volume of available capital (Skaggs 2003, 368–369).

18.5 Evaluation

Macleod stood in opposition not only to metallists but also to classical economists who assumed in the neutrality of money in the long run. According to Macleod, the view that banks merely act as credit intermediaries is incorrect. He reverses the explanation of money originating from exchange, instead viewing money as originating from credit (Skaggs 1998, 455–457; Skaggs 2003, 366).

This establishes Macleod as a founder of modern credit creation theory (Wagner 1937, 148–149; Werner 2014, 3), despite his status as an academic outsider. Nevertheless, he significantly influenced Ralph Hawtrey in England, Alfred

Mitchell-Innes in the USA, and Albert Hahn in Germany (Skaggs 2003, 379; Lindner 1929, 82).

Macleod also deviated from the Banking School's view that money creation is a reflection of the real economy. While the Banking School did not doubt the basic interdependency between savings and investments, Macleod reversed cause and effect. Furthermore, Macleod clearly distinguished himself from John Law by not attributing any overarching significance to the currency (Lindner 1929, 35–36).

Macleod expressed his views in a highly polemical manner, which often resulted in his writings being rejected.

Taxonomic Classification
For Macleod, money is credit. In this respect, only the means of payment function is relevant, and currency plays no role. Banks act as credit factories, actively creating credit money.

18.6 Summary of Classical Monetary Theories

The notion of a dichotomy between the real and monetary spheres is closely associated with classical economics. While this subdivision was certainly embraced by various authors from this school, in our selection it applies only to Ricardo, and even then only to a limited extent. This provides yet further evidence for the remarkable diversity of ideas that existed even during this so-called classical phase.

The Price–Specie Flow Mechanism, which describes the operation of a fixed exchange rate system, has largely survived up to the present. Nevertheless, debate as to whether the current account is of overriding importance (as argued by Hume) or whether the capital account should be of central concern (as posited by Ricardo) remains relevant to this day, not least against the backdrop of significant macroeconomic imbalances, including those in the Eurozone.

Another key issue of discussion was how to best safeguard the currency. Despite the many arguments in favor of a fiat money system, the idea of gold backing remained predominant. Clearly, many authors did not trust political institutions to guarantee a stable currency without a precious metal backing.

This phase in the history of Great Britain was characterized by the development of a market-based financial system and the adoption of credit instruments for payment transactions. Discussions about the importance of credit money continued throughout the nineteenth century, beginning with the Bullion Controversy and Currency School–Banking School debate, and continuing with discussions regarding the role of the Bank of England as a central bank. Macleod, for his part, found little resonance when he proposed a monetary system consisting exclusively of credit money.

References

Fryer, S. E., and John Maloney. 2004. Macleod, Henry Dunning (1821–1902). In *Oxford Dictionary of National Biography*. Oxford: Oxford University Press. [www.oxforddnb.com/view/article/34787].

Lindner, Martin. 1929. *Die Kredittheorie von Henry Dunning Macleod*. Görlitz: Görlitzer Nachrichten und Anzeiger.

Macleod, Henry Dunning. 1892. *The Theory and Practice of Banking*. Vol. 1. 5th edition. London: Longmans, Green and Co.

Meyer, Ingeborg. 1957. Geldbewußtsein und Münzpolitik. In *Das sogenannte Gresham'sche Gesetz im Lichte der Verhaltensforschung*. Forschungsberichte des Wirtschafts- und Verkehrsministerium Nordrhein-Westfalen. No. 437.

Schäffle. 1864. Die Macleod'sche Kredittheorie. *Zeitschrift für die gesamte Staatswissenschaft* 20 (3): 549–558.

Skaggs, Neil T. 1998. Debt as the basis of currency: The monetary economics of trust. *American Journal of Economics and Sociology* 57 (4): 453–467.

Skaggs, Neil T. 2003. H.D. Macleod and the origins of the theory of finance in the economic development. *History of Political Economy* 35 (3): 361–384.

Wagner, Valentin F. 1937. *Geschichte der Kredittheorien. Eine dogmen-kritische Darstellung*. Vienna: Springer.

Werner, Richard. 2014. Can banks individually create money out of nothing?—The theories and the empirical evidence. *International Review of Financial Analysis* 36:1–19.

References

Part V
German-Speaking Authors

The German-language debate on monetary theory that occurred prior to the twentieth century is generally considered backward by present-day scholars. This is partly due to the lack of national unity prior to 1871: in a politically and economically fragmented empire, there was no single national currency or central fiscal authority. Accordingly, there was comparatively less incentive to develop abstract monetary theory. German scholars also had difficulty keeping up with developments in English and French theory. It was not until the end of the nineteenth century that an analytical monetary theory by German authors came into existence (Häuser 1998, 69). Consequently, various earlier debates were often a delayed echo of discussion in English (Rieter 2001).

Nevertheless, the German-language debate had a few peculiarities. Since the beginning of the Thirty Years' War, there had been frequent and massive currency devaluations. These crises created the impression of an unstable monetary system.

Inquiry into the essence of money emerged as a concern of the Historical School and their predecessors like Pufendorf, and the notion of money as more than just a standardized commodity, or *numéraire*, was a central element of contemporary monetary debates (Häuser 1998, 70). In additional, issues in monetary theory were frequently couched in broader social contexts.

References

Häuser, Karl. 1998. "Dogmengeschichtliche Betrachtungen zur deutschen Währungsunion von 1871–1876." *Studien zur Entwicklung der ökonomischen Theorie XVII. Die Umsetzung wirtschaftspolitischer Grundkonzeptionen in die kontinentaleuropäische Praxis des 19. und 20. Jahrhunderts*. Vol. 2. Berlin: Duncker & Humblot. 67–94.

Rieter, Heinz. 2001. "Deutsche Geldtheorie im 19. Jahrhundert – mehr als nur ein Echo englischer Debatten?" *Exogenität und Endogenität. Die Geldmenge in der Geschichte des ökonomischen Denkens und in der modernen Politik*. Marburg: Metropolis. 13–55.

Chapter 19
Johann Heinrich Gottlob Justi (1717–1771): The Fight Against Shadow Money

19.1 Biography[1]

Johann Heinrich Gottlob Justi was baptized on December 28, 1717, in Brücken an der Helme (in present-day Thüringen) and attended grammar school in Quedlinburg. His time in the Saxon military (1741–1742) in a regiment under Lieutenant Colonel Wigand Gottlob von Gersdorff exerted a major influence on his life. The lieutenant colonel recognized that Justi's talents were not of a martial nature, and thus made him his private secretary. Additionally, after the war, Gersdorff provided Justi with the means to study law in Wittenberg from 1742 to 1744.

Justi began to engage with economic issues and was appointed to a professorship at the Theresianum in Vienna in 1750. In 1753, Justi returned to Saxony. Beginning in 1755 he worked as a police director and *Bergrat* on behalf of Hanover and also taught cameralism, yet without a professorial appointment. He published his main works during this period, releasing *Staatswirthschaft* in 1755 followed by *Grundsätze der Policey–Wissenschaft* in 1756. Justi reached a large readership with the latter work, which was a bestseller.

Justi left Göttingen in June 1757, shortly before its occupation by French troops in the Seven Years' War. Justi subsequently sought employment in Prussia. In 1762 Justi built a particularly efficient furnace in Wandsbeck for fine smelting the silver contained in the many token coins brought into circulation because of the war.

In 1765, Frederick II admitted Justi into the Prussian bureaucratic service as a mining captain (Berghauptmann). Justi was tasked against his will with managing glass, steel, and smelting works in Neumark. Justi's ongoing financial problems were the cause of numerous conflicts, including a legal dispute regarding a possible misuse of state funds. Justi was imprisoned at Küstrin Fortress during these

[1] This biography follows Reinert (2009, 35–44) and Greitens (2020, 240–242).

J. Greitens, *Currency and Credit Money*, Springer Studies in the History of Economic Thought, https://doi.org/10.1007/978-3-032-24113-9_19

proceedings. He died prior to the end of the trial on July 21, 1771, at the age of 54. There is no evidence he was granted noble status.

19.2 Selected Text

Justi, Johann Heinrich Gottlob. 1766. *System des Finanzwesens*. Halle: Rengerische Buchhandung.

All translations provided here were performed by the author.

19.3 Historical Background

Justi was a prolific writer, a widely read late-cameralist of considerable reputation. While there are numerous recurring themes in his books, he did not publish a single seminal work. His ideas are spread across numerous writings, and some of his works show considerable overlap, with passages repeated verbatim. Justi's *System des Finanzwesens* of 1766, which discusses the right of coinage, is his most concise work.

The book deals implicitly with Graumann's coin reform of 1750 and the upheavals in the Prussian coinage system experienced after the Seven Years' War. In 1750, Frederick II ("the Great") commissioned Johann Philipp Graumann to make the devalued Prussian *Reichstaler* a leading currency in the German states and to increase seigniorage revenues. The project had to be abandoned in 1755 and the war, which started in 1756, caused the coins known in the vernacular as *Ephraimites* to further devalue. Justi implicitly attacks Graumann, but also Friedrich, for their dovish monetary policy (Greitens 2020, 236–239, 251–253) (Fig. 19.1).

19.4 Discussion

19.4.1 The Essence of Money

According to Justi, gold and silver emerge as a general means of exchange in trade due to the double coincidence of wants and their natural properties. He asserts the state has an obligation to ensure the quality of the coins, and the minting of the coins should vouchsafe for their quality (1766, 300–304).

Justi explicitly defines money as "pieces of gold and silver brought into a certain form, on which, according to the credible testimony of the highest authority, the true value or content contained therein is noted, so that one can use them with

Fig. 19.1 Reichsthaler (1750) (Münzkabinett der Staatlichen Museen Berlin, 18219377, Saczewski)

foreigners and locals as a general means of compensation for all kinds of goods" (Justi 1766, 305). Justi thus views money in a purely metallistic fashion as a mere commodity.

Justi explains that gold and silver prices were rising because coins were being poorly minted; mines were increasing their profits as a result. Nominal increases in metal prices encouraged further debasement, causing silver prices to rise even further in a mutually reinforcing process. "This increase in the price of gold and silver will also continue forever; as long as one follows the principle that the right to mint coins [*Münzregal*] can be used as a source of income" (Justi 1766, 337).

According to Justi, bad money from abroad is the initial cause of rising prices, which has many negative effects on workers and creditors (Justi 1766, 322–3). However, the greatest damage is caused by a falling exchange rate, as the lower silver content of coins in comparison to full-value coins means greater expense for foreign goods: "and the more money that goes out of the country annually to pay for the trade balance; the more significant is the damage it suffers in the exchange rate" (Justi 1766, 323).

Similar problems were being faced by many countries in Europe. However, according to Justi, the situation in Germany was particularly bad because there were too many authorities with minting rights. Justi compares this situation to that of the *Kipper und Wipper* period at the beginning of the Thirty Years' War, when hyperinflation led to collapse. Justi notes that no single state can withdraw from this race to the bottom; all are forced to participate in the devaluation of the coinage. Justi hopes the princes will realize that a well-ordered coinage system is more important than income from minting, as it is a prerequisite for healthy economic development (Justi 1766, 337).

19.4.2 The Value of Money

For Justi, any deviation from a coin's metallic value is harmful: "It is in the preceding principles and explanations often talked about the intrinsic content and value of money, and of low-value coins, which do not have this intrinsic content. This assumes that coins can have two values, an intrinsic and an external one" (Justi 1766, 321). However, people cannot evaluate the quality of the metal, and therefore trust in the nominal value, which is only a "shadow image" (Justi 1755, 12).

For Justi, it is already a sign of degeneration in the coinage system that there is such a distinction at all: "I do not know if my readers will agree with me when I say that the external or numeraire value that is attributed to money is the only great source of all disorders of the coinage system" (Justi 1766, 324). Bad coinage is a "plague that has inflicted unspeakable harm on commerce" (Justi 1766, 322).

Even domestically, the apparent benefit of minting bad coins is outweighed by the damage caused. Although the prince makes a profit by issuing inferior coins to his soldiers and servants, he receives them back as tax payments. In addition, prices rise, meaning the ruler has to pay higher wages. Ultimately, the prince damages himself by damaging his subjects. These effects cannot be separated; the happiness (Glückseligkeit) of the princes and of the people are interconnected (Justi 1766, 310–311).

"If the costs of minting are to be borne by the coin itself, the coin must, as a natural consequence, have two types of value, namely its true, or intrinsic, value, and the extrinsic value, which is also called the numeraire value of the money" (Justi 1766, 321). This problem would not exist if the prince did not seek to generate seigniorage revenues. Accordingly, for Justi, disorder will cease when the intrinsic value of the coins, as determined by their metal content, and the extrinsic nominal value of the coins, as determined by the minting authority, coincide once again (Justi 1766, 324).

Nominal values that deviate from underlying metal values thus lead to disorder in the coinage system, which harms the economy. In line with this insight, Justi calls for units of coinage to once again correspond with units of weight: "The supreme power, to which an entire people has entrusted the care of its happiness, is the guardian of public faith and trust" (Justi 1766, 305). If the state debases the coinage, this is "not much better than open fraud" (Justi 1766, 342). In connection with the question of wealth distribution, Justi writes: "One can regard this invention of money as the source of all evil and all misfortune in the world" (Justi 1766, 36).

19.4.3 Foreign Trade

Justi also argues from a metallistic perspective with regard to foreign trade. Full value coins will result in exchange rates becoming equal once again, he asserts, as fewer coins will need to flow abroad to purchase foreign goods. This is because foreign countries only accept coins according to their intrinsic value, whereas "token coins" (whose face value exceeds their intrinsic value) are only usable domestically and, according to Justi, are not really money in the strict sense. One cannot add value to metal by minting with it, Justi asserts (1766, 310, 316–317, 326).

"A ruler is very much mistaken if he believes that he can issue his low-grade coins in neighboring states, or to foreigners in general, at the same value that he has marked on them. These, even if they do not proceed to actual devaluation, and thus pretend to accept them at full value, know how to arrange it through agio, exchange rate, commission, and especially through the price of goods in such a way that they actually do not pay more than the true intrinsic value. Yes, they rather deduct too much than too little, so that they remain without damage with certainty" (Justi 1766, 36). In a similar vein, Justi notes: "If a country is constantly losing precious metal, this is not due to the coinage standard, but to the overall economic condition. But if more and more money is leaving the country through foreign trade, and a wise ruler does not know how to put the commerce in any other state; then things look gloomy for such a country" (Justi 1766, 340).

Without explicitly referencing John Locke or the Great Recoinage of 1696, Justi presumably alludes to them while addressing the question of how good coins can be kept in circulation. He argues entirely in the tradition of mercantilism, maintaining that the state should enact and enforce strict laws against the export of coins. "The main objection usually comes down to the belief that such good coin types would soon be taken out of the country; and the ruler would therefore be forced to constantly mint new similar coin types at his great expense. [...] The export of the good coin types happens solely because all kinds of poor token coins are valid in the country" (Justi 1766, 339).

Therefore, the state should only permit foreign token coins to circulate at their intrinsic value, and must enforce the long-standing prohibition on melting down good coins, then "one can be quite sure that the good national coins will not be lost from circulation" (Justi 1766, 339–340).

19.4.4 Monetary Policy

Justi argues that the primary responsibilities of monetary policy lie not in the management of exchange rates or foreign relations, but rather in the domestic economy. Monetary policy should seek not only to increase the domestic money supply, but also promote its circulation. Justi draw the analogy to blood in a body, which benefits from improved circulation (Justi 1766, 571).

Justi argues that all factors hindering the circulation of money should be eliminated, including the minting of inferior coins. In this context, Justi does not distinguish between the money supply and the velocity of circulation. Instead, in a manner similar to Cantillon, he describes a transmission mechanism that responds to an increase in the money supply (Sommer 1920, 257–259).

According to Justi, the fundamental error of rulers is the desire to run the coinage system for profit, when the goal should be to stimulate the economy: "that one wants to make a financial prerogative out of the coinage system, which should yield important revenues; that even those states that do not have mines want to exercise this prerogative profitably, regardless of the nature and purpose of the coins, which should primarily be established for the benefit of commerce, does not allow this at all, that one does not mint gold and silver purely, but makes additions of lesser metals, as a result of which the low-quality minting is concealed" (Justi 1766, 323).

Justi defines his right of coinage as follows: "It is the high right of the supreme power to determine the value of all foreign coins circulating in the country, to make laws and regulations about it, and to direct all related matters, as well as to mint the gold and silver obtained either from the mines or designated by its subjects for the trades into money, in order to facilitate commerce by giving the coin types, because of their true intrinsic content, the to provide the necessary faith" (Justi 1766, 313).

The right to mint coins stems from the right to mine. While the mining right is intended to generate income, the right to mint coins is intended to facilitate trade by providing a public and credible state guarantee of the metallic value of the coinage. Therefore, it does not generate short-term income for the state, but incurs costs. In order to exercise the right to mint coins profitably, a country would need its own mines. Otherwise, the sovereign must "buy the raw silver and gold in other countries, and especially from his subjects, and have it minted profitably. I answer to that, that this is a pure impossibility, if not the nature and the ultimate purpose of money, as well as justice and fairness are disregarded, and constant disorder and ruin in the coinage system is facilitated" (Justi 1766, 308).

A country without its own mines cannot mint good coins profitably because the raw gold and silver must be worth the same as the gold and silver in the coins, and the cost of minting must be covered. In this way, the price of newly minted gold and silver coins is often higher than the underlying metal price. Therefore, if a fair price is paid, no profit can be made from coinage. Justi argues that in order to promote the economy through increasing the money supply rather than generate income, the state should operate loss-making mines (Justi 1766, 228–229, 308–309).

Justi hopes that the princes will recognize that a stable coinage system is more important for economic development than income from minting coins. The princes thus have two options for covering the costs of minting: they can cover these costs from other state revenues, or rely on profits made from minting token coins solely intended for domestic use. Justi also warns of potential misbehavior by masters of the mint and calls for their strict supervision. Justi asserts that masters of the mint seek to make profits by adding other metals to the coins, citing the need to harden the metal as a pretext for fraud. He notes that the cost of removing the alloy reduces the value of the coin compared to pure metal (Justi 1766, 332–333, 343).

France made short-term profits by minting undervalued coins under strict enforcement, but harmed itself in the long run. Justi thus advises against such approaches. Instead, a country without mines should cover the cost of minting through other means and produce coins of full value, as is the case in England (Justi 1766, 328–330).

19.5 Evaluation

Justi is a representative of a narrow and strict metallistic understanding of money, according to which the state's role is to guarantee the quality of currency, which for Justi was merely a commodity. For Justi, anything else would constitute theft and a breach of good faith. Based on historical experience, including the economic distortions caused by John Law's monetary scheme, he concluded that an even stricter form of metallism was necessary. This led him to advocate a restrictive monetary policy that was focused on ensuring stability. Justi follows in the footsteps of fourteenth-century Nicolaus Oresme and seventeenth-century John Locke, according to whom the state must guarantee the quality of the currency. Justi rejected political projects that sought to achieve short-term advantage. In formulating this judgement, Justi was taking aim at Frederick II and Johann Philipp Graumann, who were responsible for the coinage reform of 1750; he was also criticizing the financing of the Seven Years' War of 1756–1763. Due to England's implementation of free coinage without seigniorage, the quality of coins would increase, and it was not possible for the right of coinage to be abused.

Justi's conception of long-term economic development was paired with a liberal understanding of economic and trade policy. However, his strict metallism obscured his understanding of exchange rates and the balance of payments system. For Justi, trade was an act of barter, and he gave insufficient consideration to the capital account or credit system.

Nevertheless, Justi's demand for a coinage system without seigniorage revenues in the Holy Roman Empire was unrealistic. Comparing Justi's views with those of his English contemporaries confirms the backwardness of German monetary theory at this time. Justi was trapped by the real economic situation of the many small German states, whose monetary and financial systems lagged behind those of England and France. The backwardness of Germany's monetary and financial systems at that time conditioned the backwardness of monetary theory. Indeed, the debates in which Justi was involved partially echoed older English debates between 1666 and 1717.

Taxonomic Classification

Justi stands entirely in the tradition of Oresme and Locke. He focused on currency as a store of value. He did not consider credit money.

References

Greitens, Jan. 2020. Geldtheorie und -politik in Preußen Mitte des 18. Jahrhunderts. *Jahrbuch für Wirtschaftsgeschichte* 61 (1): 217–257.

Justi, Johann Heinrich Gottlob. 1755. *Entdeckte Ursachen des verderbten Münzwesens in Teutschland, nach ihren ersten und wahren Quellen*. Leipzig.

Justi, Johann Heinrich Gottlob. 1766. *System des Finanzwesens*. Halle: Rengerische Buchhandung.

Reinert, Erik S. 2009. Johann Heinrich Gottlob von Justi—the life and times of an economist adventurer. In *The Beginnings of Political Economy. The European Heritage in Economics and the Social Sciences*, vol. 7, 33–74. Boston, MA: Springer.

Sommer, Louise. 1920. *Die österreichischen Kameralisten. Reprint*. Aalen: Scientia Verlag. 1967.

Chapter 20
Adam Müller (1779–1829): The Power of Unity in Money

20.1 Biography[1]

Adam Müller was born on June 30, 1779, in Berlin to Protestant parents; his father was a Prussian finance official. After completing high school, he pursued studies in philosophy, history, law, and political science at the University of Göttingen between 1798 and 1801. During this time, he became acquainted with the writings of Adam Smith, Edmund Burke, and Gustav Hugo. He was particularly influenced by the contrast between rationalist natural law and historical approaches to jurisprudence. In Göttingen, Müller also formed a lifelong friendship with Friedrich von Gentz, 15 years his senior, who would later become secretary to Klemens von Metternich at the Congress of Vienna.

Following a brief period of service as a legal trainee in the Prussian War and Domain Chamber (1802–1803), Müller moved to southern Prussia. There he wrote *Die Lehre vom Gegensatze* (1804), which laid the foundation for his universalist and dialectical mode of thinking. In 1805, during a visit to Vienna, he converted to Catholicism under Gentz's influence. From 1806 to 1809, Müller lived in Dresden as an educator and private scholar. His well-received lecture series culminated in the publication of his major work, *Die Elemente der Staatskunst* (1809), considered the "Magna Carta" of political Romanticism and a cornerstone of his economic thought.

Müller's political economy was defined by a sharp critique of the abstract rationalism of classical economics. While he acknowledged Adam Smith's contributions, he rejected the exclusive focus on markets and individualism, instead emphasizing the organic growth of institutions, the socially embedded nature of economic activity, and the responsibility of the state. His ideas defended feudal and estate-based social structures and linked economic arguments with broader cultural, religious, and philosophical reflections.

[1] This biography follows Harada (2004) and Müller-Schmid and Paul (2002).

J. Greitens, *Currency and Credit Money*, Springer Studies in the History of Economic Thought, https://doi.org/10.1007/978-3-032-24113-9_20

In 1811, Müller co-founded the *Deutsche Tischgesellschaft* with the Romantic poet Achim von Arnim. The society, which became part of the German national movement, partially reflected the problematic anti-Semitic elements within that movement. Around this time, his initial support for Prussian reforms turned into open opposition. He emerged as a spokesperson for the reactionary noble opposition against Chancellor Karl August von Hardenberg, with whom he broke in late 1811. Müller then moved permanently to Vienna, marking his transition from rationalist liberalism to conservative Romanticism and ultimately to a theocratic Catholic worldview.

From 1811 onward, Müller gradually entered Austrian service. He worked as a publicist in Vienna and as a commissioner in Tyrol during the Wars of Liberation (1813–1815). Later, he served as Austrian general consul in Leipzig, where he edited the *Deutsche Staatsanzeigen*, and subsequently as envoy and councilor in the Viennese State Chancellery. In 1826, he was ennobled by the Austrian Empire. Müller died in Vienna on January 17, 1829.

Müller's literary and theoretical output was extensive. With his works, Müller gave nineteenth-century conservative political economy a distinctive profile. He stands as one of the most important representative of political Romanticism in Germany, advocating an organic, estate-based economic and social order rooted in cultural and religious traditions. His thought exemplifies Romanticism's broader intellectual project: a reaction against the individualism of industrialization, rationalism, utilitarianism, and the ideals of the French Revolution, while seeking to restore a unified vision of body, mind, and soul through the idealization of medieval and organic forms of community.

20.2 Selected Text

Müller, Adam. 1816. *Versuche einer neuen Theorie des Geldes mit besonderer Rücksicht auf Großbritannien*. Leipzig und Altenburg: F. A. Brockhaus.

All translations from the German are performed by the author.

20.3 Historical Background

Triggered by the Bullion Controversy in England, *Versuche einer neuen Theorie des Geldes* aimed to spread the discussion in German-speaking world. Müller wrote the text in Vienna in 1810/1811, but did not publish it until 1816. While Müller praises Gentz's writings on the topic as "masterful," he asserts that theoretical discussion was necessary to expand upon their practical focus. Müller's intention was integrate these ideas into a comprehensive economic theory (Müller 1816, 3).

Müller's engagement with Adam Smith and his reception in Germany is central. Müller frequently quotes Smith, referencing his distinction between value and price.

While he concurs with Smith's emphasis on the importance of the division of labor, he rejects his "idolization of things" (Müller 1816, 170) and repudiates his conception of the labor theory of value. Smith saw labor as the crucial touchstone for economic analysis; for Müller, by contrast, the overriding determinant was the state and its laws (Müller 1816, 31, 157–166, 224; Kautz 1860, 661; Stephinger 1909, 134–147).

Like Smith, Müller rejects mercantilism, a term that appears consistently throughout the text. Evidence of Müller's Romanticism can be seen in his explicit references to Novalis (Friedrich von Hardenberg) and Friedrich Schlegel. He also repeatedly idealizes the Middle Ages as a better time. Like his friend Gentz, Müller sought to inherit the legacy of the conservative Edmund Burke (Müller 1816, 85–89, 225–226, 197–281; Kozik 2018, 131–133, 167–169; Liefer 1922, 311).

Müller's rejection of English political economy is most evident in his methods. He asserts that one cannot view reality in a purely quantitative fashion because numerical determinations are like "dream images" (Müller 1816, 13) and do not deliver results. There is an "unfortunate delusion in this calculating age" (Müller 1816, 52); he views the theory of political economy expounded to date as "a rather arbitrary mixture of mathematical and historical components" that "lived in a state of open hostility" (Müller 1816, 64). Abstract models like those advanced by the Physiocrats or classical economists were thus not helpful. Ultimately, Müller sought to achieve a reconciliation of all "differences between mathematical and historical truths and return both to the one eternal source of all human knowledge" by "vindicating the qualities of things, their nature as types, and interactions with each other" (Müller 1816, 65–66). In his view, this could be achieved by reuniting political economy and jurisprudence. According to Müller (1816, 125), economic insights can only be gained through a truly historical and empathetic human engagement with social and economic reality, and not through any static theory (Müller 1816, 164; Stephinger 1909, 16–17).

However, at the center of his writing on monetary theory is his criticism of metallism (Müller 1816, 90). During the time of the Napoleonic Wars, Müller, a German patriot, associated paper money with the hope of financing wars of independence from France (Palyi 1916, 111–112).

20.4 Discussion

Müller's starting point is property in the legal sense, which distinguishes him from "Locke, Hume, and Adam Smith" (Müller 1816, 23). He deliberately elaborates a legal theory, explaining that in the Middle Ages, there were two types of property, the *feod* (feudal, common property) and the *allod* (full ownership, private property). The present day, by contrast, was marked by the "absolute rule of private property" (Müller 1816, 25). For Müller, this restricts the freedom of the individual, because private property is not restrained by "true feudalism" (Müller 1816, 29) in which "the good merchant does not work to gain things but rather to give more, to expand the sphere of his credit [e.g., personal importance]" (Müller 1816, 173; Stephinger 1909, 61). In this way, Müller fundamentally rejects a self-interested, individualistic, and capitalistic economy. For Müller, the degree of creditworthiness means the degree of personal significance (Stephinger 1909, 61).

Müller acknowledges the benefits of a division of labor. In a specialized economy, money is used to facilitate exchange; it acts in lieu of the state, which would otherwise have to organize the exchange of goods. In this sense, money is a *feod*, and therefore a public good. Müller asserts that there are two types of money: money as a personal means (i.e., as a promise or credit) and money as a material means (i.e., as a universally accepted good) (Müller 1816, 33–36, 139; Stephinger 1909, 40–42, 62–63).

Throughout the text, Müller invokes the image of a sphere, which he uses in his whole oeuvre as a symbol for the holistic. In a sphere, all forces revolve in reference to the center; it is a symbol for balance and universalism, rather than individualism (Müller 1816, e.g., 60, 141–145).

Müller asserts that the division of labor leads to individualization: "To conquer the world, he must isolate it [...] he must divide it to possess it; he must give up its wholeness. [...] Nevertheless, this need for abundance, and this need for unity can be satisfied" (Müller 1816, 106). However, humans have a need for community: "All individual needs can be [...] reduced to a single main need: man wants to complete himself, to perpetuate himself. [...] he needs the state; indeed, he needs the union of states in a world-encompassing faith, i.e. the church" (Müller 1816, 105–106).

For Müller, anything else—that is, a purely economic man—is a violation of nature: "For even if a man can devote his entire life to a single economic function, he would first have to renounce all other needs, and only be able to retain the one that is satisfied by his particular activity in order to be able to separate himself from the society of the rest" (Müller 1816, 155). Based on these considerations, Müller advances his version of a Social-Legal Theory of Credit (Wagner 1937, 51–71). For Müller, the state represents the universality in which the individual is absorbed and in which he is immortal (Stephinger 1909, 25–26); the state itself is the community.

Müller asserts that the economically isolated man depends on the state: "He can only work insofar as the whole society works for him: he needs the entirety of the rest and their forces everywhere; in short, society, the union of all economic functions, the state—remains the need of all needs" (Müller 1816, 155). In this way, money is the instrument through which humanity is unified: "All of this is presented to the senses in the functions of money: the desire for money is a mere imperfect representative of the higher desire for union, for the state [...] money is actually nothing more than the essence of sociability" (Müller 1816, 156).

With reference to the Bullion Controversy, Müller writes: "So if in recent times the matter has been presented as if state paper is a mere substitute for metals, or as if a promise of the state could only represent the metals, and as if the same without reference to the metals is meaningless, then things have been reversed: the metals are the representatives; the great need for cohesion, which even before all division of labor prevented the individual organs of man, then later sees all the different economic functions constantly returning to their origin and to union; that which elevates metals to money through the stamp, as if through a kind of credit, and which is ultimately forced upon on the further development of citizen life through state paper money—that is the principal" (Müller 1816, 156–157). Money is therefore not a commodity, but rather a representative of or substitute for the state (Stephinger 1909, 58–59).

Müller ascribes a role to both metallism and nominalism: "Money is nothing else than the economic expression of this need for union or for the state; just as laws are the legal expression of it. The unification of things is achieved in each sphere separately; in the realm of things, the precious metals accomplish this union; in the realm of man, this is achieved by the word [...] The word and precious metal are thus the two great forms under which money appears [...]. Neither of the two alone and by itself expresses the essence of money completely" (Müller 1816, 158–159). In this way, both forms of money are interdependent; paper money must be "mixed with metal money, which, in a way, confirms it" (Müller 1816, 160).

However, for Müller, the law dominates: "if metal money is to become real money, the word must press a seal, its stamp on it: it must become a coin" (Müller 1816, 161). Without a stamp—that is, without the law—metal is not money. Müller asserts that the metallists only see private property and therefore view paper money merely as a representation of metal. "Thus, the two ruling forms of money can only assert themselves to the extent that they form an indissoluble alliance, to the extent they mutually guarantee each other; in other words, insofar as they enter into the aforedescribed mutual dependency" (Müller 1816, 162).

Müller then draws again on his analogy of the sphere. *Wortgeld* (roughly, "money as word) and metal money stand at opposite poles: namely, the material pole, with precious metal as the medium of exchange (*Guinee*), and, at the other end, the personal pole with faith or credit as the unit of account (*Bank*) (Müller 1816, 164–165). Müller is particularly fond of thinking in terms of opposites, a tendency that we find manifest here (Gray 2000, 96).

For Müller, credit forms "the center point of the economic sphere and thus represents the actual, true money" (Müller 1816, 183). However, it must remain in balance with money as a commodity. Müller ascribes supreme importance to the function of a standard, to the unit of account. However, metals cannot fulfil this function because they remain commodities that fluctuate in value. For a standard to be established, it must be fixed by law (Fig. 20.1).

In the second part of the text, Müller addresses the English debate. Although coins had almost completely disappeared from circulation in England, they were still present *de jure*. "Whoever sees nothing more in the minted Guinee than the current commodity price of the metals contained therein, has not understood the essence of money at all" (Müller 1816, 198).

Müller also discusses market prices for gold and silver and how they relate to the fixed ratio in gold and silver coins. In this way, he addresses the core problem of bimetallism. Müller asserts that the state should choose an average market ratio, a normal ratio based on market developments over time (Müller 1816, 211–214).

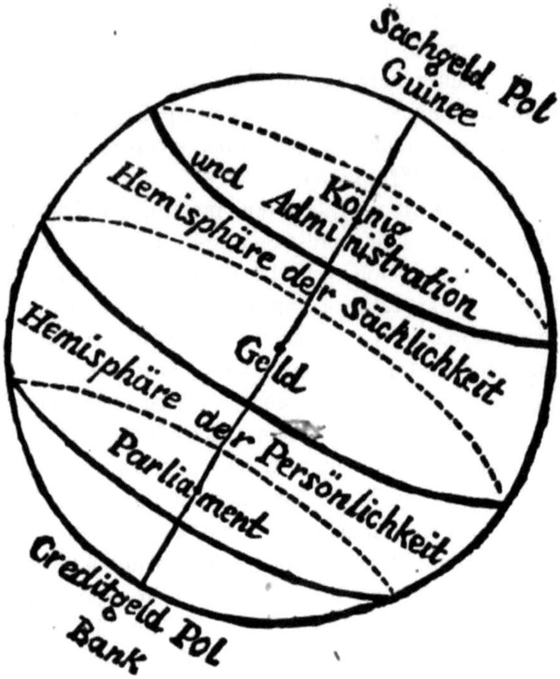

Fig. 20.1 The analogy of the sphere (Müller 1816, 308)

According to Müller, the representatives of metallism deny "the miracle of the coin stamp, that is, the authority of the law" (Müller 1816, 220). Accordingly, "instead of values they weigh silver and gold; instead of money, they invent weights" (Müller 1816, 236). While coins can become worse, *Wortgeld* remains pure; it has the "higher, firmer value" (Müller 1816, 219). In this way, paper money is an "essential element of the value standard" (Müller 1816, 260). For this reason, Müller did not view the abolition of convertibility in 1797 as a problem, because "the momentary absence of the precious metals was nothing more than proof of their dispensability" (Müller 1816, 292). A similar discussion influenced by John Locke took place during the Great Recoinage of 1696 (Müller 1816, 249–251).

Müller posits a three-stage process: initially, a period of commodity exchange prevails; this is supplanted by a period of trade; finally, one arrives at the period of credit (Müller 1816, 204; Stephinger 1909, 55). This rough sketch seems to have been later picked up and expanded upon by Hildebrand (1864).

Müller clearly separates credit money from currency and addresses their relationship to each other. He calls *Wortgeld* "elastic" in relation to the national product (Müller 1816, 263), while metal currency reacts in an inelastic fashion (Müller 1816, 276). This passage clarifies that Müller understands *Wortgeld* to mean "elastic credit money" given the direct contrast to scarce currency usually made of metal (Liefer 1922, 320; Stephinger 1909, 81). "The elasticity of credit was thus a corrective to the inelasticity of precious metals" (Müller 1816, 267). In this way, both metal and paper money must be combined.

In England, where precious metal has disappeared from circulation, Müller assigns a dual role to *Wortgeld*: First, it served as a replacement for currency: "The bank behaves like the faithful administrators of a king who is absent for a while [...] thus the notes represent the Guineas completely" (Müller 1816, 271); "they are the temporary representatives of the vanished gold" (Müller 1816, 275). Second, *Wortgeld* also fulfilled its normal role as private credit money. "In the present state of affairs, banknotes perform two functions; the personalization of all credit as banknotes, and the realization of all material values as representatives of gold, as currency" (Müller 1816, 277). Thus, under these circumstances, paper money is both private credit money and currency. Similar to Smith's Real Bills Doctrine, Müller calls paper money stable and thus usable as a unit of account, as long as there is sufficient collateral, i.e. provided the bills of exchange are secured (Müller 1816, 269).

Müller asserts that the "government cannot increase commodity money without increasing credit money" (Müller 1816, 303). However, credit increases in a decentralized and uncontrolled manner. This creates the risk of credit-financed speculation. "Thus, on the other side, an equally artificial and apparent private credit will arise, which will primarily manifest itself in usury and speculation. This economic facade of life will ruin the entire internal relations of the household; the organization of the state itself will be thrown into disorder. But not the sum, not the quantity of money signs must be considered as the cause of these evils; rather, it is the arbitrariness in the creation of the money signs" (Müller 1816, 303). The emission of credit money must therefore be controlled: "thus, the power of private credit must not be increased by increasing the money signs, without the public credit also increasing in the same measure" (Müller 1816, 304). Metal money serves the purpose of undergirding credit money, of avoiding arbitrariness (Stephinger 1909, 91, 102).

20.5 Evaluation

Müller's monetary theory has often been negatively received. He writes in very flowery and digressive manner, making it difficult for the reader to take away something tangible. His methodological approach also means his assertions cannot be subjected to any empirical verification (Eisermann 2009, 371). It is thus understandable that his holistic economic theory has been referred to as "metaphysical irrationalism" (Winkel 1977, 51). His ideas regarding the subsumption of the individual in an overarching organic unity are simply too far removed from present-day thought.

However, what is often overlooked is that Müller distinguishes between credit money and currency with remarkable clarity. He addresses paper money in its dual function as government paper money and as the credit money of banks, and discusses the necessary interaction between credit money and currency. This does not yet have great analytical depth, but his holistic approach prevents him from giving simple, one-sided answers. This thinking in opposites, which characterizes Müller's entire work, was influenced by Johann Gottlieb Fichte (Palyi 1916, 102).

Müller always considers the legal aspects of economics; as his perspectives are partially sociological, he can be said to elaborate a sociological theory of money. For Müller, precious metal money can be replaced by state-regulated paper money. Therefore, he has a predominantly nominalistic understanding of money, which could make him a predecessor of Georg Friedrich Knapp (Heisenberg 2024, 321). However, these contrasts in Müller are only relative, and the two classes of money—that is, money as word and money as metal—are closely interconnected.

In light of Müller's opposition to anything associated with the French Revolution, John Law's failed experiment in France, and the assignats of the Jacobins, it is remarkable that he supports paper money at all (Gray 2000, 300).

From today's perspective, he is a difficult source, as he was a reactionary who romanticized the Middle Ages, supported the feudal system, and criticized industrialization. Shaped by the experiences of the French Revolution and the subsequent wars, he rejected anything that did not correspond to his understanding of holistic balance, not least out of fear of revolution and violence; this included Smith's economic theory and the Prussian reforms (Kautz 1860, 661, 665).

Karl Marx read Müller and criticized "two circumstances in particular that enabled A. Muller to arrive at a so-called *higher* conception of political economy: first, his extensive ignorance of economic facts and second, his purely amateurish infatuation with philosophy" (Marx 1859, 73). However, Müller's theory, which attributes great power to the state and rejects individualism in favor of a broader sociological approach, certainly has a proximity to socialist ideas. Indeed, Müller's reading of the individual as severed from a primordial or communal unity has parallels to the Marxist critique of the "alienated" worker (Gray, 2020, 298).

Taxonomic Classification

Müller does not have a well-defined theory of the value of money or a clear understanding of credit money. However, he emphasizes the connections between commodity money, which has a medium of exchange function (metal money), and legally determined paper money (*Wortgeld*) as a means of payment. He also highlights the connection between currency and credit money, and the necessity of maintaining a stable, balanced relationship between the two.

References

Eisermann, Gottfried. 2009. Rückblick auf Adam Müller. In *Studien zur Entwicklung der ökonomischen Theorie XXII*, 363–385. Berlin: Duncker & Humblot.

Gray, Richard T. 2000. Hypersign, Hypermoney, hypermarket: Adam Muller's theory of money and romantic semiotics. *New Literary History* 31 (2): 295–314.

Harada, Tetsushi. 2004. *Adam Müllers Staats- und Wirtschaftslehre*. Marburg: Metropolis.

Heisenberg, Thimo. 2024. Adam Müller on money. In *The Palgrave handbook of philosophy and money*, 307–322. Cham: Palgrave Macmillan.

Hildebrand, Bruno. 1864. Naturalwirthschaft, Geldwirthschaft und Creditwirthschaft. *Jahrbücher für Nationalökonomie und Statistik* 2:1–24.

Kautz, Julius. 1860. *Theorie und Geschichte der National-Oekonomik. Part 2*. Vienna: Carl Gerold's Sohn.

Kozik, Walther. 2018. *Adam Müllers, "Elemente der Staatskunst"*. Marburg: Metropolis.

Liefer, Helene. 1922. Anmerkungen. In *Versuche einer neuen Theorie des Geldes*, 287–325. Jena: Gustav Fischer.

Marx, Karl. 1859. A contribution to the critique of political economy. Trans. W. Ryazanskaya. Ed. Maurice Dobb. Moscow: Progress Publishers. 1977.

Müller, Adam. 1816. *Versuche einer neuen Theorie des Geldes mit besonderer Rücksicht auf Großbritannien*. Leipzig und Altenburg: F. A. Brockhaus.

Müller-Schmid, and Peter Paul. 2002. Adam Müller (1779–1829). In *Politische Theorien des 19. Jahrhunderts*, 109–138. Berlin: Akademie Verlag.

Palyi, Melchior. 1916. Die romantische Geldtheorie. *Archiv fur Sozialwissenschaft und Sozialpolitik*89–118.

Stephinger, Ludwig. 1909. Die Geldlehre Adam Müllers. In *Tübinger staatswissenschaftliche Abhandlungen*. Stuttgart: Enke.

Wagner, Valentin F. 1937. *Geschichte der Kredittheorien. Eine dogmen-kritische Darstellung*. Vienna: Springer.

Winkel, Harald. 1977. *Die deutsche Nationalökonomie im 19. Jahrhundert*. Darmstadt: Wissenschaftliche Buchgesellschaft.

Chapter 21
Georg Friedrich Knapp (1842–1926): Money as a Legal Entity

21.1 Biography[1]

Georg Friedrich Knapp was born in Giessen, Germany, in 1842 into an academically distinguished family. His uncle, the chemist Justus Liebig, had a strong influence on his intellectual development. Knapp studied political science in Munich, Berlin, and Göttingen, completing his dissertation on the economist Johann Heinrich von Thünen in 1865. Two years later, he became the head of the statistical office in Leipzig, a position he held until 1874. He then accepted a professorship at the University of Strasbourg in the newly annexed Alsace, where he remained until 1919. Knapp died in 1926 in Darmstadt.

Knapp was a co-founder of the renowned *Verein für Socialpolitik* and is considered a member of the Younger Historical School, primarily due to his contributions to statistics and historical research. Knapp's scholarly work can be divided into three phases. In the first phase, drawing on his experience in the statistical office, he developed methods for measuring mortality. In the second phase, he turned to agrarian history and the study of rural working conditions. It was only later in life that he devoted himself to monetary theory, producing his influential book *The State Theory of Money* (1905). Throughout his career, Knapp cultivated the image of a detached, apolitical scholar who pursued his studies without polemical intent.

21.2 Selected Text

Knapp, Georg Friedrich. 1905. *The State Theory of Money*. Abridged and translated by H. M. Lucas and J. Bonar. London: Macmillan. 1924.

[1] This biography follows Greitens (2022).

J. Greitens, *Currency and Credit Money*, Springer Studies in the History of Economic Thought, https://doi.org/10.1007/978-3-032-24113-9_21

21.3 Historical Background

Knapp wrote *The State Theory of Money* at a time when the importance of coinage was decreasing. In 1910, Reichsbank notes became legal tender and, like the coins before them, were generally required to be accepted without limitation. The silver *Vereinstaler*, which was still based on the Graumann coin standard of 1750, lost value as the price of silver fell, and was abandoned in 1907. Meanwhile, the practical importance of paper and credit money grew significantly, meaning that the commodity theory of money increasingly failed to reflect the actual situation. However, the decisive motivator for Knapp's work on monetary theory was the Austrian currency reform of 1892, which introduced an inconvertible paper currency. *The State Theory of Money* is filled with examples from Austria. Knapp consistently emphasized the importance of the Austrian monetary system for his thinking.

His ideas were the most significant contribution to monetary theory in German at the beginning of the twentieth century, and were the subject of intense debate for many years (Greitens 2022).

21.4 Discussion

The central concept of *The State Theory of Money* is found in the first sentence: "Money is a creature of law. A theory of money must therefore deal with legal history" (Knapp 1905, 1).[2] The entire book elaborates on the idea of money as a legal entity and this nominalistic understanding of money. Knapp's aim is to overcome the backwardness of metallism. "The natural man is a metallist; the theorist, on the other hand, is forced to become a nominalist" (Knapp 1905, 10).

The first part of the book presents a taxonomy of the various historical and theoretical forms of money. Based on this taxonomy, Knapp concludes there is a developmental trend toward nominalistic monies (Fig. 21.1).

Knapp begins by defining the term means of payment, which he views as a *Geschöpf* (entity) agreed to by the relevant payment community for use in

[2] The German original is *"Das Geld ist ein Geschöpf der Rechtsordnung,"* which translates literally to "Money is an entity of the legal order." This misleading translation, along with many others, has led to a significant misinterpretation of Knapp's work in English-speaking literature. Translating it as "creature" might suggest that the state can always determine the amount of currency in circulation. While Knapp does not rule out this possibility, it is not mandatory. The state or the relevant decision-making body can also legitimize a private unit of account, the quantity of which is governed by other regulations or mechanisms. The distinction between "law" and "legal order" in "Rechtsordnung" is important because "law" refers to the state in a narrower sense, focusing mainly on the legal code set by legislative entities. However, Knapp has the broader term "legal order" in mind, which includes orders established not only in legal terms, but also in different subsystems of society (including private contracts and judicature), which are governed by corresponding institutions or authoritative bodies that can establish and enforce legal orders as normative powers (Greitens 2022).

<table>
<tr><td colspan="4">Means of payment are</td></tr>
<tr><td colspan="2">Pensatory
(can only be hylogenic).</td><td colspan="2">Proclamatory
(can only be morphic).</td></tr>
<tr><td>Amorphic.</td><td>Morphic.</td><td colspan="2" rowspan="2"></td></tr>
<tr><td>Autometallism comes here.</td><td>The example of the ducats (p. 28) comes here.</td></tr>
<tr><td rowspan="3">I</td><td rowspan="3">II</td><td colspan="2">These means of payment are Chartal. Chartal means of payment = money.</td></tr>
<tr><td>Hylogenic.</td><td>Autogenic.</td></tr>
<tr><td>III & IV
(see below).</td><td>V & VI
(see below).</td></tr>
</table>

Fig. 21.1 Knapp's taxonomy of money forms (Knapp 1905, 44)

circulation, based on convention. He distinguishes means of payment from goods that are occasionally used for exchange, but not for this purpose. "When, however, in any society, for example, a State, it is a custom gradually recognized by law that all goods should be exchanged against definite quantities of a given commodity, e.g. silver, then in this instance silver has become an exchange-commodity in a narrower sense. It is called, therefore, within the range of its use, a general exchange-commodity. The general exchange-commodity is, accordingly, an institution of social intercourse; it is a commodity which has obtained a special use in society, first by custom, then by law" (Knapp 1905, 3). Knapp goes on to note: "A man who can employ the exchange-commodity he has received for some craft, but cannot pass it on in circulation, owns a commodity, but not a means of payment" (Knapp 1905, 6). Knapp uses the term lytric (from Greek: lytron = ransom) for means of payment.

Ultimately, the social recognition of a means of payment in a modern society is a legal act. "All money, whether of metal or of paper, is only a special case of the means of payment in general. In legal history the concept of the means of payment is gradually evolved, beginning from simple forms and proceeding to the more complex" (Knapp 1905, 2).

In a second step, Knapp distinguishes between "pensatory" and "proclamatory" means of payment. Pensatory (from Latin: pensare = to weigh) means that the value of the means of payment is determined by the weight of the metal. Therefore, these means of payment can only be "hylogenic" (from Greek: hyle = metal), i.e., made of metal.

Within the category of pensatory means of payment, Knapp distinguishes between "morphic" and "amorphic." Amorphic (I)—i.e., without shape—are metals that have not been brought into any specific form, so they can also be ingots. Only the inner value of the substance, which must be determined by weighing, applies. "The bar form is sufficient. The form of coins is not excluded, so long as we mean coin only in the technical sense. But the form of the coins must not have any legal significance" (Knapp 1905, 3).

Knapp calls this auto-metallism or authylism, i.e., the validity of the means of payment is determined by physical dimension. The legal order determines the commodities that are recognized as authylic means of payment. Accordingly, even in this seemingly pure category of metallism, we find a "nominalistic" component in this seemingly pure metallistic system.

Following Knapp's taxonomy further, pensatory means of payment can also be morphic (II), i.e., shaped, including (in particular) coins. Knapp speaks of "full-value coins," which are used according to their weight of the precious metal, e.g., grams of gold. But "not any gramme of gold of the fineness prescribed for the coining of ducats, for that would be autometallism, but the gramme of gold coined into ducat form. The gramme of gold in this form is a totally different concept from the gramme of gold of which ducats could be made" (Knapp 1905, 28–29). Because of this distinction, Knapp considers this variant to be purely theoretical, because in this case coins would only serve to simplify weighing by counting.

"Proclamatory" (from Latin: pro clamare = to proclaim, announce) means of payment have a value independent of their material value, such as stamps or theater tokens. Knapp also speaks of chartal means of payment (from Latin: charta = leaf/paper), by which he means tokens. "Perhaps the Latin word 'Charta' can bear the sense of ticket or token, and we can form a new but intelligible adjective—'Chartal.' Our means of payment have this token, or Chartal, form. Among civilised peoples in our day, payments can only be made with pay-tickets or Chartal pieces" (Knapp 1905, 32).

The token's material is thus no longer essential. What is essential is the codification of the token by the state or legal order. Therefore, all proclamatory means of payment must be morphic, as they must be marked with legally relevant signs. "We pay with pieces that have a legal significance. Our law lays it down that only pieces formed in such and such a manner are to be admitted as means of payment, and the significant marks of the pieces are prescribed by law" (Knapp 1905, 27).

Only now does Knapp introduce the concept of money, which he exclusively restricts to proclamatory means of payment: "Money always signifies a Chartal means of payment. Every Chartal means of payment we call money. The definition of money is therefore 'a Chartal means of payment'" (Knapp 1905, 38). According to Knapp, the decoupling of money from material properties and its nominal characteristics are what make it a means of payment.

The central concept here is "recurrent connection."[3] Money is a chartal means of payment that is used to settle debts. Knapp writes: "Let us assume that the transition has been made from copper to silver; the process will be as follows. First, the State describes the new means of payment by saying it shall consist of the metal silver. Secondly, the State ordains that the new unit shall be called a 'pound of silver,' and for the description of the new means of payment it lays down the rule in this special instance, that it shall be formed by the physical experiment of weighing. Each quantity of silver is called legally as many 'pounds of silver' as it weighs pounds. Thirdly, the State says that the unit 'pound of silver' takes the place of so many earlier units, e.g. fifty pounds of copper. That is the legal definition of the new unit. As soon as all this has been done, the transition from copper to silver is complete" (Knapp 1905, 22).

In this connection, Knapp also explains: "The State therefore treats the older debts as if the unit of value, a pound of copper, were only a name by the use of which the relative amount of the debt was indicated, and which does not mean that in reality copper was to be delivered. The State reserves to itself the right to order that 'a pound of copper' should now mean that a given weight of silver was to be paid. At the moment of transition from copper to silver, the State treats existing debts as nominal debts and immediately adds what other material, and how much of it, shall in future represent the unit of the means of payment" (Knapp 1905, 14).

For Knapp, debts are not absolute, but relative. Following a currency reform, conversion factors to the previous means of payment are fixed, after which debts are settled using the new means of payment. Trust in the future currency is established through the legal obligation to accept it. In a currency reform, old debts are legally connected to the new currency, regardless of any intrinsic value (e.g., from metal).

Even chartal means of payment can be hylogenic, i.e., related to metal. Only this money allows weighing, i.e., a pensatory use. The means of payment here is based on its material. However, the value is no longer determined by the means of payment itself; it only serves as a comparison object. It is just "juridical precious metal."[4]

Hylogenic money is divided into two types: orthotypic (III), where cash is issued, and non-orthotypic (IV), where precious metal is present, but does not circulate itself. For example, gold-backed banknotes are used as a representation.

The other chartal means of payment are autogenic, i.e., money out of itself. Here we find pure paper money, where there is no longer any hylic (i.e., material) basis. "We presupposed the hylogenesis of the means of payment, for only hylic means of payment allow of pensatory use. (2) Then morphism appears; only morphic means of payment can be proclamatory and therefore Chartal. (3) Finally, it is only in the

[3] The concept of "recurrent connection" represents a core idea in *The State Theory of Money*. However, it is omitted from the 1924 English translation and only circumscribed. Furthermore, the paraphrase does not sufficiently emphasize the central importance of this point for Knapp, for which he invented this special term.

[4] "Juristisches Edelmetall," omitted in the 1924 translation.

case of Chartal means of payment that the hylic basis can disappear; they alone, therefore, can be autogenic" (Knapp 1905, 38–39).

Autogenic money is further sub-divided into: metalloplastic money (V), where there are still metal coins, but these only represent any amount of the paper currency; and non-metalloplastic money (VI), which is autogenic paper money without any connection to a substance.

21.5 Evaluation

Knapp presents a legal theory of money, for he defines money as an "entity of the legal order." In a developed society, the state proclaims the convention of what constitutes money. Money itself has no intrinsic value, but it serves to settle debts. In order to achieve his goal of overcoming metallism, Knapp considerably sharpens his theory. He borrows unique, artificial Greek and Roman terminology to establish his unique monetary taxonomy. Knapp was well aware of the dangers of state power over money, and its potential for abuse. He opposed state financing under normal conditions and favored stable exchange rates. He would only accept such financing in an emergency, such as in war.

Knapp's influence remains significant to this day. Max Weber called Knapp's writing "brilliant" (Weber 1921, 163), and he partially adopted his terminology. Modern Monetary Theory (MMT) refers to Knapp's chartalism and identifies itself as "neo-chartalist" because of its emphasis on state financing. However, one can debate whether Knapp was truly a founding father of MMT, or whether Neo-Chartalists are really Knappians (Greitens 2022).

In 1917, Ludwig von Mises responded to Knapp's theory by distinguishing between catallactic and acatallactic money theories. Catallactic theories of money attempt to identify "the essence of money in the mediation of exchange transactions" (von Mises 1917, 199, my translation) and to explain "its value from the laws of exchange transactions" (von Mises 1917, 199, my translation).

Catallactic monetary theories are compatible with value theories and are therefore economic theories in the narrower sense. Acatallactic monetary theories, on the other hand, do not seek to understand the essence of money within a circular economy as an economic theory; rather, they have legal, historical, or sociological explanations for money. In this sense, the *State Theory of Money* is "not at all a bad money theory, it is not a money theory at all" (von Mises 1924, 249). Mises presents Knapp as an example of a definite acatallactic position.

Taxonomic Classification

For Knapp, money is a legally defined convention for means of payment. He focused on currency, and failed to publish anything about the value of money.

21.6 Summary of German-Speaking Monetary Theory

The eighteenth and nineteenth centuries are considered a low point in the history of German-speaking monetary theory. Unlike in England, there were no systematic theoretical developments or lines of reception (Krohn 1986, 3–4). This was largely due to the ongoing influence of the economic and political backwardness of the Holy Roman Empire (Krohn 1986, 3–4). Schumpeter explains: "That period failed to develop and systematize its conquests in a form readily accessible to all economists, with all implications and applications nicely worked out and displayed on a silver platter. These conquests therefore did not penetrate into the common run of literature, especially into the textbooks, so that derogatory criticism, while it arouses just indignation in scholars like Professor Marget, is at the same time in a position to justify itself by quotations from the common run—even from such well-known, successful, and (in their way) meritorious books as Karl Helfferich's *Das Geld* (1903), or J. L. Laughlin's *Principles of Money* (1903), or Horace White's popular *Money and Banking* (1st ed., 1895; 5th ed., 1914), or David Kinley's *Money* (1904), or Alfred de Foville's *La Monnaie* (1907). Even Adolf Wagner's *Sozialökonomische Theorie des Geldes* (1909), which takes a higher flight and contains several original points, is not in much better case, and Karl Knies's *Geld und Credit* (1873–9), important though it is in other respects, added but little to the topics covered by its title" (Schumpeter 1954, 1081).

However, certain aspects should not be overlooked in narratives about German-speaking monetary authors. A strand of orthodox thought can be observed in various thinkers from Oresme to Biel within the German-speaking world. This tradition continues to this day, with authors such as Justi acting as one bridge between the past and the present.

Adam Müller wrote during the Congress of Vienna under conditions that were completely different from those experienced by Georg Friedrich Knapp at the beginning of the twentieth century. Although Müller's language and approach may seem unusual to us today, he belongs to a broader nominalist tradition that also encompasses Knapp, and his work is still widely read today (Krohn 1986, 11).

Taking this historical background into account, it could be argued that Anglo-Saxon monetary literature was generally more hostile to paper money in the nineteenth century, whereas German-language literature tended to favor it (Rieter 2001, 39). It was not until Knapp that the backward phase of German-language monetary theory came to an end.

References

Greitens, Jan. 2022. Georg Friedrich Knapp und die modern monetary theory. *Wirtschaftsdienst* 102 (3): 193–198.

Knapp, Georg Friedrich. 1905. *The State Theory of Money*. Abridged and translated by H. M. Lucas and J. Bonar. London: Macmillan. 1924.

Krohn, Claus-Dieter. 1986. Geldtheorien in Deutschland während der Inflation 1914 bis 1924. In *Die Anpassung an die Inflation*, 3–45. Berlin: De Gruyter.

Rieter, Heinz. 2001. Deutsche Geldtheorie im 19. Jahrhundert—mehr als nur ein Echo englischer Debatten? In *Exogenität und Endogenität: Die Geldmenge in der Geschichte des ökonomischen Denkens und in der modernen Politik*, 13–55. Marburg: Metropolis.

Schumpeter, Joseph. 1954. In *History of economic analysis*, ed. Elizabeth Boody Schumpeter. New York: Oxford University Press.

von Mises, Ludwig. 1917. Zur Klassifikation der Geldtheorie. *Archiv fur Sozialwissenschaft und Sozialpolitik* 44:198–213.

von Mises, Ludwig. 1924. *Theorie des Geldes und der Umlaufsmittel*. 2nd ed. München: Duncker & Humblot.

Weber, Max. 1921. *Economy and society: A new translation*. Trans. K. Tribe. Harvard University Press, Cambridge, MA 201+++9

Part VI
Marxist Authors

Chapter 22
Karl Marx (1818–1883): Money-Commodity as a Mirror of all Values

22.1 Biography[1]

Karl Marx was born in 1818 in Trier as the third of nine children of Heinrich Marx, a lawyer. Both his paternal and maternal families came from long rabbinical lineages, yet his father converted to Protestantism in order to continue practicing law. Marx attended high school in Trier and, in 1835, began studying law in Bonn. From 1836 to 1841, he pursued philosophy in Berlin, where he became associated with the Young Hegelians. In 1841, he received his doctorate in absentia from the University of Jena, but his attempts to secure an academic position were unsuccessful.

In 1842, Marx turned to journalism, first as a contributor and later, from October onward, as editor-in-chief of the liberal *Rheinische Zeitung* in Cologne. The paper was suppressed in March 1843 under threat of a ban. That same year, in June, Marx married Jenny von Westphalen, his fiancée since 1836. By October, the couple had moved to Paris, where Marx established contacts with figures such as Heinrich Heine. In 1844, he began his lifelong friendship and intellectual collaboration with Friedrich Engels, the son of a textile manufacturer.

At the request of the Prussian government, Marx was expelled from Paris in 1845 and settled in Brussels. Together with Engels, he drafted a programmatic statement for the reorganization of the Communist League, culminating in the publication of *The Communist Manifesto* in London in February 1848.

During the revolutionary upheavals of 1848–1849, Marx returned to Cologne to publish the *Neue Rheinische Zeitung*. Following the failure of the uprisings, he was expelled from Germany in May 1849 and took refuge in London. There, he and his family often lived in poverty, relying on his journalism, financial support from Engels, and occasional inheritances from Jenny's family. In 1864, Marx played a

[1] This biography follows Sperber (2013).

J. Greitens, *Currency and Credit Money*, Springer Studies in the History of Economic Thought, https://doi.org/10.1007/978-3-032-24113-9_22

central role in establishing the International Workingmen's Association, later known as the First International.

While in London, Marx devoted himself to the study of political economy. In 1859, he published *A Contribution to the Critique of Political Economy*, followed in 1867 by the first volume of *Capital*, the only volume of his major work to appear during his lifetime. After his death in 1883, Engels edited and published the second and third volumes from Marx's manuscripts.

22.2 Selected Text

Marx, Karl. 1867. *Capital: A Critique of Political Economy*. Volume One. Translated by Ben Fowkes. Penguin Books. 1982. 152–187.

22.3 Historical Background

Interpreting Karl Marx is a difficult undertaking, not least because of the large and diverse body of secondary literature devoted to his work. Accordingly, this chapter does not attempt to present or discuss the many perspectives offered by scholars. Rather, it only examines Marx's value-form analysis from the opening section of the first volume of *Capital*, which discusses how *Geldware* (money-commodity) comes into being.

Only the first volume of *Capital* was published solely by Marx. As money is discussed in this volume as a medium of exchange, this should also be the focus of our analysis. Further Marxist ideas on money as means of payment and on paper money are discussed with reference to Hilferding, who built on Marx's work.

22.4 Discussion

Marx develops the core principles of his political economy in the value-form analysis undertaken in the opening sections of *Capital*. At the heart of this analysis is the labor theory of value, which also explains how money emerges as a commodity—a process that Marx viewed as concealed within standard economics. For Marx, money only emerges at the end of a process, so it cannot be taken for granted as an inevitable feature of exchange. According to Marx, money is an expression of the value of other commodities: "as soon as it enters into circulation as money, its value is already given" (Marx 1867, 186).

It is not the natural properties of a certain commodity that make it money. Rather, a commodity that represents value is elevated to the status of a general equivalent. "What appears to happen is not that a particular commodity becomes money because all other commodities express their values in it, but, on the contrary, that all other commodities universally express their values in a particular commodity because it is money" (Marx 1867, 186).

Marx understands the development toward money as a process caused by the contradictions in exchange: "Money necessarily crystallizes out of the process of exchange, in which different products of labour are in fact equated with each other, and thus converted into commodities. The historical broadening and deepening of the phenomenon of exchange develops the opposition between use value and value which is latent in the nature of the commodity. The need to give an external expression to this opposition for the purposes of commercial intercourse produces the drive towards an independent form of value, which finds neither rest nor peace until an independent form has been achieved by the differentiation of commodities into commodities and money. At the same rate, then, as the transformation of the products of labour into commodities is accomplished, one particular commodity is transformed into money" (Marx 1867, 181).

22.4.1 Use Value and Exchange Value

Marx begins his explanations with the famous sentence: "The wealth of societies in which the capitalist mode of production prevails appears as an 'immense collection of commodities'; the individual commodity appears as its elementary form" (Marx 1867, 125).

He begins by analyzing the commodity, which, in a capitalist system, has both use value and exchange value: "A thing can be a use-value without being a value. This is the case whenever its utility to man is not mediated through labour. Air, virgin soil, natural meadows, unplanted forests, etc. fall into this category. A thing can be useful, and a product of human labour, without being a commodity. He who satisfies his own need with the product of his own labour admittedly creates use value, but not commodities. In order to produce the latter, he must not only produce use values, but use-values for others, social use-values" (Marx 1867, 131). Use value and exchange value depend on each other; they are two sides of the same coin. In capitalist societies, which are marked by a division of labor, the production of use value also produces exchange value.

Exchange value manifests itself as a quantitative relation; the exchange values of commodities must therefore be reduced to a common element, of which they represent a greater or a lesser quantity. "This common element cannot be a geometrical, physical, chemical or other natural property of commodities. Such properties come into consideration only to the extent that they make the commodities useful, i.e. turn them into use-values. But clearly, the exchange relation of commodities is characterized precisely by its abstraction from their use values. Within the exchange relation, one use value is worth just as much as another, provided only that it is present in the appropriate quantity" (Marx 1867, 127).

The abstract quantitative aspect of exchange value in a commodity is explained by Marx through a second distinction: that is, between useful labor and abstract labor. "All these things now tell us is that human labour-power has been expended to produce them, human labour is accumulated in them. As crystals of this social substance, which is common to them all, they are values—commodity values [*Warenwerte*] [...] If then we disregard the use-value of commodities, only one property remains, that of being products of labour. But even the product of labour has already been transformed in our hands. If we make abstraction from its use-value, we abstract also from the material constituents and forms which make it a use-value" (Marx 1867, 128).

As with commodities, labor can be viewed in two ways: as qualitative useful labor, or as quantitative abstract labor. When it comes to the exchange of commodities, abstract labor is the relevant dimension: "With the disappearance of the useful character of the products of labour, the useful character of the kinds of labour embodied in them also disappears; this in turn entails the disappearance of the different concrete forms of labour. They can no longer be distinguished, but are all together reduced to the same kind of labour, human labour in the abstract" (Marx 1867, 128).

For Marx, abstract labor means socially necessary labor time. In other words, it is "the labour-time required to produce any use-value under the conditions of production normal for a given society and with the average degree of skill and intensity of labour prevalent in that society" (Marx 1867, 129). Complex labor is thus reduced to a multiple of simple labor.

Building on these fundamentals, Marx explores monetary theory. The quantities of abstract labor contained in commodities cannot be observed directly. Therefore, they must take on an objective form of appearance that renders them observable and comparable—a process that occurs during exchange (Harvey 2010, 25–27).

22.4.2 Simple Form of Value (Form I)

With the simple form of value, Marx describes the comparison of commodities in isolated or accidental exchange. It is the first and simple form of relative value: x commodity A = y commodity B.

For an exchange, two commodities with very different use values must be made comparable. This is done by comparing the labor values in the commodities. The value of one commodity (A) is then reflected in the value of the other commodity (B).

- Commodity A is in the relative value-form: it is the active side, which is considered not quantitatively, but qualitatively.
- Commodity B is the simple equivalence, in the equivalent form: it is the passive side, which is considered not qualitatively, but only quantitatively.

"The whole mystery of the form of value lies hidden in this simple form. Our real difficulty, therefore, is to analyze it. Here, two different kinds of commodities (in our example, the linen and the coat) evidently play two different parts. The linen expresses its value in the coat; the coat serves as the material in which that value is expressed" (Marx 1867, 139). Commodity B thus becomes the cellular form of money, the starting point of money.

"I cannot, for example, express the value of linen in linen. 20 yards of linen = 20 yards of linen is not an expression of value. [...] The value of the linen can therefore only be expressed relatively, i.e. in another commodity. The relative form of the value of the linen therefore presupposes that some other commodity confronts it in equivalent form" (Marx 1867, 140).

22.4.3 Relative Form of Value (Form II)

In the relative or expanded value-form, Marx describes the comparison of commodities in exchange as a social process. It is the second form of relative value: x commodity A = y commodity B = z commodity C and so on. In this way, "the isolated expression of A's value is thus transformed into the indefinitely expandable series of different simple expressions of that value" (Marx 1867, 154).

There is a series of commodity equivalents, in which the commodity A is reflected in countless other commodities. The value of commodity A is compared with any other labor. "The value of a commodity, the linen for example, is now expressed in terms of innumerable other members of the world of commodities. Every other physical commodity now becomes a mirror of the linen's value" (Marx 1867, 155).

22.4.4 General Form of Value (Form III)

Regular exchanges mean that a commodity is increasingly chosen in its equivalent form. In exchange, the third general form of relative value develops: x commodity A = y commodity B and z commodity C = y commodity B and so on. One commodity is set apart as the general equivalent. "The new form we have just obtained expresses the values of the world of commodities through one single kind of commodity set apart from the rest, through the linen for example, and thus represents the values of all commodities by means of their equality with linen. Through its equation with linen, the value of every commodity is now not only differentiated from its own use-value, but from all use-values, and is, by that very fact, expressed as that which is common to all commodities. By this form, commodities are, for the first time, really brought into relation with each other as values, or permitted to appear to each other as exchange-values" (Marx 1867, 158).

All commodities are in the general value-form; their value is expressed in commodity B. Commodity B is the general equivalent; it is the social expression of expended labor. "The general form of value, on the other hand, can only arise as the joint contribution of the whole world of commodities. A commodity only acquires a general expression of its value if, at the same time, all other commodities express their values in the same equivalent; and every newly emergent commodity must follow suit. It thus becomes evident that because the objectivity of commodities as values is the purely 'social existence' of these things, it can only be expressed through the whole range of their social relations; consequently the form of their value must possess social validity" (Marx 1867, 159).

"A commodity is only to be found in the universal equivalent form [...] if, and in so far as, it is excluded from the ranks of all other commodities, as being their equivalent. Only when this exclusion becomes finally restricted to a specific kind of commodity does the uniform relative form of value of the world of commodities attain objective fixedness and general social validity" (Marx 1867, 162).

22.4.5 Money Form (Form IV)

In the final step, the general equivalent becomes the money-commodity: x commodity A = y gold and z commodity C = y gold and so on. "The specific kind of commodity with whose natural form the equivalent form is socially interwoven now becomes the money-commodity, or serves as money. It becomes its specific social function, and consequently its social monopoly, to play the part of universal equivalent within the world of commodities. Among the commodities which in form B figure as particular equivalents of the linen, and in form C express in common their relative values in linen, there is one in particular which has historically conquered this advantageous position: gold" (Marx 1867, 162).

The general equivalent is the mirror of all values and, as the money-commodity, it has "to exist as a non-use-value, as a quantum of use-value superfluous to the immediate needs of its owner" (Marx 1867, 182). In this vein, Marx also asserts: "That money is a commodity is therefore only a discovery for those who proceed from its finished shape in order to analyse it afterwards" (Marx 1867, 184).

Nevertheless, the specific properties of precious metals as money commodities also play a role in their selection, Marx notes. They are the commodities that "are by nature fitted to perform the social function of a universal equivalent. [...] The money-commodity acquires a dual use-value. Alongside its special use-value as a commodity (gold, for instance, serves to fill hollow teeth, it forms the raw material for luxury articles, etc.) it acquires a formal use-value, arising out of its specific social function" (Marx 1867, 183–4).

For Marx, money is a commodity, and only as a commodity can it be measure of value and therefore money: "Gold confronts the other commodities as money only because it previously confronted them as a commodity. Like all other commodities it also functioned as an equivalent, either as a single equivalent in isolated exchanges or as a particular equivalent alongside other commodity-equivalents. Gradually it began to serve as universal equivalent in narrower or wider fields. As soon as it had won a monopoly of this position in the expression of value for the world of commodities" (Marx 1867, 162–163). Here, Marx sets forth a strictly metallic theory of money.

22.5 Evaluation

A central question in the debate surrounding Marx's monetary theory is whether the different forms of value should be understood as an expression of a historical process or rather as a logical argument. A similar dispute arose, e.g., in relation to Carl Menger's monetary theory: is his argument logical or historical? For Hong, both Marx and Menger assumed that commodity money formed spontaneously within the economic sphere (Hong 2000, 92–93). While it may be true that Marx does not put forward a historical argument, he does develop a metallistic definition of money.

Marx advocated a metallistic theory of money and presupposed reliance on a gold-backed currency with "token money" (*Geldzeichen*) circulating as a representative of gold. As a commodity, money-commodity enters circulation with its value determined by labor. Therefore, the amount of money-commodity in circulation fluctuates in line with the commodities being exchanged. The money supply adapts to the circulation of commodities through the hoarding of gold (e.g., as jewelry) or, alternatively, through its reintroduction to circulation. Therefore, the amount of money in circulation is endogenous.

The monetary theorist Karl Knies was a prominent contemporary critic of Marx's ideas. Like Marx, Knies agrees that it is difficult to compare different use values being exchanged. However, he explicitly rejects Marx's abstract approach to labor value. "The following objections are precisely directed at the question to be resolved here: whether the equalization of two different 'use-values' in exchange can be explained by the equalization of two quantities of labor or two equal durations of simple labor required to produce those commodities. I must decisively reject this" (Knies 1885, 155, my translation).

Based on Marx's discussion of exceptions, such as natural meadows or unplanted forests, which have a use value but no exchange value, Knies derives a fundamental rejection of labor value theory. "If, as Marx expressly affirms, 'there are use-values that are not exchange values because their existence is not mediated by labor, such as wild-growing wood, etc.,' then the specific essence of use-value [...] cannot be related to a quantum of human labor at all" (Knies 1885, 155, my translation). For Knies, goods must have an independently determined, marketable use-value (Trautwein 2002, 197): "The equalization of different types of 'use values' for the satisfaction of human needs can only be explained by reducing them to a common use value" (Knies 1885, 160, my translation).

Taxonomic Classification

A recurring question is whether Marx's theory of money is a metallistic one. Marx emphasizes that money is both a commodity and a set of social relations. This would make his theory nominalistic (e.g., de Brunhoff, 2015). However, Marx derives money from a commodity whose value is determined by labor time. Even if money has social functions, these functions must be fulfilled by a commodity. The same applies to other metallic theories of money, e.g., those of Menger, which focus less on the social aspect of money. In the text under discussion, Marx addresses the commodity that serves as currency; he defines money from a metallistic perspective. Money, which has intrinsic value as a store of value, enters or exits circulation as money depending on market requirements; the money supply is therefore determined endogenously. In the third volume of *Capital*, Marx discusses other forms of money.

References

De Brunhoff, Suzanne. 2015. *Marx on money*. London: Verso.

Harvey, David. 2010. *A companion to Marx's capital*. London: Verso.

Hong, Hoon. 2000. Marx and Menger on value: As many similarities as differences. *Cambridge Journal of Economics* 24:87–105.

Knies, Karl. 1885. *Das Geld. Darlegung der Grundlehren von dem Gelde*. 2nd ed. Berlin: Weidmannsche Buchhandlung.

Marx, Karl. 1867. *Capital: A Critique of Political Economy*. Volume One. Translated by Ben Fowkes. Penguin Books. 1982. 152–187.

Sperber, Jonathan. 2013. *Karl Marx: Sein Leben und sein Jahrhundert*. München: Beck.

Trautwein, Hans-Michael. 2002. The credit theory of Carl Knies: Knowledge, truth and the history of economic thought. In *Is there Progress in economics?* 193–214. Cheltenham: Edward Elgar Publishing.

Chapter 23
Rudolf Hilferding (1877–1941): Marxist Eclecticism

23.1 Biography[1]

Rudolf Hilferding was born in Vienna in 1877. During his student years, he became involved in socialist circles. While studying medicine in Vienna, he also devoted himself to political economy. After receiving his doctorate in 1901, he initially worked as a physician. In 1906, he became a lecturer in political economy at the newly established SPD party school in Berlin, but left the following year after the Prussian police threatened him with expulsion.

From 1907 to 1915, he worked as a political editor and later as the editor-in-chief of the SPD newspaper *Vorwärts*. Between 1915 and 1918, he served as a military doctor in the Austro-Hungarian armed forces.

In 1917, Hilferding joined the SPD splinter party USPD. From 1918 to 1923, he worked in Berlin as the editor-in-chief of the USPD newspaper *Freiheit*. He advocated strongly for the reintegration of the USPD into the SPD, which was achieved in 1922. During the period of hyperinflation, Hilferding served as Minister of Finance under Chancellor Gustav Stresemann from August to October 1923. From 1924 to 1933, he was a member of parliament for the SPD, and under Chancellor Hermann Müller (SPD), he again assumed the post of Minister of Finance from 1928 to 1929.

Stripped of his citizenship in 1933, Hilferding fled first to Zurich and later, in 1938, settled in France. There he worked with the SPD leadership in exile and played a key role in drafting the Prague Manifesto of 1934. After the German occupation of France, Hilferding was arrested by the French authorities in Marseille and handed over to the Gestapo on February 9, 1941. Two days later, he died in a Gestapo prison in Paris.

[1] This biography follows Greitens (2018, 223–278).

J. Greitens, *Currency and Credit Money*, Springer Studies in the History of Economic Thought, https://doi.org/10.1007/978-3-032-24113-9_23

Hilferding considered himself a Marxist and, as a close friend and intellectual successor of Karl Kautsky, shaped the ideological orientation of the SPD for many years. In his magnum opus, *Finance Capital* (1910), Hilferding systematically developed several of Karl Marx's ideas on money and finance that had been presented in fragmentary form in the third volume of *Capital*, which was published posthumously by Engels.

23.2 Selected Text

Hilferding, Rudolf. 1910. *Finance Capital*. Translated by Morris Watnick and Sam Gordon, edited by Tom Bottomore. London: Routledge and Kegan. 1981.

23.3 Historical Background

Published 1910, *Finance Capital* focuses on economic conditions in Germany and Austria. Following German unification in 1871, there had been there a massive increase in the monetization of the economy, and a specific form of financial system had emerged that did not exist in Anglo-American countries. In this bank-based financial system, universal banks carried out all financial transactions, from payments and deposits to the large-scale financing of industry. The system was characterized by close links between banks and industry, including the formation of numerous cartels. Hilferding's *Finance Capital* was one of the first systematic scholarly examination of this kind of financial system. He begins his analysis by presenting a theory of money, which forms the basis for the entire work (Greitens 2018, 187–223).

23.4 Discussion

Hilferding builds on Karl Marx's explanation of money as medium of exchange, in which a money-commodity emerges from circulation to ease the exchange of goods. Hilferding adopts Marx's value-form analysis—and, by extension, the metallistic position with his value theory. The explanations regarding means of payment, i.e., credit money, contained in the third volume of *Capital* are less systematic. Nevertheless, Hilferding uses these ideas as a framework for his exposition (Greitens 2018, 27–30).

23.4.1 Gold Money

Hilferding quotes Marx to assert that the supply of money is dependent on its value: "the quantity of the medium of exchange is determined by the sum of the prices of commodities in circulation and the average velocity of circulation of money can also be expressed by saying that 'given the sum of the values of commodities and the average rapidity of their metamorphosis, the quantity of precious metal current as money depends on the value of that precious metal'" (Hilferding 1910, 37).

Hilferding explains that the money supply regulates itself endogenously. If the amount of gold in circulation is too high, it is hoarded as treasure and withdrawn from circulation. Conversely, if the supply of gold is too low, hoarded gold is released back into circulation. "We have seen that money is a social relationship expressed in the form of an object. This object serves as a direct expression of value. In the sequence C-M-C, however, the value of a commodity is always exchanged for the value of another commodity, and money is a transitory form or a mere technical aid, the use of which causes expense which should be avoided as far as possible" (Hilferding 1910, 37–38).

As money only functions as a technical medium of exchange, attempts are made to keep its quantity as small as possible, for otherwise, money that can serve as capital—i.e., that can be invested—remains idle. When hoarded, money acts as a store of value.

23.4.2 Paper Money

"Money can be dispensed with as an expression of equivalence. But it is indispensable as a symbol of value [*Wertkristall*] because it is a necessary means of giving society's sanction to the value of a commodity. Thanks to money, it is possible for value to be reconverted from its monetary form into any other commodity" (Hilferding 1910, 38). Thus, gold cannot be replaced with paper money as a store of value. However, paper money can fulfil the function of being a medium of exchange, representing the money-commodity, because the value of money vanishes immediately into the next commodity through exchange.

Therefore, paper money does not need to have its own value because it is not hoarded, but only acts as a medium of exchange for other goods. In this case, paper money represents the value of the commodity with which it is exchanged, thereby reducing the costs of circulation. As a consciously organized organ of the commodity-producing society, the state can establish such paper notes.

23.4.3 *Minimum Circulation*

The circulation of goods fluctuates according to the price sum of exchanges goods and the business cycle. Yet a certain minimum level of circulation will always take place. Within this minimum circulation, the state can issue paper money. "For this reason, money and precious bullion, such as gold, can never be replaced completely by mere money tokens without introducing disturbances into the process of circulation. Hence, in practice, even under a system of exclusive paper currency, full value money is always available in circulation, if only for the purpose of making payments abroad" (Hilferding 1910, 54). Hilferding also notes: "Hence, the volume of paper money must always be kept down to the minimum amount of money required for circulation. This minimum can, however, be replaced by paper, and since this amount of money is always necessary for circulation there is no need for gold to appear in its place. The state can therefore make paper money legal tender" (Hilferding 1910, 38).[2]

Hilferding asserts that under a monetary order organized by the state, the anarchic economy is supplanted by consciously organized societal relations; state paper money serves as a means of organizing the economy. According to Hilferding, the introduction of state paper money overcomes the anarchic form of society. However, if the minimum circulation is exceeded, paper money loses its value. "Since the circulation amount always fluctuates, gold money must always be able to flow into and out of circulation alongside paper money. If this is not possible, deviations of the nominal value of the paper from its real value occur, we have paper money devaluation" (Hilferding 1910, 39).

23.4.4 *The Quantity Theory of Money*

To explain this devaluation within Marx's framework, Hilferding draws on a concept introduced by Marx himself—that is, the minimum amount of money required for circulation, also referred to as the "social minimum of circulation." As long as paper money remains within the minimum of circulation, paper money only represents the money-commodity. Marx writes: "If £14 million were the level below which the circulation of a country never fell […], then 14 million pieces of paper, each a token of value representing £1, could circulate. If the value of gold decreased or increased because the labour-time required for its production had fallen or risen then the number of pound notes in circulation would increase or decrease in inverse ratio to the change in the value of gold, provided the exchange-value of the same

[2] Incorrect translation of „Bewußt geregeltes gesellschaftliches Verhältnis "(consciously organized societal relations), as the state can make paper money legal tender. This translation makes Hilferding sound similar to Knapp, from whom Hilferding distances himself sharply (Greitens, 2020).

mass of commodities remained unchanged. […] The number of pieces of paper is thus determined by the quantity of gold currency which they represent in circulation, and as they are tokens of value only in so far as they take the place of gold currency, their value is simply determined by their quantity. Whereas, therefore, the quantity of gold in circulation depends on the prices of commodities, the value of the paper in circulation, on the other hand, depends solely on its own quantity" (Marx 1859, 118–119).

Although Hilferding fundamentally rejects the Quantity Theory of Money, the next step builds on it. In the case of irredeemable paper currencies that exceed the minimum circulation level, their value fluctuates based on the amount of money and goods in circulation, as well as the velocity of circulation. "The quantity theory being rightly regarded as refuted, there is a reluctance to give due recognition to the influence of quantity on the value of money even where it really is the determining factor, as in the case of paper money and depreciated currency" (Hilferding 1910, 50).

23.4.5 The Role of the State

According to Hilferding, the state's first involvement in the monetary system is to mint gold coins, which makes handling gold money easier, without influencing its value. The state guarantees and sanctions the existing medium of exchange. In the second step, the state—as the "conscious organ of the commodity-producing society"—produces paper money, which represents gold money. The state then regulates the function of paper money as a means of payment. This guarantee is necessarily bound by the borders of the state.

Hilferding thus asserts that Knapp did not actually write a theory of money, noting: "Claims to the social product issued by society are no more money than is a theatre ticket which is a claim to a reserved seat. It is the nature of commodity production which makes money necessary as a measure of value and a medium of circulation" (Hilferding 1910, 67). In contrast to Knapp, Hilferding contends that without a link to gold as the money-commodity—and, by extension, without a value theory—no real money can exist.

23.4.6 Means of Payment

Building on Marx and the Banking School, Hilferding introduces a means of payment concept that is separate from the concept of money as a medium of exchange. Here, sale and payment are separated; the W-G-W process is divided into two parts through credit. "The function of money as a means of payment, therefore, presupposes a mutual agreement between buyer and seller to defer payment. The economic relation arises in this case from a private act. Purchase and sale have their counterpart in a second relationship between creditor and debtor, an obligation between two private individuals" (Hilferding 1910, 61).

In this way, money is no longer just a medium of exchange; as a means of payment, it independently brings the exchange process to conclusion. Direct and socially necessary exchange using state-guaranteed money is a societal act. However, a promise to pay, such as a bill of exchange, is a purely private guarantee, the value of which only becomes apparent when converted into money. If it has sufficient credibility, this bill can act as a means of payment created privately, i.e., credit money. Unlike state paper money, these bills must always be convertible into money.

23.4.7 Credit Money

Hilferding asserts that credit money arises from private relationships between debtors and creditors; it is limited in quantity by the price sum of the goods to be paid with credit money as a bill of exchange. Currency and credit money thus stand in a substitutional relationship to each other. Credit is a further development of money. However, the end of a credit term always concludes with a cash payment.

Due to the societal guarantee, state paper money can only lose value in toto. By contrast, the value of credit money depends on the respective debtor's payment pledge, i.e., its individual convertibility into money. Hilferding rules out the devaluation of credit money based on the quantity of such money in circulation, as it remains limited to specific circulation processes.

In the area of credit money, Hilferding assumes an endogenous money supply: The amount of credit money in circulation depends on the quantity of goods that stand behind and cover the promise to pay. Debtors can only fulfil this promise if they are able to sell the goods in question. Disruptions to this process affect credit, meaning that trade crises goes hand in hand with credit crises.

23.4.8 The Components of Money

Hilferding essentially describes not one but three monetary theories, which he tries to combine.

1. On the one hand, Hilferding's approach is based on the Marxian theory of the intrinsic value of gold money as a medium of exchange.
2. On the other hand, Hilferding adds state-issued paper money, which he allows to exist up to the minimum level of circulation as a representation of gold; paper money prices are, if the amount exceeds the minimum, determined by quantity theory.

3. Thirdly, he emphasizes his connection with the Banking School and embraces the notion that the money supply is endogenously self-regulated through credit processes.

All three of these components have their own logic. Gold and state paper money belong to the domain of currency and are supplemented with credit money, which is conceived in line with Marx's understanding of the Banking School, meaning that credit money elastically expands the money supply.

23.5 Evaluation

Overall, Hilferding fails to convincingly link the various conceptions of money that he presents. Since all of the components are largely interchangeable in their functions, it is unclear why their value determination should be so different. For instance, the inflation of state paper money reduces, among other things, the value of credit claims, since these can be settled with money at a fixed nominal rate. A comparable tension has been identified by Foley (1983) in Marx's own monetary theory, where the value of money appears both as the expression of abstract labor and as the value of the money commodity, without a fully articulated mediation between the two.

Unlike Marx, he does not derive the emergence of money-commodity from the simple to the general form of value, but rather summarizes this process in a few words. Consequently, Hilferding focuses on the quantitative level. For Hilferding, money is thus primarily a technical means of simplifying transactions. Marx's strictly elaborated dialectical process thus recedes to the background.

Taxonomic Classification
Hilferding combines a production cost theory of money for precious metals with a state paper theory of money that draws on quantity theory. He also incorporates a credit money theory based on the Real Bills Doctrine and the Banking School. He thus has both a narrow and broad conception of the money supply; each are considered separately.

23.6 Summary of Marxist Monetary Theories

Marxist theory focuses on the real economy. Marx derives money from the real exchange of goods, or sees it as a reflection of it; money cannot permanently disentangle itself from the real economy; it merely reflects it. The development of money is described in a manner similar to that of Menger, for example. However, everything beyond this, such as credit money, is vague and has been interpreted in many different ways, beginning with the third volume of *Capital* by Engels. Hilferding thus exhibits an eclectic approach.

References

Foley, Duncan K. 1983. On Marx's theory of money. *Social Concept* 1 (1): 5–19.

Greitens, Jan. 2018. *Finanzkapital und Finanzsysteme. "Das Finanzkapital" von Rudolf Hilferding*. Vol. 40. 2nd ed. Beiträge zur Geschichte der deutschsprachigen Ökonomie.

Hilferding, Rudolf. 1910. *Finance Capital*. Translated by Morris Watnick and Sam Gordon, edited by Tom Bottomore. London: Routledge and Kegan. 1981.

Greitens, Jan. 2020. Geldtheorien während der Hyperinflation von 1923: Die Rezeption von Georg Friedrich Knapps Staatliche Theorie des Geldes. In *Entwicklung der Konjunkturforschung im frühen 20. Jahrhundert*, 135–173. Studien zur Entwicklung der ökonomischen Theorie XL.

Marx, Karl. 1859. A contribution to the critique of political economy. Trans. W. Ryazanskaya. Ed. Maurice Dobb. Moscow: Progress Publishers. 1977.

Part VII
Neoclassical Authors

Monetary theory only plays a subordinate role in answering the fundamental neoclassical questions of efficiency and allocation. Nevertheless, new theoretical developments have emerged in monetary theory within a widespread gold standard. For example, quantity theory has been refined through a more specific analysis of individual money supply and demand, and a clearer distinction between the short and long term. Theory regarding the macroeconomic effects of money has also been significantly expanded. Three main areas can be identified: the relationship between money and the business cycle (which is discussed in particular by Marshall and Wicksell); the neutrality of money (especially Walras and Fisher); and subjective value theory and money (especially the Austrian School, including Menger, Wieser, Mises, and Hayek) (Claassen 1980, 5–6).

Reference

Claassen, Emil-Maria. 1980. *Grundlagen der Geldtheorie*. 2nd edition. Berlin: Springer.

Chapter 24
Carl Menger (1840–1921): Metallism in Neoclassical Economics

24.1 Biography[1]

Carl Menger was born on February 23, 1840, in Neu Sandez, Galicia. He studied in Vienna, Prague, and Krakow, earning his doctorate in 1867. After working as a journalist and later for the newspaper *Wiener Zeitung*, Menger published his groundbreaking work *Principles of Economics* in 1871, in which he laid the foundation of marginal utility theory, arguing that the value of goods depends on individual utility assessments.

In 1872 he completed his habilitation and was appointed *Privatdozent* in Vienna, despite initial opposition from Lorenz von Stein; he received an extraordinary professorship the following year. From 1876, Menger served as tutor and travel companion to Crown Prince Rudolf, before taking up the newly established chair of political economy at the University of Vienna in 1879, a position he held until his retirement in 1903 due to poor health.

During the 1880s, he engaged in the famous *Methodenstreit* (methodological dispute) with Gustav von Schmoller over the proper approach to economics. From 1900 onward, Menger was a member of the Austrian House of Lords. He died in Vienna in 1921.

Menger is regarded as the founder of the Austrian School of Economics, which influenced economists such as Eugen von Böhm-Bawerk, Friedrich von Wieser, Ludwig von Mises, and Friedrich von Hayek.

[1] This biography follows Schumacher and Scheall (2019).

J. Greitens, *Currency and Credit Money*, Springer Studies in the History of Economic Thought, https://doi.org/10.1007/978-3-032-24113-9_24

24.2 Selected Text

Menger, Carl. 1909. "Money." Translated by Leland B. Yeager with Monika Streissler. *Carl Menger and the Evolution of Payments Systems*. Originally from *Handwörterbuch der Staatswissenschaften*. Cheltenham: Edward Elgar. 2002. 25–107.

24.3 Historical Background

Menger's engagement with monetary policy, which dates back to the 1870s, culminated in his 1892 article "Money," which was published in the *Handwörterbuch der Staatswissenschaften*. The essay was revised twice, for a second time in 1909, and became increasingly extensive, showcasing his vast knowledge on the subject. The bulk of the essay is devoted to an extensive exploration of the history and concept of money, which markedly outweighs its opening theoretical considerations. With this essay, which sought to apply a subjective theory of value to money, Menger greatly influenced economic discourse, including the debate leading up to Austria's currency reform of 1892.

24.4 Discussion

Menger states that his goal is to understand the "essence of money" (Menger 1909, 76), to explain the "origin of generally used intermediaries of exchange" (Menger 1909, 26). In this way, from the very outset he describes money's function as a medium of exchange as constitutive.

He seeks to clarify his subject matter with a thought experiment, asking why someone would take the risk of accepting a commodity that they actually do not want: "we are confronted with the same phenomenon requiring explanation: the phenomenon that economizing persons are willing to accept certain goods, even when they do not need them" (Menger 1909, 26).

24.4.1 Double Coincidence of Wants

Menger takes barter exchange as a starting point, arguing that the problem of money only arises "with that stage of development of human societies when 'the no-exchange economy' has already made the transition to 'the economy with barter'" (Menger 1909, 27). This means that production is achieved through a division of labor and specialization. In a barter economy, goods are often indivisible and also heterogenous, complicating their exchange. However, for Menger, these problems seem "to be greatly exaggerated in theory" (Menger 1909, 27).

For Menger, the actual problem for barter exchange lies in the double coincidence of wants: "the fact that on barter markets pairs of contracting parties who need each other's commodities are actually present only in a relatively small number of cases, and it is therefore anything but easy for a person offering a commodity to find another market participant who is offering the commodity he is looking for and at the same time wants the commodity he is offering. But this is a difficulty that only keeps increasing with the progress in the division of labour and with the multiplication of the kinds of goods brought to market" (Menger 1909, 27–8). One must find a suitable trading partner—that is, "suitable pairs of contracting parties" (Menger 1909, 101, footnote).

In this way, the "direct exchange of goods is basically restricted to those relatively rare cases when each of the contracting parties actually needs the very goods offered by the other" (Menger 1909, 28). In a barter economy, the number of possible exchange relations increases exponentially with the number of goods.

24.4.2 Marketability and Indirect Exchange

With an increasing number of barter transactions, the market develops a solution to this problem. "Everyone must make the observation, which at this very stage of development of trade is of practical significance, that for certain goods there is only a slight or occasional demand, while for other goods there is a more general and constant demand, so that someone who brings goods of the first kind to market to trade for goods that he particularly needs is as a rule less likely to achieve this goal or must at least make greater efforts and greater economic sacrifices than someone who goes to market with goods of the latter type" (Menger 1909, 29).

Different goods experience divergent levels of demand. Menger thus speaks of goods having varying levels of *Marktgängigkeit* ("saleability" or "marketability"): "In this situation it will occur to everyone bringing goods to market to exchange them for goods meeting his special need that if his goal is not directly attainable because of the limited marketability of his goods, he could exchange them for goods that are considerably more marketable than his own even if he has no direct need for them" (Menger 1909, 29).

Thus, if one possesses goods with limited marketability, the obvious solution is to acquire goods with high marketability for the purpose of intermediate exchange. "He does not thus attain the ultimate goal of his intended exchange (acquisition of the goods he especially needs!) immediately and directly. But he comes closer to this goal. In the roundabout way of an intermediary exchange (by giving up his less marketable goods for more marketable ones), he gets the chance of reaching his ultimate goal in a surer and more economical way than by restricting himself to direct exchange" (Menger 1909, 29).

Experience shows that goods are particularly marketable when there is a general and consistent demand for them that is not fully met. Furthermore, the marketability of such goods increases even further through their use as a medium of exchange. "As soon as one or more goods have become generally used media of exchange on a country's markets, a profound and striking transformation of market relations occurs. Above all, the fact that one good becomes the generally used medium of exchange substantially increases its marketability [...]. Now whoever goes to market with a commodity that has become money is [...] able to acquire at any time and as he likes and chooses such quantities of all other goods on the market as are in proportion to the amounts he possesses" (Menger 1909, 33).

24.4.3 Generally Used Media of Exchange

The emergence of a universal medium of exchange occurs without state intervention, though the state can take action to promote or hinder this development: "The interest of individual economic agents in their supply of goods and the increasing recognition of this interest led them to pursue their individual economic ends more and more by means of intermediary acts of exchange, without mutual agreements, without the force of law, indeed without any regard for the common interest, and eventually to regard these as a normal form of exchanging goods" (Menger 1909, 30).

The generally used medium of exchange thus emerges spontaneously in the market due to individual utility considerations: "The fact that one good becomes the generally used medium of exchange causes its acceptability to differ increasingly from that of all other commodities—a difference that can no longer be called merely one of degree but in a certain sense already a difference in kind" (Menger 1909, 34).

The universal medium of exchange becomes further entrenched as the accepted standard because prices become more comparable and thus lower. Furthermore, through habit, practice and/or imitation of its use as the medium of exchange, transaction costs decline. Menger calls this universal medium of exchange—which was initially only accepted based on the intention of further exchange—money. "Only in this way did the phenomenon of money come into existence (money in the sense of a generally used intermediary of exchange)" (Menger 1909, 32). Menger asserts that precious metals are the most common medium of exchange for cultural reasons and for their special material properties, including low transport costs relative to their value, near-perfect durability, easy divisibility, and substitutability (fungibility).

With the introduction of money, "a profound and striking transformation of market relations occurs" (Menger 1909, 33). Competition in the supply and demand of goods increases significantly, and influences general price formation. "Current market prices are formed, and from now on the valuation of goods in money terms is incomparably more exact and economic than on barter markets" (Menger 1909, 35). Money is thus a sine qua non for efficient price formation in an economy. Money prices significantly improve market efficiency, as they are an indispensable tool for economic calculation and the rational allocation of resources in a dynamic world.

24.4.4 Nominalism

Menger then rejects nominalism and the ideas forwarded by Knapp. "The possibility, observable precisely with money, of an arbitrary regulation of its (nominal) value by government, and also the often misunderstood phenomenon of document money, whose substance is valueless, have considerably fostered the above error and induced many students of monetary theory to regard money as a mere token of value, as a mere (immaterial) pledge of an expected return performance, as something valueless in itself (like a trading ticket!) whose actual exchange value derives only from an agreement among the people, from custom, or from a government order" (Menger 1909, 36). This false doctrine "has also become pernicious for the coinage policies of many states" (Menger 1909, 36).

Menger also clarifies that a commodity's exchange value as money, rather than its use value as a commodity, is decisive for determining value: "We seek to acquire money for the goods we bring to market not on account of the useful properties of the money material but rather [...] for the sake of its exchange value. All this, however, only points to the medium-of-exchange function of money, that is, to the distinctiveness of the 'commodity' that has become money; it is not evidence against the character of money as a commodity as such. It is without fundamental significance for the question under discussion: whether money is a commodity at all in the sense that is relevant here. Indeed, it does not even touch upon the essential feature that distinguishes money from other commodities; for in addition to the merchant especially the speculator acquires commodities not in order to hold them nor with direct regard to their useful properties but rather in order to sell the commodities again, and only for the sake of their exchange values" (Menger 1909, 37).

Even though, in jurisprudence, money is distinct from other objects of trade, the government cannot regulate its value through declarations. Coins are stamped by the state for convenience and efficiency. The circulation of weighted metal pieces first happened in the market, i.e., without any action or intervention by a public authority (Semenova 2014, 117–118).

24.5 Evaluation

Menger's purely theoretical deductions regarding the origins of money are a special feature of his argument. Menger does not argue inductively or historically, as there is no historical evidence to support the Mengerian supposition of a premodern barter economy without money. According to Menger, convention, agreement, or state intervention are not necessary for the emergence of money; rather, the pursuit of economic advantage is the essential motive force. Menger's theory represents the orthodox view that is still widely held, not least due to his systematic and persuasive method of argumentation, which was highly influential (Brandl 2015, 49).

A key question, however, is what significance does clarifying the origins have for explaining money as an economic phenomenon? Some anthropologists, such as David Graeber (2011), reject the idea that money originates from a barter economy. Others defend Menger's ideas, presenting a barter narrative that does not require *homo oeconomicus* or established market systems (Ganev 2025). In view of the whole text, Menger probably intended to present a theoretical argument within a broader narrative of how money developed.

Central to the definition of money is its function as a medium of exchange rather than as a store of value or unit of account. However, Menger does not consistently apply marginal utility theory to the value of money. He only hints at functional value theory, which attempts to explain the essence of money based on its functions rather than its material nature. While the value of money is related to the commodity used as money, its value lies more specifically in its utility or use value as a medium of exchange (Brandl 2015, 48).

The use value of money as a commodity is determined by its purchasing power, i.e., the quantity of goods that can be exchanged for a unit of money. This purchasing power, in turn, depends on the market price of money. Thus, we find a case of circular reasoning: The market price of money is explained by its subjective use value, but this subjective use value is determined by the market price (Hülsmann 2018, 40–41). Mises responded to this criticism of Menger with his regression theorem: "The problem is to conceive the determination of the purchasing power of the immediate future, of the impending moment. For the solution to this problem we refer to the purchasing power of the immediate past, of the moment just passed. These are two distinct magnitudes. It is erroneous to object to our theorem, which may be called the regression theorem, that it moves in a vicious circle. But, say the critics, this is tantamount to merely pushing back the problem. For now one must still explain the determination of yesterday's purchasing power. If one explains this in the same way by referring to the purchasing power of the day before yesterday and so on, one slips into a regressus in infinitum. This reasoning, they assert, is certainly not a complete and logically satisfactory solution of the problem involved. What these critics fail to see is that the regression does not go back endlessly. It reaches a point at which the explanation is completed and no further question remains unanswered. If we trace the purchasing power of money back step by step, we finally arrive at the point at which the service of the good concerned as a medium of exchange begins. At this point yesterday's exchange value is exclusively determined by the nonmonetary—industrial—demand which is displayed only by those who want to use this good for other employments than that of a medium of exchange" (von Mises 1912, 409).

Yet if the monetary value of today is traced back to the monetary value of yesterday, and so on, then this raises the question as to the original determining factor—that is, the first monetary value. The oldest monetary value that has been passed down through history is clearly the value of goods when they were first used as a general medium of exchange due to their usefulness in satisfying non-monetary needs. When individuals first acquired an object for use as a medium of exchange rather than for their own consumption, they valued it according to its exchange value on the market due to its usefulness, as well as for its potential use as a medium of exchange. The oldest monetary value can be traced back to the commodity value of the monetary substance. From this day on, the monetary demand was added, and the subjective money value was derived from the already existing purchasing power of the commodity.

However, there is a distinction between Menger's monetary theories and those of his more radical Austrian School followers, such as Hayek and Mises. According to Menger, states play an important and desirable role in shaping, perfecting, and administering monetary systems at advanced stages of development (Semenova 2014, 138).

Taxonomic Classification

Menger is interested in the role of money as a medium of exchange. For him, it is the function of money, rather than the commodity itself, that is relevant. He does not consider credit money.

References

Brandl, Felix. 2015. *Von der Entstehung des Geldes zur Sicherung der Währung*. Wiesbaden: Springer Gabler.

Ganev, Georgy. 2025. Has the barter theory of the origins of money been rejected? *Bulgarian Economic Papers*. No. 2025-02.

Graeber, David. 2011. *Debt. The first 5,000 years*. New York: Melville House.

Hülsmann, J. G. 2018. Mises' Monetary Theory. In *Banking and Monetary Policy from the Perspective of Austrian Economics*, 25–48. Wiesbaden: Springer.

Menger, Carl. 1909. "Money." Translated by Leland B. Yeager with Monika Streissler *Carl Menger and the Evolution of Payments Systems*. Originally from *Handwörterbuch der Staatswissenschaften*. Cheltenham: Edward Elgar. 2002. 25–107.

Schumacher, Reinhard, and Scott Scheall. 2019. Karl Menger's unfinished biography of his father: Insights into Carl Menger's life through 1889. https://asu.elsevierpure.com/en/publications/karl-mengers-unfinished-biography-of-his-father-new-insights-into

Semenova, Alla. 2014. Carl Menger's theory of money's origins: Responding to revisionism. *The European Journal of the History of Economic Thought* 21 (1): 107–141.

von Mises, Ludwig. 1912. *The theory of money and credit*. New Haven: Yale University Press. 1953.

Chapter 25
Knut Wicksell (1851–1926): Quantity Theory in a Pure System of Credit

25.1 Biography[1]

Knut Wicksell was born in Stockholm in 1851 into a large, middle-class family. Following the early death of his parents, he was raised in an environment that fostered his enduring interest in literature and music. His intellectual formation was marked by an extended period of religious reflection under the influence of Lutheran teaching; however, after a personal crisis in 1874, he abandoned Christianity and declared himself an atheist, adopting a lifelong critical stance toward orthodox theology.

Wicksell began his formal studies in mathematics, Latin philology, Scandinavian languages, and philosophy. Initially a model student, he soon became involved in student politics, gaining prominence through his involvement in issues such as alcoholism and population growth. His discovery of neo-Malthusian ideas in the late 1870s proved decisive, as it shifted his intellectual trajectory away from the natural sciences—which he pursued belatedly, completing an advanced degree in mathematics in 1885—toward the social sciences and ultimately economics.

Between 1885 and 1890, he studied in London, Strasbourg, Vienna, and Berlin. While he valued the statistical and historical contributions of the German Historical School, he criticized what he saw as its anti-theoretical orientation. It was his intensive engagement with Eugen Böhm-Bawerk's writings that proved particularly crucial for his development, as they provided the theoretical basis for his later contributions to capital and interest theory.

Upon his return to Sweden in 1890, Wicksell completed his transition to the field of economics, publishing his doctoral dissertation in 1895, which laid the foundation for his 1896 publication of *Finanztheoretische Untersuchungen* (Studies in the Theory of Public Finance). Another period of study in Berlin preceded the 1898

[1] This biography follows Lindahl (1958) and Hansson (1997, 38–47).

J. Greitens, *Currency and Credit Money*, Springer Studies in the History of Economic Thought, https://doi.org/10.1007/978-3-032-24113-9_25

publication of *Geldzins und Güterpreise* (Interest and Prices). His academic career progressed slowly due to his republican and anti-monarchical views, but in 1904 he was appointed Professor of Economics at Lund University, a position he held until his retirement in 1916.

His marriage to Anna Bugge was shaped by his skepticism toward social institutions, while his outspoken radicalism in political and social debates culminated in a conviction for blasphemy in 1908. He maintained close ties to the Social Democratic movement, though he was never a formal member.

As a professor, Wicksell exercised considerable influence through his lectures and seminars; he was also a prolific contributor to newspapers and journals. Even after retiring, he continued to advise policymakers, particularly at the Riksbank, and remained active in public debate on finance and monetary stability. Following the First World War, he advocated a return to pre-war price levels for reasons of distributive justice, but later refined his political recommendations into a more pragmatic program designed to stabilize employment. He died in Stockholm on May 3, 1926, leaving behind a legacy that continues to influence economic thought to this day.

25.2 Selected Text

Wicksell, Knut. 1898. *Interest and Prices: A Study of the Causes Regulating the Value of Money*. Translated by Richard F. Kahn. London: Macmillan. 1936.

25.3 Historical Background

In the preface to *Interest and Prices*, Wicksell notes that the book was prompted by the persistent deflation of his time, and the related debate over bimetallism that occurred between 1873 and 1896. This period, often referred to as the Long Depression, began with the global financial panic of 1873, which was triggered by the collapse of speculative bubbles in railways and real estate. The result was a prolonged phase of falling prices and slower economic growth in many parts of the world.

Following Sweden's adoption of the gold standard in 1874, the issuance of private banknotes was a recurring subject of debate. In 1881, a parliamentary banking committee proposed prohibiting the issuance of private notes; however, this proposal was never implemented. A second banking committee formed in 1889 recommended the complete withdrawal of private notes by the end of 1898, but this plan also remained unimplemented. Despite the lack of legislative action, note issuance became an increasingly uncertain business. Over time, private commercial banks shifted their funding structure toward deposits, gradually reducing their reliance on note issuance. The Bank of Sweden Act of 1897 gave the Riksbank the exclusive right to issue banknotes, thus transforming it into a modern central bank. However, private banks were permitted to continue issuing their own notes until the end of 1903 (Grodecka-Messi and Zhang 2025, 7–8).

Against this backdrop, Wicksell's book aimed to explain fluctuations in the money supply and prices. He was particularly concerned with preventing further deflation. A crucial prerequisite for his analysis was the development of modern financial systems; his conception of a "pure system of credit" would have been unthinkable without the greatly increased role of banks in the late nineteenth century.

25.4 Discussion

For Wicksell, both rising and falling price levels are harmful (Wicksell 1898, 1–2). Therefore, he favored truly constant prices over slightly rising ones (in contrast to Hume). "Those people who prefer a continually upward moving to a stationary price level forcibly remind one of those who purposely keep their watches a little fast so as to be more certain of catching their trains. But to achieve their purpose they must not be conscious or remain conscious of the fact that their watches are fast; otherwise they become accustomed to take the extra few minutes into account and so after all, in spite of their artfulness, arrive too late" (Wicksell 1898, 3–4).

According to Wicksell, any metallistic conceptions of money should be rejected. "No theorist can to-day lend his support to the traditional conception that money possesses in itself an independent, and more or less invariable, intrinsic value, against which the exchange values of real commodities are, as it were, compared or measured; though echoes of this doctrine are sometimes observed even in modern monetary literature" (Wicksell 1898, 29). Since precious metals are used almost exclusively as money, their commodity value is irrelevant. "But the case is a different one where the employment of the money commodity as an article of use, and particularly its *actual* consumption (in gilding, silver-plating, etc.), have come to occupy a position altogether secondary to its employment as a medium of exchange, and where, in addition, the yearly production results only in a relatively slow increase in monetary stocks" (Wicksell 1898, 30). The development of the financial system was therefore decisive for the rejection of a metallist conception of money. In his critique of metallism, Wicksell singles Karl Marx out in particular, describing him as a metallist (Wicksell 1898, 35).

Wicksell cites David Hume when introducing the Quantity Theory of Money (Wicksell 1898, 38). He criticizes both David Ricardo and Thomas Tooke for their interpretation of the theory:

- Wicksell considered Ricardo's Quantity Theory of Money to be valid only in a pure cash economy (Leijonhufvud 1997, 92). The relationship between the money supply and prices becomes more indirect and less clear when the pure cash economy expands to include a banking system, creating a mixed system involving bank money. Like Schumpeter later on, Wicksell considers all the necessary variables to be uncertain; for example, the velocity of circulation fluctuates and money is hoarded (Wicksell 1898, 41–42). Only a limited insight remains: The Quantity Theory of Money "consists of more than a mere 'truism,' i.e. a truth which is self-evident but barren; it consists of more than the rule that the sum of the quantities purchased, each multiplied by its respective price, must be equal to the amount of money paid for them" (Wicksell 1898, 41).

- On the other hand, Wicksell also sees Tooke's alternative very critical. "I already had my suspicions [...] that, as an alternative to the Quantity Theory, there is no complete and coherent theory of money. If the Quantity Theory is false [...] there is so far available only one false theory of money, and no true theory. In the criticisms advanced by the school of Tooke, there is on the negative side much that is correct and instructive, but in a positive sense they do not amount to more than a few aphorisms" (Wicksell 1898, xxiii). "It is usual to speak of a Credit Theory of Money, which is supposed to originate from Thomas Tooke and provide a scientific antithesis to the Quantity Theory. But I find myself unable to say where such a theory is developed in Tooke's writings. His monetary contributions [...] are on the theoretical side purely critical in general outlook and negative in concept. It is quite impossible, I think, to construct out of them a positive theory of money. He frequently mentions factors—and usually quite correctly—as being *without* influence on the value of money, but he never mentions the factors on which the value of money must ultimately depend" (Wicksell 1898, 43–44).

However, Wicksell wishes to retain the Quantity Theory of Money, which he argues "cannot just be thrown overboard" (Wicksell 1898, 50). However, he aims to reestablish it in a new and improved way for a credit economy, noting it is "far easier to criticise the Quantity Theory than to replace it by a better and more correct one" (Wicksell 1898, 43).

Wicksell's starting point is the idea that the price level does not increase simply as a result of an increase in the money supply, but rather as a result of the demand caused by the additional money supply. "It is not as though a man who accidentally possesses twice as many ten-mark pieces as usual would now proceed to bid double the price for every commodity. But he will probably desire to complete some purchase that he would otherwise have postponed, or he will be more hesitant in disposing of some commodity that necessity would otherwise have compelled him to sell. In short, the result of the increase in the quantity of money is a rise in the demand for commodities, and a fall in their supply, with the consequence that all prices rise continuously—until cash balances stand once again in their normal relation to the level of prices" (Wicksell 1898, 40–41).

Wicksell goes on to envision a pure credit system without currency in which all transactions take the form of book transfers between banks: "We intend therefore, as a basis for the following discussion, to imagine a state of affairs in which money does not actually circulate at all, neither in the form of coin (except perhaps as small change) nor in the form of notes, but where all domestic payments are effected by means of the Giro system and bookkeeping transfers" (Wicksell 1898, 70).

This famous model of a pure credit economy addresses the hypothetical extreme case of an historical evolutionary process (Leijonhufvud 1997, 93). "For the sake of simplicity, let us then assume that the whole monetary system of a country is in the hands of a single credit institution, provided with an adequate number of branches, at which each independent economic individual keeps an account on which he can draw cheques" (Wicksell 1898, 71). Here we find Wicksell's ideal bank concept, which presumes a single bank and monetary system that exclusively relies on credit money, without currency.

Wicksell then asks how the exchange value of money and the general level of commodity prices are determined within this system. This is followed by his explanation regarding a "cumulative process" in which low rates of interest on loans lead to more loans and, consequently, more credit money. This increases "moneyed demand," in turn pushing up prices (Wicksell 1898, 96). The same process also occurs in reverse. Whether the interest rates on loans are low or high depends on their relation to the natural rate of interest on capital. "There is a certain rate of interest on loans which is neutral in respect to commodity prices, and tends neither to raise nor to lower them. This is necessarily the same as the rate of interest which would be determined by supply and demand if no use were made of money and all lending were effected in the form of real capital goods. It comes to much the same thing to describe it as the current value of the natural rate of interest on capital" (Wicksell 1898, 102).

The arbitrage principle informs these ideas. Specifically, the price neutral rate of interest on loans is found when no one is able to make a profit through countertrades. This means that the nominal purchasing power must increase by the same percentage as the real goods. If the natural rate of interest on capital is higher, loans are taken out and invested in capital because the return is higher than the cost of the loan. Conversely, if the natural rate of interest on capital is lower than the rate on loans, loans are repaid.

The entire model is fundamentally based on the quantity equation. However, prices are not absolute, but relatively stable. "The analogous picture for money prices should rather be some easily movable object, such as a cylinder, which rests on a horizontal plane in so-called neutral equilibrium. The plane is somewhat rough and a certain force is required to set the price-cylinder in motion and to keep it in motion. But so long as this force—the raising or lowering of the rate of interest—remains in operation, the cylinder continues to move in the same direction" (Wicksell 1898, 101).

Like Hilferding, Wicksell notes an increasing level of concentration among banks, and he considers the potential consequences: "The various practical obstacles which stand in the way of ideally perfect mobility of money are gradually being removed as a result of concentration in the hands of the banks of cash holdings and of the business of lending, and of the use of bills and notes, cheques and clearing methods. Money is continually becoming more fluid, and the supply of money is more and more inclined to accommodate itself to the level of demand. We have seen that in our ideal state every payment, and consequently every loan, is accomplished by means of cheques or giro facilities. It is then no longer possible to refer to the supply of money as an independent magnitude, differing from the demand for money. No matter what amount of money may be demanded from the banks, that is the amount which they are in a position to lend (so long as the security of the borrower is adequate)" (Wicksell 1898, 110).

In a pure system of credit, where all payments are effected through bank bookkeeping entries, the money supply is theoretically unlimited. Banks would be able to grant loans of any amount at any time, depending only on the demand for money. "It is then no longer possible to refer to the supply of money as an independent magnitude, differing from the demand for money" (Wicksell 1898, 110).

25.5 Evaluation

Wicksell regarded his work as a refinement of Ricardo's Quantity Theory of Money that incorporated Tooke's ideas while addressing his criticisms. He contrasts a pure cash economy with a pure credit system. Although he emphasizes that reality is a mixture of the two, he offers no synthesis of the two approaches (Leijonhufvud 1997, 94–96).

For Wicksell, precious metals should remain a monetary anchor. However, it is unclear why currency should remain as the unit of account in a pure system of credit money. Indeed, the issue of central banking remains unclear in Wicksell's work. Is he offering a theory of central banking yet without a central bank?

Wicksell describes the cumulative and self-reinforcing process of adjustment in a credit economy. He relates this to the monetary controversies arising from the debate surrounding Ricardo's Quantity Theory of Money, since the money supply must adjust to fluctuations in monetary demand at a given price level. Wicksell separates the quantity theory from the money supply mechanism, instead attributing it to the interest rate differential. Wicksell attributes a high degree of self-regulation to the system, and asserts that interest rates are the only effective lever for conducting monetary policy.

Taxonomic Classification
Wicksell discusses a pure credit system in which credit money adjusts endogenously, e.g., through passive money creation.

References

Grodecka-Messi, Anna, and Xin Zhang. 2025. *Central Bank Liquidity Support, Bank Lending, and the End of Currency Competition*. Sveriges Riksbank Working Paper Series 454. August 2025.

Hansson, Björn. 1997. Knut Wicksells Leben und Werk und sein Einfluß auf die Entstehung einer Schwedischen Schule der Ökonomie. In *Vademecum zu einem Klassiker der Preis- und Geldtheorie*, 37–69. Düsseldorf: Wirtschaft und Finanzen.

Leijonhufvud, Axel. 1997. Wicksells Erbe. In *Vademecum zu einem Klassiker der Preis- und Geldtheorie*, 91–104. Düsseldorf: Wirtschaft und Finanzen.

Lindahl, Erik. 1958. Introduction: Wicksell's life and work. In *Knut Wicksell. Selected papers on economic theory*. Reprint 2017, 9–48. Routledge.

Wicksell, Knut. 1898. *Interest and Prices: A Study of the Causes Regulating the Value of Money*. Translated by Richard F. Kahn. London: Macmillan. 1936.

Chapter 26
Irving Fisher (1867–1947): The Canonical Form of the Quantity Theory

26.1 Biography[1]

Irving Fisher was born in 1867 in Saugerties, New York. The son of a Congregational minister, he grew up in a household of modest means, but thanks to his intellectual abilities was accepted to Yale, where he spent his entire academic career. Although he initially intended to pursue mathematics, he earned his doctorate in 1891 with a dissertation on equilibrium theory, which brought him early international recognition. In 1898, his career was interrupted by a three-year battle with tuberculosis.

Fisher consistently sought to make his theories measurable and practically applicable through precise definitions. Under his influence, economics took on a new, mathematically empirical form; in 1918, he was elected president of the American Economic Association.

Through his marriage, Fisher acquired some wealth, which he expanded through various technical inventions. However, in the crash of 1929 he lost not just his fortune, but also much of his professional reputation, as he had previously dismissed the possibility of a crisis with great confidence. He died disillusioned in 1947.

A highly prolific writer, Fisher published not only on economic theory and his inventions but also authored widely read books on health and temperance, in addition to shorter pieces on eugenics.

26.2 Selected Text

Fisher, Irving. 1911. *The Purchasing Power of Money*. New York: Macmillan.

[1] This biography follows Fisher (1929) and Monissen (1989).

J. Greitens, *Currency and Credit Money*, Springer Studies in the History of Economic Thought, https://doi.org/10.1007/978-3-032-24113-9_26

26.3 Historical Background

Fisher's *Purchasing Power of Money* falls within the period between two intense debates on monetary policy in the USA: the bimetallism controversy surrounding the 1896 US presidential campaign and the passage of the Federal Reserve Act in 1913. Following the American Civil War, there was a period of economic growth, but this was accompanied by persistent deflation. The gold standard was introduced the USA in a gradual manner: in 1873 the minting of silver coins was discontinued; this was followed in 1900 by the passage of the Gold Standard Act. Due to obligations stemming from the international gold standard, it was difficult for the USA, which did not have a central bank, to accommodate pressures on money and prices (Laidler 2013, 178).

During his unsuccessful campaign for the Democratic presidential nomination in 1896, William Jennings Bryan campaigned using populist rhetoric for the reintroduction of bimetallism. During this period, silver prices were falling, not only due to increasing production, but also due to declining demand, as countries were transitioning to gold-backed currencies. On the other hand, the supply of money was limited by the availability of gold. Indebted farmers in particular hoped that a bimetallic standard would improve their situation, as the minting of large quantities of silver would increase the money supply. At the Democratic National Convention of 1896, Bryan famously pronounced: "If they dare to come out in the open field and defend the gold standard as a good thing, we shall fight them to the uttermost, having behind us the producing masses of the nation and the world. Having behind us the commercial interests and the laboring interests and all the toiling masses, we shall answer their demands for a gold standard by saying to them, you shall not press down upon the brow of labor this crown of thorns. You shall not crucify mankind upon a cross of gold."

Similar disputes over bimetallism took place in other countries. For example, in Germany, important protagonists were Otto Arendt, who supported a bimetallic standard and was backed by the East Prussian Junkers. Arendt was opposed by Ludwig Bamberger, who supported the gold standard.

In Fisher's eyes, the proponents of bimetallism advanced arguments that were based on a misreading of the Quantity Theory of Money: "It has seemed to me a scandal that academic economists have [...] been led into disagreements over the fundamental propositions concerning money. [...] The attempts by promoters of unsound money to make an improper use of the quantity theory—as in the first Bryan campaign—led many sound money men to the utter repudiation of the quantity theory. The consequence has been that, especially in America, the quantity theory needs to be reintroduced into general knowledge" (Fisher 1911, viii). Fisher aimed to defend the idea that money is neutral over the long term and that a stable monetary system is important (Dimand 2011, 132) (Fig. 26.1).

Fig. 26.1 Illustration from the Bryan campaign, in which a flourishing world of bimetallism is contrasted with the poverty endemic to a gold standard (Harvey 1894, 21)

Beginning in 1889, gold production costs fell due to new cyanide leaching techniques. This significantly increased gold production and helped to end the period of deflation. The banking crisis of 1907 sparked discussions about establishing a central bank to manage future crises. These discussions entered a final phase around 1911.

Fisher dedicated his book to Simon Newcomb, whom he called an "inspiring friend" and "pioneer in study of Societary Circulation." Newcomb was a mathematician and astronomer who published the *Principles of Political Economy* in 1885. In this work, Newcomb presented his "equation of societary circulation," which describes the circulation of money while distinguishing between flow and stock. Newcomb's equation of exchange furnished the basis for Fisher's monetary theory (Newcomb 1885, 316–328, 350–355).

26.4 Discussion

Fisher sought to empirically account for the Quantity Theory of Money while also reintroducing it to economic discourse. "The purpose of this book is to set forth the principles determining the purchasing power of money. [...] The main contentions of this book are at bottom simply a restatement and amplification of the old 'quantity theory' of money. With certain corrections in the usual statements of that theory, it may still be called fundamentally sound" (Fisher 1911, vii).

26.4.1 The Monetary System

Fisher's division of money into types is central to his overall theory. He considers all means of circulation to be relevant, using the term "currency" to describe them. He further subdivides this category into "money" and "bank deposits."

"If we confine our attention to present and normal conditions, and to those means of exchange which either are money or most nearly approximate it, we shall find that money itself belongs to a general class of property rights which we may call 'currency' or 'circulating media.' Currency includes any type of property right which, whether generally acceptable or not, does actually, for its chief purpose and use, serve as a means of exchange. Circulating media are of two chief classes: (1) money; (2) bank deposits" (Fisher 1911, 10).

He defines currency as a "commodity generally accepted in exchange, such as gold coins" (Fisher 1911, 10). Money therefore has its own intrinsic value, but only exists as highly liquid, circulating assets, i.e., not as real estate, for example. In contrast to Knapp, it is irrelevant to him whether this money is officially authorized by the state: "We define money as what is generally acceptable in exchange for goods. […] The general acceptability may be reinforced by law, the money thus becoming what is known as 'legal tender'; but such reinforcement is not essential" (Fisher 1911, 8).

Fisher also considers as money circulating deposits such as banknotes or small change. "Of real money there are two kinds: primary and fiduciary. Money is called 'primary' if it is a commodity which has just as much value in some use other than money as it has in monetary use. Primary money has its full value independently of any other wealth. Fiduciary money, on the other hand, is money the value of which depends partly or wholly on the confidence that the owner can exchange it for other goods, e.g. for primary money at a bank or government office, or at any rate for discharge of debts or purchase of goods of merchants. The chief example of primary money is gold coin; the chief example of fiduciary money is bank notes" (Fisher 1911, 11).

Fisher thus distinguishes between bank deposits, that are disposable via banknotes, and bank deposits, that are disposable via checks or bills of exchange. According to him, the latter are not money, but rather circulation medium or circulating credit. "By means of checks, bank deposits serve as a means of payment in exchange for other goods. A check is the 'certificate' or evidence of the transfer of bank deposits" (Fisher 1911, 10).

"But while a bank deposit transferable by check is included as circulating media, it is not money. A bank note, on the other hand, is both circulating medium and money" (Fisher 1911, 10). For him, deposits that circulate via checks or bills are not money, because acceptance depends on the recipient. "Yet while a note is generally acceptable in exchange, a check is specially acceptable only, i.e. only by the consent of the payee" (Fisher 1911, 10).

26.4.2 Fisher's Equation of Exchange

Fisher then aims to formulate the Quantity Theory of Money more precisely than Locke, Hume, or Ricardo: "Overlooking the influence of deposit currency, or checks, the price level may be said to depend on only three sets of causes: (1) the quantity of money in circulation; (2) its 'efficiency' or velocity of circulation (or the average number of times a year money is exchanged for goods); and (3) the volume of trade (or amount of goods bought by money)" (Fisher 1911, 14).

To this end, Fisher sets out his equation of exchange: "The quantity theory will be made more clear by the equation of exchange, which is now to be explained. [...] The equation of exchange is a statement, in mathematical form, of the total transactions effected in a certain period in a given community. It is obtained simply by adding together the equations of exchange for all individual transactions" (Fisher 1911, 15–16).

His presentation always follows a three-part approach: First, he gives an arithmetic example, which he then illustrates with a mechanical metaphor (a scale), before offering an algebraic expression (Fig. 26.2).

$$MV = \Sigma pQ$$

- *M*: Quantity of money.
- *V*: Velocity of circulation.
- *p*: Price of a single good in exchange.
- *Q*: Quantity of a single good in exchange.

The sum of all individual exchanges within a certain period and community must correspond to the circulation of money, i.e., the money that was exchanged for goods.

"This equation contains on the money side two magnitudes, viz. (1) the quantity of money and (2) its velocity of circulation; and on the goods side two groups of magnitudes in two columns, viz. (1) the quantities of goods exchanged (loaves, tons, yards), and (2) the prices of these goods. The equation shows that these four sets of magnitudes are mutually related. Because this equation must be fulfilled, the prices must bear a relation to the three other sets of magnitudes – quantity of money,

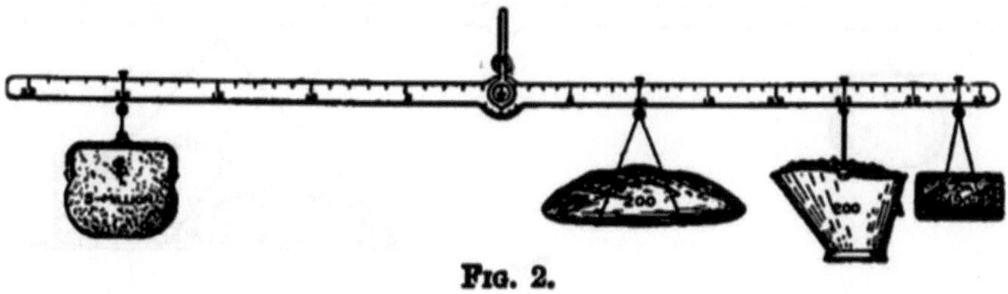

FIG. 2.

Fig. 26.2 Fisher's depiction of Quantity Theory (only money, without bank deposits) (Fisher 1911, 21)

rapidity of circulation, and quantities of goods exchanged. Consequently, these prices must, as a whole, vary proportionally with the quantity of money and with its velocity of circulation, and inversely with the quantities of goods exchanged" (Fisher 1911, 18).

Fisher notes that prices adjust to increases in the money supply: "but whether all prices increase uniformly, each being exactly doubled, or some prices increase more and some less (so as still to double the total money value of the goods purchased), the prices are doubled on the average" (Fisher 1911, 19).

However, the quantity of goods can also adjust: "if there is a simultaneous change in two or all of the three influences, i.e. quantity of money, velocity of circulation, and quantities of goods exchanged, the price level will be a compound or resultant of these various influences. If, for example, the quantity of money is doubled, and its velocity of circulation is halved, while the quantity of goods exchanged remains constant, the price level will be undisturbed" (Fisher 1911, 21).

$$MV = PT$$

- *M*: Quantity of money.
- *V*: Velocity of circulation.
- *P*: Price index of goods in exchange.
- *T*: Transaction volume of goods in exchange.

Fisher then combines the quantity of traded goods into a transaction volume and the individual prices into a measurable price level. "This averaging of prices is represented in Fig. 26.3, which visualizes the fact that the average price of goods (right arm) varies directly with the quantity of money (left weight), and directly with its velocity of circulation (left arm), and inversely with the volume of trade (right weight)" (Fisher 1911, 23–24). "We may [...] further simplify the right side by writing it in the form PT where *P* is a weighted average of all the *p*'s, and *T* is the sum of all the Q's" (Fisher 1911, 27).

Based on the foregoing, Fisher emphasizes the core principle underlying the Quantity Theory of Money. "To recapitulate, we find then that, under the conditions

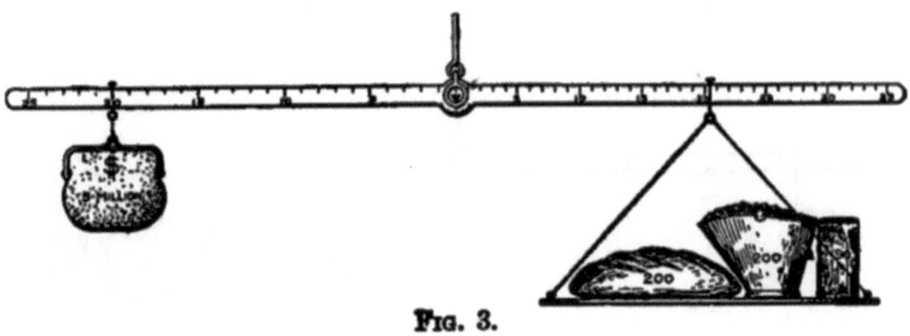

Fig. 3.

Fig. 26.3 Fisher's depiction of Quantity Theory (with the transaction volume and a price index) (Fisher 1911, 23)

assumed, the price level varies (1) directly as the quantity of money in circulation (*M*), (2) directly as the velocity of its circulation (*F*), (3) inversely as the volume of trade done by it (*T*). The first of these three relations is the most important. It constitutes the 'Quantity Theory of Money'" (Fisher 1911, 29). In this context, it is evident that money has no inherent value; its worth is determined solely by its purchasing power. "The Quantity Theory of Money thus rests, ultimately, upon the fundamental peculiarity which money alone of all goods possesses—the fact that it has no power to satisfy human wants except a power to *purchase* things which do have such power" (Fisher 1911, 32) (Fig. 26.4).

The next section begins with a description of how credit money is created, including legally required reserves, as found in textbooks today. However, according to Fisher, this credit money is not actually money, but merely a medium of circulation. Fisher then incorporates credit money into the quantity theory (Fisher 1911, 33–47).

"The analysis of the balance sheets of banks has prepared us for the inclusion of bank deposits or circulating credit in the equation of exchange. We shall still use *M* to express the quantity of actual money, and *V* to express the velocity of its circulation. Similarly, we shall now use *M'* to express the total deposits subject to transfer by check; and V to express the average velocity of circulation. The total value of purchases in a year is therefore no longer to be measured by *MV*, but by $MV + M'V'$. The equation of exchange, therefore, becomes: $MV + M'V' = \sum pQ = PT$" (Fisher 1911, 48).

- T / $\sum Q$: The transaction volume depends on needs and the degree of specialization/division of labor in the economy.
- V / V': The velocity of circulation depends on payment habits, population density and transport routes, among other things, and is therefore independent of *M* or *M'*. Furthermore, it only changes over the long term (Dimand 2011, 136).
- *M*: The money supply is exogenously determined by the import or production of precious metals or by the issuance of notes by the state and banks.
- *M'*: The supply of circulating media depends on the development of the banking system. *M'* is always a multiple of *M* and the ratio of the two sizes is constant. "But the fact is that the quantity of circulating credit, *M'*, tends to hold a definite relation to *M*, the quantity of money in circulation; that is, deposits are normally a more or less definite multiple of money. Two facts normally give deposits a more or less definite ratio to money. The first has been already explained, viz.,

FIG. 4.

Fig. 26.4 Fisher's depiction of Quantity Theory (with money and bank deposits) (Fisher 1911, 48)

that bank reserves are kept in a more or less definite ratio to bank deposits. The second is that individuals, firms, and corporations preserve more or less definite ratios between their cash transactions and their check transactions, and also between their money and deposit balances. These ratios are determined by motives of individual convenience and habit" (Fisher 1911, 50).

Based on these assumptions, the price level is proportional to the exogenous money supply. In chapter 4, Fisher discusses "transition periods," during which slower changes in nominal interest rates have short-term real effects (Dimand 2011, 131). In chapter 13, Fisher presents his first proposal for a currency reform: the Compensated Dollar Plan.

26.5 Evaluation

Today, Fisher's equation of exchange is widely regarded as the pinnacle of modern quantity theory. Fisher developed it to defend the quantity theory against misuse by bimetallists and the populists. For Fisher, the primary aim of a central bank's monetary policy should be to stabilize the price level. Fisher defends the idea that long-term neutrality will prevail over any short-term stimulation (via expectations or interest rates), and in this respect, his book is more than just a reformulation of quantity theory (Dimand 2013, 288–290).

In Fisher's model, the transaction quantity (T) includes all transactions in an economy, not just the purchases of products for consumption (goods and services), but also intermediate products and assets. According to Milton Friedman, this was replaced by real gross domestic product (Y), based on the assumption of a constant relationship between T and Y.

Drawing on Hume and others, Fisher presents the equation of exchange without showcasing the steps that led to it. Departing from earlier formulations, Fisher explicitly incorporates the creation of credit money and implicitly assumes full employment. However, his theory lacks a behavioral component for individual economic agents. Furthermore, this equation does not explain the causal relationship between variables.

His efforts to empirically depict the equation of exchange and measure the velocity of circulation in relation to the money supply and prices were groundbreaking and formed the basis for twentieth-century macroeconomics (Dimand 2011, 132; Dimand 2013, 286).

Fisher believed that the central role of money in an economy was under threat as soon as its value fluctuated or these fluctuations were not properly understood. In his view, this would ultimately destroy the ethics of the monetary system and create social injustice. He thus made efforts to raise awareness for this issue and promote monetary stability, particularly with his 1928 book *The Money Illusion*. Due to this sociopolitical objective, Fisher insisted on a strict and somewhat unrealistic proportionality between the money supply and the price level (Rieter 1995, 111–113).

Despite the Great Depression and his experiences during the First World War, Fisher remained committed to the Quantity Theory of Money until his death. His 100% Money proposal of 1935 aimed to stabilize the value of money and thus avoid boom-and-bust cycles (Demeulemeester 2024).

Taxonomic Classification

Fisher does not seek to account for the origins of money but describes it as a means of payment. Rather, he seeks to explain its value using the Quantity Theory of Money, incorporating credit money as a multiple of base money to reflect banks' role in money creation.

References

Demeulemeester, Samuel. 2024. Investigating the 'debt-money prices' triangle: Irving Fisher's theoretical journey towards the 100% money proposal. *Journal of the History of Economic Thought* 46 (2): 225–243.

Dimand, Robert W. 2011. Irving Fisher's the purchasing power of money. *History of Economics Review* 54:131–143.

Dimand, Robert W. 2013. David Hume and Irving Fisher on the quantity theory of money in the long run and the short run. *European Journal for the History of Economic Thought* 20 (2): 284–304.

Fisher, Irving. 1911. *The Purchasing Power of Money*, New York: Macmillan.

Fisher, Irving. 1929. Fisher, Irving. In *Die Volkswirtschaftslehre der Gegenwart in Selbstdarstellungen*, vol. 2, 1–14. Leipzig: Verlag Felix Meiner.

Harvey, William Hope. 1894. *Coin's financial school*. Chicago: Coin Publishing Company.

Laidler, David. 2013. Professor Fisher and the quantity theory—A significant encounter. *European Journal of the History of Economic Thought* 20 (2): 174–205.

Monissen, Hans G. 1989. Irving Fisher (1867–1947). In *Klassiker des ökonomischen Denkens*, vol. 2, 211–230. Munich: Beck.

Newcomb, Simon. 1885. *Principles of political economy*. New York: Harper.

Rieter, Heinz. 1995. Fisher, Irving (1867–1947). In *Von Aktie bis Zoll: Ein historisches Lexikon des Geldes*, 110–114. Munich: Beck.

Chapter 27
Joseph A. Schumpeter (1883–1950): Money as an Endogenous Token

27.1 Biography[1]

Joseph A. Schumpeter was born in 1883 as the only child of the cloth manufacturer Joseph Alois Karl Schumpeter and his wife Johanna in Triesch. After the early death of his father, the five-year-old moved with his mother in 1888 to Graz and then in 1893 to Vienna, where he was admitted to the Theresianum. In 1901 Schumpeter began studying economics at the University of Vienna, graduating in February 1906. He subsequently spent a year in Berlin, London, and Oxford before going to Cairo. He obtained his habilitation in Vienna in 1909 and became an associate professor at the University of Czernowitz. From there he went to Graz, assuming a position as full professor in 1911.

In 1919, Schumpeter became a member of the first Socialization Commission in Germany. Despite his lack of party affiliation, he was appointed minister of finance to Austria's socialist government in March of 1919. His unsuccessful tenure ended just 6 months later. He then switched from politics to business, becoming president of the Biedermann Bank, but lost his fortune and position due to inflation and the economic crisis of 1923. In 1925 he was appointed chair of economics in Bonn; from there, he went to Harvard in 1932. He died on January 8, 1950, following a stroke.

His economic reasoning was eclectic due to his extensive knowledge of contemporary sociology and economics, including the ideas of the Austrian School, German Historical School, and Lausanne School.

[1] This biography follows Naderer (1990) and Legrand (2024).

J. Greitens, *Currency and Credit Money*, Springer Studies in the History of Economic Thought, https://doi.org/10.1007/978-3-032-24113-9_27

27.2 Selected Text

Schumpeter, Joseph. 1918. "Money and the Social Product." *International Economic Papers 6*. 1956, 148–211. Translation by A.W. Marget of "Das Sozialproduct und die Rechenpfennige." *Archiv für Sozialwissenschaft und Sozialpolitik*. 44. 627–715.

27.3 Historical Background

Schumpeter wrote *Money and the Social Product* in the final phase of the First World War, as war-induced inflation was becoming increasingly difficult to contain. The inflation spikes experienced during the war, which ultimately culminated in the hyperinflation of 1923, challenged established monetary theory and sparked intense debate, to which Schumpeter was a notable contributor.

Schumpeter wanted to overcome the deficits in prevailing monetary theory: "It is altogether regrettable that our science has proved completely incapable of contributing to the discussion of practical problems what can rightfully be demanded of it, namely a foundation of principle, clarity on the basic questions and on the nature of monetary interrelations" (Schumpeter 1918, 148).

Drawing on his comprehensive knowledge of economics, Schumpeter wished to reconcile the disputes regarding proper methods that had erupted in the wake of Knapp's theory. "All serious workers in the field are nearer to one another than they admit. This is true also of the conflict which has split the German workers in this field, and which has no analogy in the literature of other nations, namely the conflict between the supporters and the opponents of Knapp" (Schumpeter 1918, 149).

Schumpeter positions himself as an eclectic: "The view that we are dealing here with two standpoints which differ *toto caelo*, which lead to completely different results and are irreconcilable, is as superficial as is the belief that the ideas involved are of a novelty which places them beyond and completely interrupts all doctrinal development. [...] I hope to show that the 'dominant' doctrine should, and can, make its peace with the State Theory and absorb its achievements, even though some of it may have to be discarded" (Schumpeter 1918, 149).

"The present essay nevertheless follows the lines which have been traced in German by Menger, Wieser, Wicksell and Schlesinger; in Italian by Del Vecchio and Fanno; in French by Walras and Aupetit; in English by Marshall, Keynes, and in some points by Irving Fisher and Kemmerer" (Schumpeter 1918, 149). This list illustrates the large and diverse range of thinkers who influenced his ideas on monetary matters.

To avoid excessive complexity, Schumpeter deliberately limits his analysis to a closed national economy with a monometallic monetary standard; he thus avoids the need to consider exchange rates and bimetallism (Schumpeter 1918, 150).

27.4 Discussion

27.4.1 Metallism Versus Nominalism

Schumpeter attached great importance to the history of economic thought; *Money and the Social Product* engages in continuous dialog with older texts (Naderer 1990, 232). Referencing Menger, Wieser, and Mises, Schumpeter rejects metallism while nevertheless allowing that "recognition of the inadequacy of the basic idea underlying the commodity theory by no means invalidates all the work of the 'metallists.' [...] One may indeed be a 'metallist' and still a very capable monetary theorist and currency policy expert" (Schumpeter 1918, 158).

While Schumpeter rejects metallism as a theory, he recognizes the benefits of metal-backed currencies, that is, of practical metallism: "the tying of money to a valuable material [...] may nevertheless be of the greatest practical importance; the point is merely that this importance lies elsewhere than it has usually been sought. [...] The special kind of 'claim ticket' which is called money has the peculiarity that no one guarantees its commodity content. If, therefore, money consists of a valuable material, its owner does have such a guarantee, which, though not completely certain, constitutes a kind tangible pledge of convertibility into a commodity [...] [This] can provide protection against the danger of an arbitrary increase in quantity" (Schumpeter 1918, 159).

Schumpeter also opposes Knapp: "It is also wrong to believe that something has been gained, and that the abandoned commodity theory is replaced, by characterizing money as a creature of the law and attempting to explain its position in the market simply through its being declared legal tender. In the first place, money is as little and in no other sense a creature of the law than is any other social institution such as marriage or private property. The comparison is instructive. Marriage and property, too, are regulated by law and to that extent their concrete forms are of course creatures of the prevailing legal system. But no-one can explain marriage or property by this legal system. Rather, the relevant legal provisions themselves are comprehensible only on the basis of the social nature and the social functions of the relations and modes of behaviour which these legal provisions regulate and which, to be sure, never exist without them, but also never exist only through them: the essential nature of marriage relations explains the legal provisions which regulate them, but the legal provisions do not explain the essential nature and causes of marriage relations. Similarly, money transactions are regulated or shaped by the legal system, but as an object of regulation they retain a separate existence apart from the legal system itself and can be explained only by their own nature or by the inner necessities of the market economy" (Schumpeter 1918, 160–161).

Schumpeter thus reinforces the criticism that Knapp's theory lacks an economic basis, and that, by extension, it cannot explain the essence of money. "Hence, a sharp distinction must be drawn between 'nominalism' and the 'State theory.' The nominalist idea has received in the latter a special form which is not essential to it, and which exposes it to objections that would otherwise not apply. It is an open question which is the worse aberration: overestimation of the importance of the value of the money material, or overestimation of the importance of the role of the State in relation to money" (Schumpeter 1918, 161).

Schumpeter refers to Irving Fisher throughout the text, sometimes approvingly, sometimes disapprovingly. For example, the fixed ratio of currency and credit money (*M* and *M'*) assumed by Fisher in his equation of exchange is not tenable for Schumpeter: "it must assume that other payments media react to the impulse proceeding from gold money by automatically increasing or decreasing in approximately the same proportion, so that the ratio between gold and the credit which is described as its 'superstructure' is a constant, or at least changes only slowly over time. [...] Nor is the ratio between bank reserves and bank deposits nearly as fixed as he assumes" (Schumpeter 1918, 174).

However, Schumpeter also frequently discusses Marx and the Banking School in the context of quantity theory—a term he uses so loosely, he might have well called it the "quantity equation." For Schumpeter, quantity theory is "only a monetary theorem which in itself says nothing about the nature and the value of money. It is entirely compatible with the 'cost-of-production theory'. This was argued already by Mill; it therefore need not be repeated here. Mill won the argument against Marx in advance. The quantity theory is, moreover, completely compatible with the 'credit theory' of money—which, incidentally, has just as little right to be regarded as a theory of money if it is understood to contain only what can be found in Tooke and Fullarton" (Schumpeter 1918, 163). Schumpeter does not understand the term quantity theory to refer to a strict proportional relationship between the exogenous money supply and endogenous price level, but rather as all forms of compliance with the equation of exchange, even by hoarding, as it was understood by Marx—or, if one reverses the causality, as it was understood by the Banking School.

Although Schumpeter leans predominantly toward nominalism, he later developed his own version of claim and token theory, seeking connections to metallism and commodity theory. "There are only two theories of money worthy of that name: the commodity theory and the claim theory. The basic ideas of these two theories are not compatible, although in very many cases they lead to the same results. [...] In this controversy, the champions of the theoretically more correct basic idea of the claim theory do not always have right on their side" (Schumpeter 1918, 163).

27.4.2 Token Theory

The idea of circular flow lies at the center of Schumpeter's monetary theory. "It is clear that the function of money in the economy is in principle of a merely technical nature, i.e. money is essentially a device for carrying on business transactions, a mere satellite of commodities, a servant of the processes in the world of goods" (Schumpeter 1918, 150). He also notes: "In the last analysis, only commodities are exchanged against commodities in the economy; money is always only an intermediate link without independent significance" (Schumpeter 1918, 171).

Schumpeter begins his analysis of circular flow by envisioning a static economy (Naderer 1990, 126–127): "The basic process of economic life is clearly a continuous circular flow of production expenditure and consumption uses within each economic period" (Schumpeter 1918, 150).

The term "social product," which in 1918 had not yet been standardized in its modern form, is defined by Schumpeter as follows: "The social product of an isolated economy—Marshall's National Dividend—consists of all the material and non-material consumer goods which are made available for consumption in an economic period, including the depreciation quotas of durable goods" (Schumpeter 1918, 151).

As one cannot distinguish between the production and distribution of the social product as processes, consumer goods also represent income. "In this way every productive contribution in the exchange economy automatically implies a definitive quantity of consumer goods. This is the real income. [...] Accounting in terms of money, which we now have introduced, changes little as the use of chips changes the essential nature of a game" (Schumpeter 1918, 152). From this, it follows that "given stationary equilibrium, the money value of all consumer goods should equal the money value of all producer goods, and both identically equal the sum of all money incomes" (Schumpeter 1918, 153).

For Schumpeter, money is a token, a "claim ticket" to the reservoir of goods (Schumpeter 1918, 201). Everyone receives as much from the quantity of consumer goods in terms of value as they have contributed to production. And the share of the money supply that one possesses determines the share of goods one can acquire with that money. "Everybody must submit to the condition that a money income is obtainable only against an equivalent contribution to production, and everybody looks upon money income from the point of view of the commodities which can be acquired with it—exactly as in the case of a claim ticket—and hence from the point of view of the real income [...] which money income represents" (Schumpeter 1918, 155). Money is thus an instrument for the appropriation of goods, a certification of value added; in this way, it is a *Rechenpfennig*, an "accounting token" (a historical calculation aid for bookkeeping), as in the German title of the text. Schumpeter also compares money to an *Eintrittskarte*, a ticket that allows entrance to the theater (Schumpeter 1918, 162). While Schumpeter does not mention Galiani by name, this was precisely the idea proposed by Galiani, who envisioned a special form of social accounting by token. In its purest form, we could imagine the management of this accounting system from a central ledger.

Like Knapp, Schumpeter elaborates a nominalistic theory of money, yet Schumpeter's theory is catallactic, while Knapp's is acatallactic. Besides the function as a token, i.e., as a unit of account, he considers all other functions to be secondary: "We are not going into a discussion of other functions of money, none of which are essential" (Schumpeter 1918, 155). The least relevant function of money is its use as a store of value: "We do not count the 'store-of-value' function among the distinguishing characteristics of money; if we did, we should have to include a whole series of commodities" (Schumpeter 1918, 168).

27.4.3 The Value of Money

For Schumpeter, the problem of determining money's value is essentially a problem of determining the purchasing power of income: "What does the worth of the income unit in the market depend upon? This is the basic theoretical and practical question of any theory of money" (Schumpeter 1918, 157).

His definition of money as a token allows a connection to be drawn to the Quantity Theory of Money: "Whatever the short-comings of the latter and of its various formulations, it is beyond doubt that the real importance of 'claim tickets' giving title not to definite objects but to shares in the mass of goods, must decisively depend upon the number of these claim tickets. The case may be likened to a game in which chips represent the players' share in the common pool; the total number of chips clearly decides the size of the share represented by each chip" (Schumpeter 1918, 162).

Purchasing power is determined by the ratio of income to the produced volume of goods. "From the point of view of the economy as a whole, increases and decreases in the sum of incomes mean something quite different from increases and decreases in the social product. The latter mean a better or worse supply of goods. Changes in the sum of incomes are in themselves a matter of indifference for the economy, and acquire real significance only if they either involve a simultaneous change in the structure of individual incomes (and therefore in the shares in the social product) or are a symptom and accompaniment of a change in the size of the social product" (Schumpeter 1918, 164).

27.4.4 The Money Supply

Schumpeter provides a detailed definition of the components of the money supply that are relevant for his equation of exchange. In this connection, he integrates "money surrogates"—that is, claims to money, i.e., credit money. Schumpeter asserts that in order to determine the money supply, everything that performs the role of money must be subsumed under the concept of money that is embraced:

- "It must include, first, commodities which in fact circulate as money. The most important case at the present time is, of course, that of full standard, freely coinable and freely demonetizable gold coins" (Schumpeter 1918, 168).
- Second, the concept of money must "include money made of a material the market price of which is less than the purchasing power of the monetary unit made of it. [...] It does not matter, for instance, whether the material, though not of full value, is still of relatively high value [...] or whether its metallic value is appreciably below its face value, as in the case of subsidiary coinage [...] or whether the material has practically no value at all, as in the case of paper money" (Schumpeter 1918, 169).

- "Third, we must include bank notes. [...] The essence of granting credit is to help someone else to disposal over goods. [...] That he has a right to gold which he normally does not exercise is a superficial legal fact which has little to do with the economic nature of the role of the bank note" (Schumpeter 1918, 169).
- "Fourth, we must include current accounts and clearing accounts [...]. There are a lot of differences of detail between deposit money and bank note money, but in essence they are the same" (Schumpeter 1918, 170).
- "Fifth, we must include the amount of all payments which are disbursements out of income and are handled exclusively by compensation" (Schumpeter 1918, 170).
- "Sixth, we have to include in the concept of money credit instruments and claim titles of all kinds, to the extent that they in fact perform the role of money" (Schumpeter 1918, 171).

Schumpeter then clarifies that other components or the use of them reduces the supply of money: "With some types of money, particularly with full-standard metallic money, there is an intermediate stage when they do not act as money but are always ready to re-emerge as such. In such cases, they remain money, but are to be excluded from the quantity of circulating money which concerns us. To this category belong, above all:

1. Hoards. [...] [Hoarded money] is temporarily dead.
2. [...] Bank notes are money and so is their gold cover, but only the former fulfil the role of money.
3. Unemployed sums waiting to be used.
4. The true cash reserves of banks, firms and private persons" (Schumpeter 1918, 173).

Schumpeter notes that this broad definition of the money supply is only determined by economic considerations, and is not limited for historical or statistical reasons. "A broad concept alone corresponds to the facts and makes possible a true conceptual representation of reality. [...] To be sure, in our formulation the quantity of money loses that easily determined magnitude which it has if it is equated, say, to the quantity of metallic money plus paper money plus bank notes. If, however, we are clear on the point that this does not encompass the actually effective quantity of money" (Schumpeter 1918, 173). Schumpeter prioritizes economic accuracy over practical applicability and data availability, even if this means that the Quantity Theory of Money cannot be empirically tested.

For Schumpeter's equation of exchange and subsequent conclusions, only money used in the market for consumer goods is considered relevant income. "Hence we must exclude the sums that circulate on the market for income-yielding assets—on the real estate market, the mortgage market, the stock market, and so on. These sums exert no direct influence on purchasing power" (Schumpeter 1918, 176). As with modern economic output calculations, purchases of assets are not taken into account. Similar to Fisher, therefore, the money supply must be defined as money used in the goods market for the social product, even though this supply fluctuates and cannot be statistically recorded.

27.4.5 The Velocity of Circulation

Schumpeter then addresses the velocity of circulation, as defined by Fisher. Schumpeter views "velocity" as an "unhappily chosen expression," asserting that "efficiency" would have been preferable (Schumpeter 1918, 177). He then explains the term, noting that "within the period in which the economic process is completed, one and the same monetary unit several times traverses the circular flow from the consumption sphere back to the consumption sphere; or, what comes to the same thing, it becomes several times an element of money income and is spent as such" (Schumpeter 1918, 179).

Schumpeter diverges from Fisher conceptually in that he only wishes to consider money that is actually used for consumption and income in the goods market (Naderer 1990, 143). Schumpeter explains that efficiency in the "velocity of circulation acts like an increase in the quantity of money" (Schumpeter 1918, 181). "The sum of incomes is the monetary expression of 'total demand'. Hence the latter, too, depends only upon the quantity of circulating money times its efficiency" (Schumpeter 1918, 182). By spotlighting the interrelated nature of production and income while drawing on the term "efficiency" Schumpeter thus links the income theory and Quantity Theory of Money (Naderer 1990, 144–145).

27.4.6 The Fundamental Equation of Monetary Theory

Schumpeter deploys a slightly modified form of Fisher's equation of exchange, based on the previous definitions, as the starting point for his subsequent analysis (Schumpeter 1918, 182–183):

$$I = MV = p_1q_1 + p_2q_2 + p_3q_3 + \ldots + p_nq_n$$

- I = Sum of the incomes of all economic subjects in an economy; income is referred to as the "anchorage of the theory" (Schumpeter 1918, 150).
- M = Circulating money supply, i.e., the amount of money used from income to purchase consumer goods.
- V = Average velocity of circulation, which Schumpeter refers to as "efficiency".
- q_1 to q_n = Quantity of individual consumer goods,
- p_1 to p_n = Respective prices.

Schumpeter attempts to equate Fisher's equation of exchange to income and thus to interrelate the quantity and income theories. "This equation is formally identical with the Newcomb-Fisher equation. In substance it differs from the latter because of the different definition of V and the corresponding limitation of the magnitudes on the right-hand side to consumer goods" (Schumpeter 1918, 182–183).

Schumpeter rejects the idea that his equation, like Fisher's, is a tautology. "Our equation is not a tautology in the proper sense. This would be the case only if both sides of the equation were expressions for the same quantity, so that a change in one side would not merely bring about but would ipso facto mean a change in the other. [...] This is not the case here: both I and the products $p_1q_1 + p_2q_2$ etc. are magnitudes which are distinguishable not only conceptually, but also practically, and are measurable on the basis of different statistical sources" (Schumpeter 1918, 183). Schumpeter notes that Fisher's equation does not sufficiently differentiate between components of the circulating money supply, includes expenditure on intermediate goods, and uses abstract indices instead of actual transactions—however, these features make it easier to implement empirically.

Schumpeter then interprets the basic equation in three steps, the central starting point of which is his subdivision into static and dynamic analysis, as in his famous *Theory of Economic Development* (1912).

27.4.7 First Proposition on the Fundamental Equation

In the static view, individual price and quantity changes cannot change the product sum. "No change in the magnitudes of which the product sum $p_1q_1 + p_2q_2 + p_3q_3 + ... + p_nq_n$ consists can directly influence the product sum itself" (Schumpeter 1918, 184).

As long as the product of M and V does not change, the product sum cannot change in a static economy. "It says only that changes in the prices and quantities of commodities which are not themselves due to changes in the magnitude *MV* can influence the product sum in no way other than through this magnitude; all it means is that, so long as *MV* remains constant, every change in the prices and quantities of some commodities must be balanced by corresponding changes in the prices and quantities of other commodities, and that it is therefore impossible for *MV* to change as a result of a prior change in the product sum at constant *MV*" (Schumpeter 1918, 184).

The individual prices result from their interplay with all other prices and the scarcities of other goods: price increases for one good are offset by other goods. "The direct influence of the commodity side always results in a shift in the relation of prices to each other" (Schumpeter 1918, 187). Changes in the value of money or price level necessarily require a monetary impulse (Naderer 1990, 150).

27.4.8 Second Proposition on the Fundamental Equation

The second proposition emphasizes the effects that result for the real economy from an increase in the money supply, given a static economy; *MV* affects the product sum: "Whatever happens on the left-hand side of the equation—that is, every effect of 'monetary causes'—directly influences *MV*, and every change in *MV* necessarily causes a corresponding change in the product sum on the right-hand side" (Schumpeter 1918, 187).

According to the Quantity Theory of Money, the changes in the product sum that result from a change in the money supply can only be associated to prices: "Now the quantity theory adds two things. The first is that the quantity of money is the driving force behind the changes in *MV* [...] secondly, that the change in the product sum which is to be brought about by changes in *MV* is effected by a change in prices, while the quantities of commodities remain constant, so that the quantity of money is the active and the price level the passive factor" (Schumpeter 1918, 189–190).

Schumpeter lists the conditions under which the Quantity Theory of Money applies with proportional prices: "If all circulating monetary units were suddenly to be doubled wherever they happened to be, if this were known to everybody, if the country were isolated, if nothing could flow out of circulation (metal, say, into industrial uses), if all contracts were changed *uno actu* so as to involve twice the sums previously mentioned therein—then we could confidently regard the matter as disposed of by what has just been said. All prices would simply double" (Schumpeter 1918, 190–191).

In this context, Schumpeter emphasizes the necessity to distinguish between individual prices and the general price level. "If a single price rises, the relevant production becomes more profitable, and one will try to expand its production. But: This would be only a temporary counter-effect which would merely intensify the result. [...] This is again the old confusion of the price level and the individual price. If an individual price rises, the corresponding production becomes more profitable and an attempt will be made to expand it by drawing means of production away from other branches. If all prices rise, no production becomes more profitable. If attempts were made to expand all branches of production, the result would be a struggle for the means of production—which after all have not increased—and everybody concerned would soon realize their error" (Schumpeter 1918, 190).

Alongside the explanation for the second proposition provided by quantity theory, Schumpeter provides a second explanation: "To begin with, increases in the quantity of money never occur uniformly for all people. Further, people are never completely aware of the nature of the process, so that, at least for some time, they act as if they received higher incomes while the sum of incomes remains constant. For both reasons, prices never rise uniformly—neither the prices for consumer goods relative to each other nor the prices of consumer goods relative to those of the means of production. Thereby the price rise ceases to be merely nominal. It means a real shift of wealth on the market for consumer goods and a real shift of power on the market for the means of production, and it affects the quantities of commodities and the whole productive process. No doubt, not all these effects are permanent" (Schumpeter 1918, 191).

Using gold prospectors as an example, Schumpeter explains what the additional money is used for. "If [...] the new gold is coined, it increases only the claim tickets to the social product and not the latter itself. It forces the economy to make unrequited deliveries to the owners of the gold pieces. To this extent, the production of gold money is not production and its effects are like those of counterfeiting [...]. The real content of the income unit is lessened, the price level rises because of the emergence of new money demand" (Schumpeter 1918, 192).

For Schumpeter, this price increase represents an act of theft from the other holders of money. "What really happens is an act of waste from the point of view of the economy as a whole, a destruction of goods without the counter-contribution which constitutes the essence of reproductive consumption, and just as unproductive, say, as an act of plunder. [...] This waste takes place at the expense of the real income, prior to the increase in the quantity of gold, of all those who do not share in this increase as gold panners or their suppliers" (Schumpeter 1918, 192–193).

The new money provides a claim to consumer goods, yet without any prior contribution to their production. "The situation would be different if our gold panner [...] did not go on a spending spree but invested their gains; for example, if they themselves acquired means of production in order to operate factories, or gave others the possibility of doing so by lending them the money, or, finally, used for this purpose the intermediary of a bank in which they deposited the amounts in question" (Schumpeter 1918, 193).

Schumpeter refers to the voluntary spending of income on investment goods as "saving," since this money is not spent on consumption. However, forced saving occurs when consumer good prices rise. "But the productive forces which are released by these groups' inability to buy as much as before, now do not serve production for immediate consumption, but production of wider scope—fewer automobiles, for example, are produced, and more machines. Many people are forced to save willy-nilly and without enjoying the fruits thereof. This forced saving is an extraordinarily important phenomenon, an essential part of the capitalistic mechanism, a key to the understanding of many phenomena of modem economic life" (Schumpeter 1918, 194).

Due to lower demand for consumer goods resulting from forced savings, investment goods are produced instead. An increase in the quantity of circulating money becomes "an important driving-belt of economic development" (Schumpeter 1918, 194). Credit money creation for investment loans therefore—unlike consumer loans—has a positive effect.

According to Schumpeter, an increase in the money supply through the issuance of government paper money is problematic because it leads to forced savings, without necessarily leading to investment. "In essence, the 'effects of paper money' are no different from the 'effects of metallic money'. We already know that if the pieces of paper simply took the place of the gold pieces, this would not set in motion any special phenomena" (Schumpeter 1918, 196). The issuance of government paper money is typically a "product of an emergency situation" and thus "subject to arbitrary government policies"; it leads to a "national excess of consumption" and to an "endless spiral" (Schumpeter 1918, 196).

"If the State used the paper money for productive purposes (a thing which never happens) or if the paper money were so used by the people into whose hands it first comes [...], the same conclusion would hold as in the case of the effects of productively employed increments of gold money" (Schumpeter 1918, 197).

27.4.9 Third Proposition on the Fundamental Equation

The third proposition considers a dynamic analysis. The real economy can influence the monetary side, and thus indirectly influence the product sum, again through a second-round effect. Schumpeter presents what Wagner (1937) calls a Development Theory of Credit. Here, the quantity theory works in reverse; there are interactions between both sides (Naderer 1990, 37). "Although, as has been shown above, changes in the prices and quantities of individual commodities, or even of all commodities, do not directly influence our product sum and hence cannot affect *MV* by way of a change in the product sum, such changes nevertheless can have an effect on the quantity of money. The change in the latter may then, in turn, affect the product sum" (Schumpeter 1918, 198).

This is an insight that stands in the tradition of the Banking School and an endogenously determined money supply. "Therefore, from a stringent quantity theory perspective, one must say not only that the quantity of gold money determines prices, but also that in principle prices likewise determine the quantity of gold money; that the purchasing power of money or its value 'depends' upon the quantity of gold, but at the same time that the quantity of gold 'depends' upon the purchasing power of money" (Schumpeter 1918, 199).

Yet Schumpeter does not see the causal relationship between the money supply and price level as unidirectional. Rather, he sees a reciprocal interrelationship between the two, in the sense of both the quantity and income theories. "This is not a circular proposition, but rather the affirmation of a two-way mutual causality, as is the rule in the field of economic relationships" (Schumpeter 1918, 199). This insight was possible because Schumpeter freed credit money from the narrow interpretation of the Real Bills Doctrine and Banking School, thus allowing him to integrate other types of credit money creation by banks.

27.4.10 Bank Money and the Price Level

Schumpeter then discusses the effect of credit money created by banks. He starts with the "much-vaunted elasticity of bank money, which is supposed to distinguish it from other types of money" (Schumpeter 1918, 199).

In line with the Banking School approach, he states: "Elasticity here means adaptability to the quantity of commodities produced, not to the prices of commodities. This follows from the very fact that another property of bank money usually comes in for praise at the same time, namely that bank money makes its appearance only when commodities appear—so that, unlike other types of money, each new 'claim ticket' to the reservoir of goods is matched by an increase in the reservoir—and disappears, according to the Fullarton principle, when commodities disappear, the credit being repaid once the consumer's payment has been received" (Schumpeter 1918, 199).

Schumpeter explicitly differentiates between the consumptive and productive use of the additional credit money created by loans, referring to "abnormal" loans for consumption and "normal" loans for investment. "When bank credit is given for consumption purposes [...] bank money has an 'inflationary' effect; and, as cannot be emphasized enough, it has such an effect however fully it may be covered by real property values" (Schumpeter 1918, 202).

To substantiate this reasoning, Schumpeter examines price level movements in relation to the business cycle: "The price rise of the upswing is characteristically general [...]. Unless by some chance new quantities of commodity money appear at the same time, the quantity of money can have been increased only by new bank money. [...] The case is quite clear: we have an increase in the quantity of bank money that normally prepares the way for an expansion of production and one that precedes the increase in commodities. The upswing consists in the creation of many new firms, the modernization and extension of old ones, and the full utilization of all productive capacity. This requires means of production and, to acquire them, increased or new bank credits. These bank credits, in turn, confront unaugmented quantities of means of production, so that the appearance of the former accentuates the entrepreneurs' struggle for the latter. The prices of means of production rise, so does the income of their owners, who eventually spend more and thereby raise the prices of consumer goods" (Schumpeter 1918, 202–203).

Inflation during an upswing is necessary and positive, as it is based on a time-delayed effect: the money supply increases immediately through additional credit money, but production only increases with a delay (Naderer 1990, 173). "If the credit is used as working capital, it will normally not be long before the corresponding commodities appear on the market and the much-praised parallelism between the flow of bank money and the flow of commodities is restored. This, however, changes nothing with respect to the 'non-simultaneity' of the movement of the two and therefore with respect to the independent effect of bank money on prices" (Schumpeter 1918, 203). In a recession, the process runs in an analogous manner in the opposite direction.

However, these temporary effects do not affect the general validity of the Banking School approach: "It would be quite mistaken to regard this, or the granting of bank credit without already existing commodities, as a deviation from sound banking principles which does not touch the essence of the matter. Rather is it one of the most important functions of the banking business to do just this" (Schumpeter 1918, 203–204).

Schumpeter then asserts that bank loans can enable "a shift in purchasing power among individuals and, if this shift favours the expansion of production, a transfer of means of production to those individuals to whom credits are granted by means of newly created money. This is what constitutes the difference between bank money and government paper money, not redeemability or 'reflux'. New men and new plans come to the forefront that otherwise would always have remained in the background. The obstacles are removed which private property places in the way of him who does not already have command over means of production. The banking world constitutes a central authority of the economy whose directives put the necessary means of production at the disposal of innovators in the productive organism. A monetary process, the creation of money which is only a 'claim ticket' and not also a 'receipt voucher,' and the rise in prices to which it leads, become a powerful lever of economic development. The essence of modern credit lies in the creation of such money. It is the specifically capitalistic method of effecting economic progress. It gives scope to the capitalistic function of money, as opposed to its market-economy function" (Schumpeter 1918, 205–206). This famous idea was initially expounded by Schumpeter in his *Theory of Economic Development* of 1912.

While Schumpeter bases much of his reasoning on the Banking School, he does not view credit money creation as limited by circular flow: "the practically unlimited demand for credit is matched by a practically unlimited supply of credit. That this is repeatedly overlooked is due only to the prejudice which regards the resources of banks as determined by objective conditions, particularly saving, and which ignores the factor of money creation. Neither the demand for credit nor the supply of it are unlimited in terms of goods" (Schumpeter 1918, 207).

On a purely monetary level, the supply and demand for money is unlimited. Schumpeter thus stands in the tradition of Macleod, who defined banks as manufacturers of credit. Banks "have no motive for issuing only as much credit money as is compatible with the existing price level. On the contrary, they do not lack a motive for a continuing credit expansion—they are driven to it by competition and by the prospect of increasing their industrial following" (Schumpeter 1918, 207). Schumpeter clarifies that the creation of money by banks is solely limited by a legal peg to a valuable substance and by the central bank's discount policy. "To this extent the currency theory is right" (Schumpeter 1918, 209).

27.5 Evaluation

Schumpeter elaborated his understanding of money as a token and sought to distinguish between different types and uses of money in an effort to integrate the quantity theory and the income theory. Schumpeter's catallactic nominalism was referred to by Wagner (1937) as a Development Theory of Credit. Here, we find Schumpeter's main criticism of Fisher, whom he accused of only considering short-term effects within a static economy.

According to Schumpeter, credit creation can either cause inflation or stimulate economic growth. The purchasing power generated through credit creation is not subject to direct limits. Real resources can be redirected toward those who receive this additional purchasing power. This process leads to what Schumpeter calls "forced saving," since scarce real resources are reallocated within the economy.

The outcome of this process depends on how the additional purchasing power is employed. If it is directed toward productive investments, the supply of goods may increase over time. When banks channel resources to entrepreneurs, this can lead to technological innovation and economic development. However, according to Schumpeter, investment requires a reduction in the consumption of limited real resources; resources can only be freed up for investment by limiting their consumption. In this sense, real saving remains a prerequisite for economic growth.

The monetary sphere facilitates this realignment, enabling the economy to evolve beyond its static state. From a macroeconomic perspective, the fact that monetary savings are not required for credit creation is irrelevant, because scarce resources have to be used differently.

Schumpeter incorporates many of the theories presented in prior chapters (including in particular metallism in the tradition of Menger, Knapp, Marx, Galiani, the Currency and Banking Schools, and Macleod). Yet he also develops his own eclectic approach to the debate.

In stark contrast to Menger, Schumpeter rejected the idea that examining the historical development of money can explain it as a phenomenon: "the historical beginnings of a phenomenon by no means always show it in its simplest and purest form, so that an attempt to get at the essential nature of the problem by genetic treatment may be easily misleading" (Schumpeter 1918, 157).

By presenting a coherent theory of money as a social accounting system, Schumpeter succeeding in resolving the theoretical deadlock that was primarily attributable to the incompatibility between metallism and Knapp's nominalism (Lakomski-Laguerre 2016, 490–491). In this respect, he resembles other contemporary authors, such as Alfred Lansburgh, who also developed eclectic, non-metallic theories to explain the dramatic changes witnessed in the monetary system after 1914 (Greitens 2022).

Taxonomic Classification

Schumpeter's understanding of money as a unit account in a social accounting system is central to his theory. Money is a *Rechenpfennig* ("accounting token"), a claim to society's production of goods and services whose value is determined by the amount of income channeled into demand and by the money supply. For Schumpeter, the money supply normally adjusts to economic activity in a passive manner, despite his assumption, in line with Macleod, that credit-money creation is theoretically unlimited.

References

Greitens, Jan. 2022. Money is a right: Alfred Lansburgh's token theory of money. *The European Journal of the History of Economic Thought* 29 (4): 619–647. https://doi.org/10.1080/09672567.2022.2063356.

Lakomski-Laguerre, Odile. 2016. Joseph Schumpeter's credit view of money: A contribution to a 'monetary analysis' of capitalism. *History of Political Economy.* 48 (3): 489–514. https://doi.org/10.1215/00182702-3638655.

Legrand, Muriel Dal Pont. 2024. Joseph a. Schumpeter (1883–1950). In *The Palgrave Companion to Harvard Economics*. Cham: Palgrave Macmillan. https://doi.org/10.1007/978-3-031-52053-2_7.

Naderer, Bärbel. 1990. *Die Entwicklung der Geldtheorie Joseph A. Schumpeters*. Berlin: Duncker & Humblot.

Schumpeter, Joseph. 1918. "Money and the Social Product." *International Economic Papers 6*. 1956, 148–211. Translation by A.W. Marget of "Das Sozialproduct und die Rechenpfennige." *Archiv für Sozialwissenschaft und Sozialpolitik*. 44. 627–715.

Part VIII
Concluding Remarks

Chapter 28
Applying the Taxonomy to the Authors Discussed in this Book

This book sought to provide the reader with a systematic history of early monetary thought. To this end, it engaged in the historical and rational reconstruction of the ideas presented in seminal works in order to develop a taxonomy of monetary theories (see Fig. 28.1).

One remaining question is whether there are lines of thought that can be examined from a diachronic perspective. For example, Neumark establishes a connection between Müller and Knapp (Neumark 1975, 263–265). Another example is Lakomski-Laguerre, who distinguishes between orthodox, money supply-oriented approaches and credit-oriented, elastic ones (Lakomski-Laguerre 2016, 490, 503).

As described in Chap. 4, the horizontal dimension of the taxonomy assigns the authors to one of three categories depending on their area of concern (i.e., the essence or value of money, or, alternatively, credit money). On the vertical dimension, the lines of tradition, distinguishing between nominalists and metallists is fairly easy; further subdivision with a view to the function of money is considerably more difficult, however. Some authors address a range of issues in the examined texts, and therefore appear in the taxonomy more than once. Explanations relevant for the subcategory assignments were provided at the end of each chapter.

Some authors present closely interconnected ideas regarding currency and credit money. This observation applies to Schumpeter, Menger, and to the Austrian School. Hilferding, by contrast, presents three more or less discrete approaches. Tooke represents income theory; however, due to historical circumstances, he only determines credit money based on the Real Bills Doctrine, without considering banks. Similarly, Copernicus follows in the tradition of Oresme, but he also discloses novel perspectives with a view to endogenous money.

In the above taxonomy, all of the authors within a given column predominantly focus on one function, and thus have a common element.

J. Greitens, *Currency and Credit Money*, Springer Studies in the History of Economic Thought, https://doi.org/10.1007/978-3-032-24113-9_28

	Metallism		Nominalism	
	Store of Value	**Medium of Exchange**	**Means of Payment**	**Unit of Account**
Theories on the **Essence of Money** (currency):	**Commodity Theory** • Oresmius (1358) • Biel (1516) • Locke (1692) • Cantillon (1755) • Justi (1766)	**Functional Theory** • Müller (1816) • Menger (1909)	**Convention Theory** • Davanzati (1588) • Müller (1816) • Knapp (1905)	**Token Theory** • Galiani (1751) • Thornton (1802) • Schumpeter (1918)
Theories on the **Value of Money** (currency):	**Cost of Production Theory** • Ricardo (1810) • Marx (1867) • Hilferding (1910)	**Functional Value Theory** • Copernicus (1526) • Bodin (1568) • Cantillon (1755) • Menger (1909)	**Quantity Theory** • Davanzati (1588) • Cantillon (1755) • Hume (1752) • Ricardo (1810) • Fisher (1911)	**Income Theory** • Copernicus (1526) • Tooke (1844) • Schumpeter (1918)
Theories on **Credit Money**:	**Real Bills Doctrine** • Tooke (1844) • Hilferding (1910)	**Covered Credit Money** • Law (1705) • Hamilton (1790)	**Active Money Creation** • MacLeod (1892) • Fisher (1911) • Phillips (1920)	**Passive Money Creation** • Thornton (1802) • Wicksell (1907) • Schumpeter (1918)

Fig. 28.1 Function-oriented taxonomy of monetary theories, including authors

- A monetary theory that prioritizes the protection of purchasing power adheres to the "store of value" line of thought. Proponents of this view place a focus on currency, and critically assess the expansion of central banks' balance sheets. Central banks should exclusively pursue stability-oriented, hawkish monetary policy, and monetary stability should be underpinned by redeemability into other assets. These ideas have retained their relevance up to the present day. For example, Shelton (2012) or White (2012) advocate the reintroduction of a gold standard, emphasizing the endogenous nature of the gold money supply. This contrasts with the mainstream Austrian School adherents (e.g., Hayek).
- Theories that focus on the "medium of exchange" function emphasize the need to maintain the exchange value of money. Here, the intellectual strands addressed in this book also remain relevant up to the present day. For example, advocates of the Sovereign Money Initiative (*Vollgeld-Initiative*) base their arguments on this line of thought (Mayer 2018, 79–92). Moreover, proponents of Bitcoin define this private currency as an artificially scarce money commodity that limits the money supply exogenously (Dodd, 2017); they assert that Bitcoin should be part of currency competition, as described by von Hayek (1976).
- The "means of payment" approach emphasizes the active role of money and its potential impact on society and the economy. Proponents of Modern Monetary Theory (MMT) associate the means of payment function with the definition of money as a social or governmental convention. Monetary financing of the state should be used to achieve political objectives, such as stabilizing aggregate demand; an exogenous money supply that meets the needs of fiscal policy is therefore necessary (Wray, 2015). From the beginning, the MMT proponents have been clear that "the currency is defined exogenously by the government" (Mosler, 1996).
- By contrast, the "unit of account" line of thought reduces money to a passive role. Money adjusts elastically to the needs of the real economy. Focusing on interest rates as the policy tool of the central bank assumes that the quantity of currency and credit money adjusts endogenously. New Keynesian theory and the Taylor rule belong to this line of thought.

The proposed taxonomy cannot be fully comprehensive, nor can it consider the macroeconomic relevance of the different theories. Categorization of this nature may elide over points of overlap and may also be partially informed by subjective interpretations of authors and their ideas. Nevertheless, such a taxonomy is a useful tool for examining monetary theories, as it reveals relevant questions while also providing context.

The explored lines of thought are logical and consistent in their underlying assumptions. The line of thought pursued by a given thinker entails a normative decision: what is the relative importance one ascribes to different monetary functions? This, in turn, often reflects political priors. This, in turn, often reflects political priorities. For instance, should the primary function of money be to maintain purchasing power (store-of-value) or to facilitate transactions (means-of-payment)?

The taxonomy presented here is based on an approach originally developed by Ehrlicher (1965). Veit attests that Ehrlicher's taxonomy "makes a lot of sense in a limited space." Yet he also writes: "No classification of monetary theories can be the sole true one" (Veit 1966, 101)—an assessment which, certainly, also applies to the present case.

References

Dodd, N. 2017. The social life of bitcoin. *Theory, Culture & Society, LSE Research Online, London* 35:35.

Ehrlicher, W. 1965. Geldtheorie. In *Handwörterbuch der Sozialwissenschaften*, vol. 4, 231–258. Stuttgart: Fischer/Mohr.

Lakomski-Laguerre, Odile. 2016. Joseph Schumpeter's credit view of money: A contribution to a 'monetary analysis' of capitalism. *History of Political Economy* 48 (3): 489–514.

Mayer, Thomas. 2018. *Austrian economics: Money and finance*. London: Routledge.

Mosler, Warren. 1996. *Currency definition (inflation)*. https://web.archive.org/web/19991003002206/http:/csf.colorado.edu/mail/pkt/96/jan96/0256.html

Neumark, Fritz. 1975. Zyklen in der Geschichte ökonomischer Ideen. *Kyklos* 28 (2): 257–285.

Shelton, Judy. 2012. Gold and government. *Cato Journal* 32 (2): 333–347.

Veit, Otto. 1966. *Reale Theorie des Geldes*. Tübingen: Mohr.

von Hayek, Friedrich August. 1976. *Denationalisation of money: An analysis of the theory and practice of concurrent currencies*. London: The Institute of Economic Affairs.

White, Lawrence H. 2012. Making the transition to a new gold standard. *Cato Journal* 32 (2): 411–421.

Wray, L. R. 2015. *Modern money theory*. 2nd ed. Basingstoke: Palgrave Macmillan.

MIX
Papier aus verantwortungsvollen Quellen
Paper from responsible sources
FSC® C105338

If you have any concerns about our products,
you can contact us on
ProductSafety@springernature.com

In case Publisher is established outside the EU,
the EU authorized representative is:
Springer Nature Customer Service Center GmbH
Europaplatz 3, 69115 Heidelberg, Germany

Printed by Libri Plureos GmbH
in Hamburg, Germany